Women on the Rope

by the same author

Bishop's Wife But Still Myself
Dear Abroad
Diary of a Decade

WOMEN
ON THE ROPE

The Feminine Share
in Mountain Adventure

Cicely Williams

London George Allen & Unwin Ltd
Ruskin House Museum Street

Printed in Great Britain
in 12 pt Fournier type by
Cox & Wyman Ltd,
London, Fakenham and Reading

In memory of
BERNARD BINER

For over thirty years
my guide, philosopher and friend

Ye who have climbed to the great white veil,
Heard ye the chant? Saw ye the Grail?

Geoffrey Winthrop Young

Contents

Contents

Acknowledgements

Many people and organisations have helped me so much in the production of this book that this paragraph can only be one big expression of gratitude. I must thank my many friends in the climbing world for the loan of photographs, especially Joan Busby, Janet Carleton, Countess Dorothea Gravina, Eveleigh Leith, Nea Morin, Frank and Babs Solari and Robert and Miriam Underhill. Much help in matters of research has come from Lady Chorley, Dorothy Walker, Felicitas von Reznicek and Mr Ronald Clark. The Seiler family and Mr Constant Cachin of Zermatt allowed me access to precious old hotel registers. The Alpine Club gave me permission to work in the library and to borrow any books I needed. Much of the book had to be written during 'official' trips abroad and my long-suffering husband never failed to find me quiet corners in which to work in many parts of the world. He later shared the task of compiling the index – a labour of love indeed! Our never-failing Jill England typed the script, as she has done so many times before, and provided great encouragement by her enthusiasm. I owe much to Mr Philip Unwin who asked me to write my fifth book and gave me the chance to fulfil one of my dearest wishes – to write a book about mountaineering. To one and all I say a very big 'Thank You'. The following kindly gave me permission to reproduce photographs: the Swiss National Tourist Office, the Ladies' Alpine Club, B. T. Batsford Ltd, Ernest Benn Ltd, J. M. Dent and Sons Ltd, Eyre and Spottiswoode (Publishers) Ltd, Methuen and Co. Ltd.

Illustrations

Chapter 1

Approach

> Only a hill: . . .
> . . . what is that to you?
> Only a hill; but all of life to me,
> Up there between the sunset and the sea.

Thus wrote Geoffrey Winthrop Young in the early years of the twentieth century. It was not always so; there was a time when mountains were looked upon with dread and when those who lived among them believed them to be inhabited by evil spirits.

In the course of his lectures on *Civilisation* Sir Kenneth Clark (now Lord Clark) explained how it was only in comparatively recent times, in the last half of the eighteenth century, that people began to get interested in mountains. No one crossing the Alps in the sixteenth or seventeenth centuries would have thought of admiring the scenery, much less of climbing the mountains.

Suddenly there came a great change: Rousseau, together with a bevy of English poets – Coleridge, Wordsworth, Byron, Shelley and, later, Matthew Arnold – ushered in the age of nature worship. There had been a great explosion of new ideas and at least a temporary abandonment of old beliefs; it all seemed very exhilarating and liberalising at first but it was not long before people began to find that they could not get on without a belief in something outside themselves. Some kind of mystical experience, however slight, seemed essential; and so the belief in the divinity of nature developed. Mountains became the abode of gods rather than of demons.

Strangely, it was botanists and scientists who first began to explore the Alps, persuading themselves that they were doing so in the interests of research rather than for their own enjoyment. This phase passed and by the nineteenth century mountaineering for its own sake was already becoming popular. Men were the first exponents but women followed almost at once and, having started, have never stopped – and this is what this book is all about.

It does not pretend to be more than a casual history, written rather for enjoyment and personal interest than as a historical survey resulting from detailed research – although there has indeed been research in plenty! But the last few years have brought together women mountaineers of all nations, many of whom have, until now, climbed in isolation and almost complete obscurity. It soon became clear to me that if justice were to be done to all women climbers of the nineteenth and twentieth centuries a vast and detailed tome would be called for, and one that could be of interest only to climbers themselves. The story of women mountaineers is so fascinating that it seemed that it should be written to appeal to the widest possible public. This is why it had to be a rather light-hearted, sometimes personal, and always essentially feminine book, dealing with personalities as well as ascents; describing the sociological aspects of the times as well as the technical difficulties of the mountains attempted and achieved.

Since 1808, when the little Chamonix maidservant, Maria Paradis, was taken by her boy friends to the top of Mont Blanc, women of all types have responded to the call of the hills. There have been reserved academics and society women of fashion; gentle, domesticated types and the early advocates of Women's Lib; wives, mothers, sisters, daughters, not to mention aunts; women famous in the world of letters and public affairs and others unknown outside the family circle; school girls, students, the young and the not-so-young; women of every colour and every race on earth – all united by their love of the mountains. Only comparatively few could be mentioned in the pages of this book. It was impossible to do more and inevitably some will be disappointed by omissions; but in writing, as in climbing, some risks have to be taken.

Times have changed, of course. The women mountaineers of

PLATE I

Henriette d'Angeville who climbed Mont Blanc in 1838
(a self-portrait)
Photo by permission of Ernest Benn Ltd

PLATE II

Lucy Walker with her guide Melchior Anderegg at Zermatt when their climbing days were past

Photo by permission of the Ladies' Alpine Club

Mrs Jackson: a kind of snow queen of Victorian times

Photo by permission of B. T. Batsford L

Tschingel and her climbing list

Photos by permission of B. T. Batsford Ltd

TSCHINGEL'S PEAKS AND PASSES.

1865.
Torrenthorn.
Tschingel Pass.

1868.
Blümlis Alps.
Balmhorn.
Nesthorn.
Mönchjoch.
Aletschhorn.

1869.
Grands Mulets.
Aiguille de Miaze.
Col de Birenger (1st passage.)
Col du Mont Tondu.
Grand Combin.
Breithorn.
Monte Rosa.

1870.
Col des Aiguilles d'Arve
Diablerets.
Brünegghorn.

1871.
Eiger.
Jungfrau (from Wengern Alp.)
Alphübeljoch.
Triftjoch.
Fusshorn (1st ascent.)

1872.
Brèche de la Meije.
Col de la Tempe.
Aletschhorn (crossed.)
Strahleck.
Mönch (from Wengern Alp.)

Jungfraujoch (descent to Wengern Alp.)
Finsteraarhorn.
Agassizjoch.
Finsteraarjoch.
Wetterhorn.
Doldenhorn.

1873.
Aiguille d'Arve (lowest peak, 1st ascent.)
Col de la Lauze.
Râteau (1st ascent.)
Col des Ecrins.
Col du Glacier Blanc.
Grande Ruine (1st ascent.)
Col de la Casse Deserte (1st passage.)
Col de la Pilatte (descent to Vallouise.)

1874.
Col du Tour
Mont Pourri.
Pic de la Grave (1st ascent.)
Brèche de St. Christophe.
Ochsenhorn.
Ochsenjoch.

1875.
Klein Schreckhorn.
Brèche de Valsenestre.
Col du Vallon (1st passage)
Pointe de Marguérite (1st ascent.)
Les Berches.
Col des Chamois (1st passage.)
Mont Blanc.

1876.
Fasshörner (1st ascent of 2nd Peak.)

today would scarcely be recognised by their predecessors. Crinolines have been exchanged for climbing breeches, nailed boots for
vibram soles, felt hats for crash helmets. Techniques have been
similarly revolutionised. The Victorians climbed with guides but
never alone with a guide; a companion of some kind, or at least a
porter, was *de rigueur*. The carefree young damsels of today have
largely dispensed with guides; lack of finance and abundance of
alpine know-how have brought them greater independence. In
the years that separate these two widely differing generations there
flourished the great guide–climber partnerships, a source of happiness to countless mountaineers. If one is put in the care of a good
guide when one is young he becomes, and remains, something of
a hero. He inspires complete confidence and in return he develops
an understanding of his young climber physically, psychologically
and spiritually. As the years go by confidence and respect become
mutual; you come to realise that while the guide carries your life
in his hands you carry something almost more precious than his
life in yours. The relationship can be near-perfect and the atmosphere in which one climbs supremely happy.

It is for this reason that this book is dedicated to Bernard Biner
of Zermatt. He was my guide from my schooldays until his death
in 1965. When the war brought my early climbing career to a
temporary halt he would send letters encouraging me to forget the
Blitz and think only of the climbs awaiting me when the Nazi
tyranny was ended. When I married, my husband joined the
rope and our mountain happiness was complete.

There has been little rivalry between men and women climbers.
Husbands and fathers brought their womenfolk to the mountains
and frequently encouraged their mountaineering careers. Women,
with a few exceptions, climbed unostentatiously; they were careful in the early days not to intrude where they sensed male
aloofness and eventually won for themselves the respect of even
the most anti-feminine members of the Alpine Club. The present
position is a happy one. There are cordial invitations to mixed
parties, there are men and women ropes and more than one
Himalayan Expedition has included a woman in its all-male team.
In the years to come there may be even greater co-operation.

Perhaps it is not too much to hope that the courage and enterprise shown by women mountaineers in the decades that have passed are indicative of greater achievements in the years that lie ahead. The spirit of adventure that inspired the women of the early nineteenth century burns as brightly today as ever it did; a new generation of climbers is ready to carry the torch forward.

What you can do or dream you can, begin it.
Boldness has genius, power and magic in it.

Chapter 2

First Beginnings

At the foot of Mont Blanc, in the year 1808, there stood a rather shabby little stall; it was scarcely more than a shack but it provided light refreshments and a few useful commodities for passing travellers; it was the property of Maria Paradis. Maria worked as a servant girl in Chamonix. Times were hard; the French Revolution had not so far improved the lot of the mountain peasants of Savoy. When she had time off from her domestic duties Maria presided over her stall to supplement her meagre earnings.

Mont Blanc had been climbed for the first time in 1786 and there had been several subsequent ascents. Maria, who was only eighteen, numbered among her boy-friends guides and porters who had been engaged in some of these early climbs. Probably it was they who suggested that she might be the first woman to stand on the top of the highest mountain in the Alps. Maria seems to have had little enthusiasm for mountains and less for climbing; but when the young men pointed out that the adventure might pay dividends in the number of people who visited her stall and that her fame would spread far beyond the confines of the Chamonix valley Maria had second thoughts.

The day came at last when she agreed to make the attempt if there were sufficient guides and porters to haul her to the top. The fact that at least one of the guides belonged to the already famous guide family of Balmat, was perhaps the deciding factor – Jacques Balmat had taken part in the first ascent of Mont Blanc in 1786.

Maria did not enjoy the climb; she suffered first from the heat and then from the intense cold; at times she could hardly speak. At one stage, however, she did manage to gasp in her local patois,

'*Licha moa dans crevasse et alla ou vo vocha,*' which, translated into colloquial English, means 'For goodness sake throw me into a crevasse and go on yourselves.'

The guides gallantly refused this request; they succeeded in dragging her to the summit, albeit in poor condition, and finally brought her safely back to Chamonix. Their prophecies were fulfilled; Maria's little stall prospered exceedingly; indeed Claire Eliane Engel goes so far as to describe it as a 'tea-room at Les Pèlerins', much advertised by the mountaineering prowess of the proprietress. Maria was as honest as the day; she admitted quite frankly that she had made the climb with an eye to the main chance and said openly, in later life, 'thanks to the curiosity of the public I have made a very nice profit out of it; and that was what I reckoned on when I made the ascent'.

Maria Paradis can hardly be acclaimed as the first woman mountaineer – she had absolutely nothing in common with those who came after her and there is no record of her ever having set foot on another mountain – but as the first woman to reach the summit of a great peak she deserves a niche among the ranks of early women climbers.

The years passed. Maria's exploit does not seem to have triggered off any passionate desire among other members of her sex to follow her example. Nevertheless women were beginning to travel among the mountains, sometimes with their scientifically-minded men-folk, sometimes by themselves. It is known that in 1822 a Mrs and Miss Campbell crossed the Col du Géant in the Mont Blanc range; this is a considerable pass and it is sad that these intrepid ladies have not left any record of their adventures. One can only assume that they enjoyed their excursions in their own quiet, unostentatious way and that it never occurred to them that generations to come would be interested in their doings.

Unobtrusive modesty was certainly not a noticeable characteristic of Mlle Henriette d'Angeville. It has been said that whereas Maria Paradis climbed for profit, Henriette d'Angeville climbed for notoriety. She certainly *achieved* notoriety with her ascent of Mont Blanc in 1838 – the first woman actually to climb, rather than be hauled, to the summit. Mont Blanc was her first climb and was, in her mind, a matter of outstanding importance. But the more we read about Henriette the more we admire and understand her and see this first ascent in its right proportions. The descriptions of her trip to the top of Mont Blanc, which have been handed down through the years, make fascinating reading even in these sophisticated days. We owe much of our knowledge of Mlle d'Angeville to Mlle Mary Paillon who knew her in her latter years and wrote much about her, not only as a climber but as an interesting character.

Henriette d'Angeville belonged to the old French aristocracy; she was born during the Reign of Terror; her grandfather was guillotined; her father was imprisoned. After these disasters the family moved away to the hilly country of the Jura. It was here that Henriette as a teenager first began to scramble about the low, limestone hills; maybe this gave her a taste for climbing but it was not until she was forty-four years of age that a visit to Chamonix fired her with a desire to climb Mont Blanc. There are many suggestions as to why and how this happened. She has been successively described as 'that thwarted maiden lady in her forties', and as 'a spinster who loved Mont Blanc because she had nothing else to love'. She has been accused of having a morbid passion for self-advertisement and Claire Engel advances the theory that she was madly jealous of the glamorous public reputation of the Baroness Dudevant (George Sand), climbing Mont Blanc by sheer willpower in order to become the lioness of the 1838 season. If this really was Henriette's object the results of her escapade must have far exceeded her expectations – her contemporaries were so carried away by enthusiasm that they called her the Bride of Mont Blanc.

If planning, forethought and attention to detail are to be commended she richly deserved her reward; for sheer tenacity she was second to none. In the first place she had to overcome tremendous opposition; almost everyone who heard of her plan was opposed to it; she could count only five supporters. An English friend, a certain Lady Cullum, implored her not to go and, in contemporary nineteenth-century style, burst into floods of her tears when she remained adamant.

Henriette d'Angeville shut her door on the public and steadily continued her preparations to make the ascent, as she originally intended, in the month of September. She consulted her doctor and made her will; she then proceeded to engage six Chamonix guides and six porters. This completed, she had to decide on an adequate stock of provisions for the party. A full inventory was preserved; this was later discovered by Mary Paillon who has handed it down to posterity.

She ordered:

  2 legs of mutton
  2 ox tongues
 24 fowls
  6 large loaves
 18 bottles of St Jean
  1 bottle of brandy
  1 bottle of *syrop*
  1 cask of *vin ordinaire*
 12 lemons
  3 lbs of sugar
  3 lbs of chocolate
  3 lbs of French plums

It hardly seems surprising that she needed six porters when one contemplates the list. But this stock of food and drink was entirely for the male members of the party – on no account must they perish from lack of nourishment whatever other discomforts they might encounter. By comparison Henriette's own needs were slight; some lemonade and a pot of chicken broth, together with a private blancmange in a flask and a few prunes; the blancmange and the prunes she insisted on carrying herself. Just how to carry a blancmange, even in a flask, to the top of a major mountain is a mystery which later generations of climbers have yet to solve.

In the matter of dress Henriette was most particular. She was heard to say that 'one cannot go to the court of the Monarch of the Alps in a simple brown holland dress and a muslin bonnet. Such a visit requires severer and, above all, warmer apparel.' The court of Louis XVI might have disappeared in the name of '*liberté, égalité, fraternité*' but in the Alps Mont Blanc still reigned supreme.

Her list of required clothing almost rivalled the bill of provisions in its overall completeness – nothing was omitted. She was arrayed in underclothing of red flannel and woollen stockings were worn over silk. Her knickerbockers of Scottish tweed were lined with flannel and with them was worn a short blouse of the same material. She had, of course, to reckon with sun and wind, with intense cold and scorching heat. To combat these extremes she had a bonnet lined with fur and a straw hat lined with a green material. Tucked away in capacious pockets were a velvet mask, a veil, green spectacles and thick woollen gloves. A plaid, a fur-lined *pelisse* and an iron-shod alpenstock completed the picture. Her appearance must have been impressive – not to say unusual.

The great day approached. Henriette retired early to her room but before she went to bed she wrote letters to her closest friends. No one was forgotten and for some, at least, these letters must have become treasured souvenirs. At 6 a.m., apparelled for the fray, she was in the foyer of the hotel, ready to be off. The galleries of the hotel were crowded with visitors, early astir in order to miss nothing of such a momentous departure. Even the soldiers stationed near by turned out to salute. Did it all just happen? Or had Henriette a publicity agent working overtime on her behalf? Nobody will ever know, but she was glad to hear later that the caravan made a deep impression on the onlookers.

Once Henriette was away she forgot, at any rate temporarily, the crowds and the publicity. Excitement lent her wings: 'I did not walk', she said later, 'I flew'. So much so in fact that the guides had to insist that she went more slowly. But quite early in the proceedings they became well aware of her prowess. She refused help over a crevasse on the Glacier des Bossons, leaping across with the greatest agility. They reported that she went as well as they did and nothing frightened her.

On the first evening they reached the Grands-Mulets; at that time there was no refuge hut so tents were pitched and the party prepared to spend the night under canvas. It proved to be a convivial evening. A certain Count Karo de Stoppen from Poland was camping near by. With the discreet formality typical of the times he sent his card with his compliments by one of his guides and asked permission to call. Count Karo de Stoppen must have been one who prepared for every contingency; not many modern climbers would equip themselves with visiting cards when kitting up for an ascent of Mont Blanc.

Henriette was charmed. She accepted the invitation with alacrity and proposed that the two parties should join forces and organise a concert. They made merry under the stars and the guides sang their national songs well into the night until the roar of a distant avalanche brought the programme to an abrupt conclusion.

We are told that before Henriette retired she prayed fervently that God would preserve her companions from misfortune; having dealt with this matter she petitioned humbly for her own success.

Early the next morning they were off again. The difficulties were considerably greater than on the previous day. At the foot of the ice on the Grand-Côte poor Henriette confessed to suffering 'suffocating palpitations of the heart' and 'a lethargic drowsiness' whenever she stopped – obviously an acute attack of mountain sickness.

For four weary hours she staggered on, pausing for breath every few minutes. Only her strength of will kept her going and at one moment of deepest despair she asked the guides to drag her body to the top of the mountain if she died before she got there. Mercifully she survived, and as she explained later, the instant she stood on the summit she recovered as by a miracle. She forgot her lassitude and her palpitations; she forgot everything and was utterly lost in the incredible wonder of the mountain world around her; her sense of peace was complete. To the uninitiated this may sound phoney and fanciful but every dedicated mountaineer from that day to this has had similar experiences on even the smallest peak. Perhaps that is one reason why we climb.

The party reached the summit at 1.30 p.m.; Henriette, staunch Royalist as she was, drank the health of the Comte de Paris – in milk – a fact she was at pains to keep from the left-wing French press of those days. Her guides, delighted at having brought the first lady to the top of the loftiest summit in the Alps, asked to be allowed to kiss her. This request (nothing more than a routine matter in these days) was a most unusual request at the time. Henriette, however, decided that the occasion was unique and gave permission, after which the guides lifted her on to their shoulders shouting: 'Now Mamselle, you shall go one higher than Mont Blanc.' When describing the incident on her return the recipient of all this affection gave it as her opinion that the kisses were so resounding that they must surely have been heard in the valley of Chamonix.

At 2.10 p.m. the guides prepared for the descent but Henriette still had one further duty to perform while she remained on the summit. It was customary for climbers to take carrier pigeons on their ascents and release them from the top of the mountain. Henriette had remembered even this detail and a pigeon had accompanied the party. With unfeigned delight she despatched it to the Comte de Paris with the news of her success. Sadly this was the one disappointment she had to endure: the pigeon failed to arrive. It was only later that they heard that it had been shot down over Les Contamines with the note telling the news still tied to its foot.

The party descended to the Grands-Mulets where they spent another night; fortunately for all concerned there were no social engagements on this occasion and they slept off the exertions of the day in total contentment. The next morning at tree-level they found a mule waiting; the muleteer explained that it had been sent by Lady Cullum who was convinced that her friend Henriette would be utterly exhausted. This was not the case at all and Henriette insisted on entering Chamonix on foot.

The correspondent of the *Journal des Débats* was waiting for her, eager to get a good story to send to his paper in Paris. According to him everyone in the village went out to meet the heroine; a cannon was fired; the enthusiasm was indescribable and he did Henriette proud by suggesting that in future the name d'Angeville would rank with those of Balmat and de Saussure.

Never before or since in the annals of mountaineering has there been such a saga; parts of it are reminiscent of comic opera. Perhaps Henriette had psychological abnormalities that caused her to embark on such an adventure; perhaps she craved for publicity and hero worship; perhaps she was unfulfilled; it has to be admitted that the first ascent of Mont Blanc by a woman bears little resemblance to the great traditions that have been established by later women climbers. But it may be that Henriette learned a lot from her climbing; she may have been the first, but she was certainly not the last, woman whose whole attitude to life has been deeply influenced by the mountains. Mont Blanc was only a beginning; she continued to climb for another twenty-five years and made no less than twenty-one further ascents, including one in the winter. At the age of sixty-nine she climbed the Oldenhorn; it was her last climb and probably, in a quiet way, one that she enjoyed as much as any. Fashions had changed since Henriette's early days; knickerbockers were out, crinolines were in. She had long discarded the flamboyant outfit she wore on Mont Blanc; she climbed the Oldenhorn in a crinoline – which unfortunately got torn to shreds during the descent.

Henriette wrote a vigorous and humorous account of her climb to her friend Mary Paillon. She mentioned that they slept in a chalet and then climbed for ten consecutive hours without a rest. She ends the letter thus, 'The Oldenhorn is my twenty-first alpine ascent, and will probably be one of the last; for it is wise at my age to drop the alpenstock before the alpenstock drops me.'

In her later years, but before she did finally 'drop the alpenstock' Henriette went to live at Ferney, a village near Geneva made famous by Voltaire. Here she was visited in 1853 by an English lady named Mrs Young who for years had longed to meet this woman mountaineer. Mrs Young was travelling with her daughters and the brilliant British climber Charles Hudson, who was later killed in the famous Matterhorn disaster. It was through Hudson that the introduction was to be effected; obviously in the course of years Henriette had been accepted by the leading climbers of the day and was a close acquaintance of Charles Hudson.

Mrs Young's impression of Henriette confirms the belief that she mellowed with the years and became a more balanced chararter. Mrs Young writes in her diary, 'She is extremely intelligent, with all the vivacity of manner and ease which characterises a French woman accustomed to mix in good society.' Henriette showed her visitors the many albums describing her famous ascent and discussed the whole adventure in a most animated manner. 'I cannot help regarding her as a marvellously wonderful being,' Mrs Young continues, 'I shall always remember my visit . . . as one of the most pleasing associations connected with Geneva.'

On 13th January 1871 Henriette died in Lausanne in her seventy-seventh year. She died just too soon to know that later that year the Matterhorn was to be climbed for the first time by a woman – an event which would certainly have rejoiced her heart. Mercifully, she passed away a few days before Paris surrendered to the Prussians – news that would have saddened her last hours. Henriette d'Angeville was a colourful character; the mountain world would have been the poorer without her.

A month before Henriette d'Angeville set out for Mont Blanc another woman mountaineer was building up a reputation in the Pyrenees. This was Miss Anne Lister, an English woman who was the *châtelaine* of Shibden Hall near Halifax. In the first half of the nineteenth century the Pyrenees attracted little attention compared with the Alps; almost nothing was known of Anne Lister and her mountaineering achievements and it is only recently that her diaries have been discovered among the Archives of Halifax Corporation. Miss Vivienne Ingham worked on these and brought to light the remarkable story of her pioneer amateur ascent of Vignemale.

Anne Lister seems to have been rather a masculine woman; a forceful personality possessed of unbounded energy. She was a great walker and visited Switzerland in 1827. This visit awakened her interest in mountains and she declared her intention of climbing Mont Blanc. Somehow she never succeeded in bringing off this project but her passion for mountains remained.

For some years she lived in Paris and in 1830, with Lady Stuart de Rothesay, the wife of the British Ambassador in Paris, and her two daughters she first visited the Pyrenees. The party stayed on French territory but Anne Lister made several *sorties* over the Spanish frontier and finally succeeded in climbing Mont Perdu. She must have been something of an embarrassment to Lady de Rothesay who, as an ambassador's wife, was acutely aware of the contemporary political situation.

The Pyrenees had captured Anne Lister's imagination and she returned in 1838 for a six-weeks' stay. She engaged her guide of 1830, Jean-Pierre Charles, and it was a chance remark of his that caused her to have designs on Vignemale. The mountain was said to be inaccessible from the French side but Charles reported that a man from Gèdre had found a way to the top. Anne Lister was not one to let the grass grow under her feet; she sent off Charles to make enquiries and while he was gone purchased a thick cape and cloak for him to wear on the expedition.

As a curtain-raiser Anne and Charles climbed the Piméné. On this mountain they met Cazaux, the Vignemale guide who had explored the mountain during the previous year. Anne engaged him on the spot at an agreed price of twenty francs, plus his food and something in which to drink her health on the summit. Unfortunately the weather broke and the expedition had to be postponed. On Sunday, 5th August, she hoped to try again but once more the clouds were low on the mountain.

It was at this point that Anne realised she had a possible rival for Vignemale. She wrote in her diary, 'The Chasseurs-Guides say that the Prince of Moscowa has engaged Cazaux to go to the top of the mountain on Thursday.' The Prince was the son of Napoleon's Marshall Ney; his presence and his plans caused Anne to set off without delay.

The guides predicted fine weather and on that afternoon, precisely at 3.55, she rode off on horse-back for Gavarnie and the *cabane des Saoussats Dabats*. She seemed to have prepared for the worst in the way of cold weather and was enveloped in a multitude of capes, cloaks, shawls and petticoats with a complex of tapes and loops adjusted to tie up her skirts. Her pockets were packed with her personal impedimenta and she took with her one hundred francs carefully tucked into the toe of a woollen stocking. The crampons she had had for Mont Perdu were included; they were probably the most useful part of the outfit. However she considered herself to be 'lightly equipped' and was in excellent spirits.

The two guides, Jean-Pierre Charles and Jean-Pierre Sanjou, also mounted, accompanied her and the cavalcade finally arrived at the cabane after a journey of four and a half hours. At the cabane they found Cazaux waiting for them, together with his brother-in-law who had been engaged to take back the horses. A bunch of shepherds shared the hut with them and they spent an uncomfortable night in cramped conditions.

Extracts from Anne's diary for 7th August are brief, but meticulous. 'Off at 2. Sent back the horses 4.55. Breakfast 4.55. Off on foot 5.20. Climbed the chimney. Rest at 7.7 for 12 minutes.' At 11.15 she records, 'Rested on top of second *crête*. I lay down a little; put on my cloak and did not feel the air cold. Off again at 11.0. Sick just before.' Her remarks on reaching the summit were as unemotional as the rest of the entries. 'At the top at 1.0 . . . Put our names in the bottle and began the descent at 2.10 . . . Back at the cabane of *Saoussats Dabats* at 8.5. Tired, but would have pushed on to Gavarnie, but Charles said it would be dangerous to attempt such a road in the dark.'

And that was that. Anne met up, by arrangement, with a woman friend; Cazaux went off to join the Prince of Moscowa; there seem to have been no jubilations of any kind. Presumably Anne Lister was not that sort of person. However, the story had a sequel which appears to have given her more pleasure than any conventional celebrations might have done.

Anne and her friend spent a few days touring along the Spanish frontier and arrived at St Sauveur on 13th August. On 14th August they went for a ride and received most disturbing news from their guide Charles. Cazaux apparently had allowed the Prince of Moscowa, whom he had accompanied to Vignemale on 8th August, to think that *he* was the first amateur to make the ascent of the mountain. He said that Anne Lister had been sick on the glacier and had not gone to the top, although the guides had done so.

Anne's entry in her diary concerning this was characteristic –

pithy and to the point. 'Annoyed; would not pay Cazaux till this was cleared. Either I had gone to the top or I had not, and if I had it should be acknowledged.' The unfortunate Charles was sent post-haste to the Prince and returned with the news that Cazaux had written to the Prince saying that Miss Lister had only reached the lower Pic. He even claimed that there was no bottle containing the names.

Anne, understandably, was furious; the quarrel became a major row. With Charles in tow she went down to Lourdes and consulted a lawyer whom she tartly described as 'rather *rotund au milieu*', but fortunately he had agreeable manners. More important still, he entirely agreed with the firm stand she was taking. A certificate was produced which Cazaux must be made to sign. The lawyer was convinced that if the fee for the climb was withheld Cazaux would soon succumb. He was proved right. Anne and Charles rode up to Gèdre and found Cazaux at home. At the local inn she ordered bread, wine and cheese for the whole party, which by now had risen to five. Cazaux talked over the whole affair most amicably, made not the slightest objection to signing the certificate and agreed that Miss Lister had indeed reached the top 'and got up very well too'. Cazaux then received his fee together with an extra five francs with two more added to insure that he looked after the precious bottle on the summit.

By this time Charles felt the time had come to give expression to his wounded feelings and proceeded to give Cazaux a piece of his mind. Anne Lister thought this to be hitting a man when he was down; she immediately shook hands with Cazaux, ordered more wine for the party and the next day poor miserable Charles was sent off to convince the Prince. This he at last succeeded in doing but in the course of the conversation, Anne reports, 'he made use of a word against Cazaux which he, Charles, could not repeat to me'.

On 25th August Anne read in her newspaper that 'the Prince of Moscowa and his brother Mons. Edgar Ney, accompanied by five guides had made a successful ascent, on the 11th instant, to the summit of Vignemale, the second highest mountain of the Pyrenees ... which had hitherto been thought inaccessible'.

Anne retaliated immediately and won the battle swiftly with a subtle stroke. She composed a paragraph which she quietly asked Galignani, the owner of the newspaper, to insert in the next convenient issue of his *Messenger*. In the afternoon edition of 3rd September the following announcement appeared:

'We noticed some days ago, the ascent of the Prince de la Moscowa and his brother Mons. Edgar Ney, with five guides to the summit of the Vignemale, hitherto thought inaccessible. We find that an English lady had, four days before, ascended with three guides to the same summit which, though inaccessible from the French side, is not more difficult from the Spanish side towards the east, than high mountains in general.'

This rather gentle, modest paragraph closed the contest decisively. Honour was satisfied; Anne had little further interest in the matter. Her victory of Vignemale had meant little to her, but the acknowledgement of what she had done – which was her due – was of paramount importance. Even before the issue was decided she had written '. . . what matters it to me? I have made each ascent for my pleasure, not for *éclat*. What is *éclat* to me?'

There is a lull of sixteen years before women began to add more to mountaineering history. Then in 1854 Mrs Hamilton with her husband and guides reached the summit of Mont Blanc. Too little importance has been attached to this event. Mrs Hamilton was the first British woman to climb Mont Blanc and she and her husband were the first exponents of husband and wife partnerships. Since then there has been a long and interesting succession of these combinations culminating in 1971 with Michel and Yvette Vaucher on Everest. Perhaps Mrs Hamilton's ascent of Mont Blanc came a little too late in the history of that mountain; it had been climbed fairly frequently by men and alpine interest was shifting to the Pennine Alps and to the Matterhorn in particular. Be that as it may, history records her ascent and she must take her rightful place among British women pioneers.

In the autumn of 1854, soon after Mrs Hamilton's ascent of Mont Blanc, another husband and wife made a joint expedition. It was less spectacular than Mont Blanc but it had its own special significance and was very rewarding. Sir Alfred Wills, already one of the famous British pioneers in the Alps, had a growing desire to give his young wife a little insight into what 'exploring the recesses of the High Alps really involved'. The young lady apparently was quite willing to be initiated and the decision was reached that the best means of doing this would be to bivouac on the Mer de Glace for a night. Detailed and very secret negotiations took place with their guide Balmat who found himself besieged with questions by the waiters at the hotel in Chamonix as to what exactly his clients were intending to do. Balmat succeeded in putting them off the scent and on the morning of 28th August they set off, soon to be joined by an old man and a *'bon garçon'* whom Balmat had engaged as porters. The amount of equipment was considerable – a mattress, sheets, blankets, a coffee pot and a supply of glasses, together with knives, forks and spoons. These were carried by the old man; the *'bon garçon'* bore the vast quantity of provisions deemed necessary for the occasion.

They spent a delightful day walking up to and across the glacier, lunched in a comfortable spot near the Trélaporte and continued up the Mer de Glace towards the Glacier de Leschaux. At four o'clock they reached their previously selected bivouac – a wild spot on the moraine near the foot of the Tacul, with views of the Aiguille de Blaitière and the approaches to the Col du Géant. The old man and the *garçon* commenced prodigious preparations while the lady of the party sat sketching contentedly.

At seven o'clock the banquet was laid – on a large, flat slab of rock below the rocky cavern which had been prepared as the sleeping quarters. Balmat, 'who always liked to do things nicely', produced a tablecloth and on this were spread such delicacies as chicken, mutton, bread, butter, cheese, biscuits and raisins. A good fire of rhododendrons was blazing near by with potatoes roasting in the ashes and the coffee pot bubbling merrily. Someone had even remembered salt, sugar and a bottle of cream; there seemed to be nothing missing. Best of all, as a nightcap, there were glasses of what we now call *Glühwein*.

'A more delightful evening was never passed', writes Sir Alfred

PLATE III

Above: Micheline Morin in a gale on the south-west ridge of the Mönch. *Above right:* Miriam Underhill, said to be the greatest lady climber America has produced, on a pinnacle in the Aiguilles Rouges. *Right:* Alice Damesme on the summit of the Matterhorn on the occasion of the first 'manless' ascent with Miriam Underhill

Photos by permission of Miriam Underhill

PLATE IV

Loulou Boulaz on
the Eiger
Photo by permission of
the Ladies' Alpine Club

Alice Damesme,
Micheline Morin and
Nea Morin in one of
the earliest and most
active *cordées
féminines*
Photo by permission of
Eyre and Spottiswoode
Ltd

Wills; mountaineers of all generations would willingly agree and wish that we could all have been invited. His description of the glacier, the snow-covered peaks, the stars and the absolute still-ness rings a bell in every climber's heart, for this is the stuff of which mountaineering is made.

The night that followed was not quite such unalloyed bliss; conditions were spartan; the temperature was well below freezing; the wind whistled through both ends of the cavern and stones protruded through the mattress. Seen in retrospect none of these things mattered at all; the pleasure outweighed any small dis-comforts and the whole expedition was voted a success.

To us today a bivouac on the Mer de Glace might hardly seem worth mentioning; but to a young bride, straight from the Vic-torian drawing-rooms of English society, it must have been the event of a lifetime and an unforgettable introduction to the mountain world.

Whenever exciting events are being played out upon the screen of history it is discovered that there are backroom boys – or girls – at work who must not be overlooked if a true picture is to be presented. Among the early women mountaineers there were at least two such girls whose names have never been forgotten and whose writings are still referred to. The first of these was a Mrs Cole who, during the years 1850–8 made a complete tour round Monte Rosa. In 1859 she published a book which she modestly called *A Lady's Tour Around Monte Rosa*. It was attractively produced, with a wild rose embellished on the fly leaf, and is still sometimes referred to by modern mountain writers.

Mrs Cole explains that she wrote the book with a view to encouraging others to follow her example. In the early pages she has quite a lot of advice to give with regard to dress.

'Don't take anything unnecessary; much luggage causes lagging behind and disgusts the rest of the party.'

'Take a broadbrimmed hat, thus making a parasol unnecessary; also a dress of light woollen material, easy to dry. Small rings should be placed inside the seams with a cord drawn through to hoist the dress to requisite heights. Take a scotch plaid or two and a mackintosh cape with a hood.'

'Most important of all – strong boots with hobnails, something like gentlemen's shooting boots.'

Mrs Cole suggests that the only books that a lady should allow herself to be burdened with are those giving information about the flora, fauna and geological structure of the district. She must, however, have slipped a volume of Ruskin's works into her own luggage for she quotes freely from *The Stones of Venice*.

On their first visit to Monte Rosa in 1850 Mrs Cole and her party approached the district via the Gemmi Pass and the Zermatt valley. In those days there were few visitors to Zermatt and she must have been one of the very early lady visitors to Lauber's Inn, the only accommodation in the village. Catering had not yet become a fine art in the alpine centres of that time and there seems to have been a certain sameness about the menu – 'mutton broth, mutton boiled, mutton roasted, and mutton boiled'! But to compensate for this she had a room with a view of the Matterhorn which enchanted her; night after night she watched it 'shining like a mass of molten silver in the moonlight'. Ruskin himself could hardly have described it more vividly.

From the Schwarzsee they had their best views of Monte Rosa and felt they had really made its acquaintance; then they were away and over the Grand St Bernard to Aosta to explore the approaches from that direction.

In 1856 the party returned to Zermatt to find that Lauber's Inn had vanished and the Hotels Monte Rosa and Mont Cervin had taken its place. On the slopes of the Riffelberg the Riffelhaus had been built; this, for many years, became the starting point for most excursions in the Monte Rosa group. They went, of course, to the Gornergrat and found the panorama breathtaking; Mrs Cole gives a detailed list of all that can be seen for the benefit of those who followed after. They left Zermatt, 'still rather a miserable village', went down to Stalden and up to Saas Fee. From here they planned to cross the Monte Moro Pass to Macugnaga with Joseph Lochmatter as guide. This was a great adventure; there were jagged rocks and icy slabs but always there was 'a hand extended and a strong arm ready to assist'. The Monte Moro showed them an entirely new aspect of Monte Rosa and they went on down to Macugnaga fully satisfied.

On her third, and last, visit in 1858 Mrs Cole had the honour of having two members of the Alpine Club as her companions. This made the whole trip memorable; they came over the Grimsel in terrible weather and eventually arrived, as so often seems to have been the case, at Aosta. Here there occurred another interesting experience. Two English ladies, 'already past the noon of life', arrived at the hotel having made the circuit of Mont Blanc with an excellent Oberland guide. They had experienced most extraordinary difficulties but these apparently had only heightened their enthusiasm for the mountains. The party left Aosta for the Val Tournanche in order to ride up to Breuil and cross the Théodule Pass back to Zermatt. Sadly Mrs Cole was prevented from doing this; it was a cruel disappointment to her but she thoughtfully includes a description given her by a friend who had successfully accomplished the trip so that her book might be complete. She put a lot of hard work into her little volume; the last paragraph shows how much she hoped it might be an inspiration to others:

'Gentle Readers! . . . let me assure you that any lady blessed with moderate health and activity . . . may accomplish the tour of Monte Rosa with great delight and few inconveniences. But I would caution against any lady suddenly undertaking a prolonged and difficult expedition without some previous training.'

The book concludes with a suitable quotation from Wordsworth who, at that time, was the mountaineers' poet *par excellence*.

In 1861 Longmans Green, the London publishing house, brought out a small book entitled *Alpine Byways* with the sub-title *Light Leaves Gathered in 1859 and 1860* by 'A Lady'. The book is a period piece in one sense; it is richly decorated with twirling leaves and is illustrated by Victorian prints. But there the analogy ceases. It is a timeless book, written with the sensitive intuition of the true mountain lover; it re-invests the crowded tourist resorts of today with the peace and the newly-discovered thrill of mountaineering that was their essential characteristic in the days when they were simple alpine villages. It is a book that can be read and re-read and almost every word could be echoed by present-day mountaineers.

The Lady who wrote it would never have dreamed of describing herself as a mountaineer; she saw herself only as an alpine traveller. In her opening chapter she explains that a wide interest in alpine travel had grown up in her family and that 'without aspiring to exploits which may be deemed unfeminine' she was able to enjoy the wildest scenes of mountain grandeur with comparative ease. During several seasons she travelled the lesser-known routes with her husband, referred to as H-, her young son D-, and a lady friend C-.

The Lady's idea of 'comparative ease' would not be shared by many people, but the family engaged a first-class guide, Michael Alphonse Couttet of Chamonix, and he brought them safely through their many adventures.

The family travels were extensive, even by modern standards. During the summer seasons of 1859 and 1860 they visited, among other districts, the Bernese Oberland, Engelberg, the valley of Sixt, the Graian Alps, the Val Tournanche and the Zermatt and Saas valleys. Transport was by horse or mule or the quaint, uncomfortable *char-a-banc* of the time; but the greater part of their travelling was done on foot. They covered incredible distances.

Their first visit was to Mürren; here they climbed the Schilthorn where D- was first on the summit. The next day they ordered horses and rode via Grindelwald and Meiringen *en route* for Engstlen. They spent the night here in preparation for the ascent of the Titlis. They crossed the Joch Pass and the party was increased by two men carrying ropes and a 'hatchet', which sent D- into transports of delight. These were the extra guides engaged by Couttet for the Titlis. The family enjoyed every moment – steep arêtes, precipitous rocky corners, a glacier and a snowfield where the snow was exceptionally deep. The summit was reached successfully and the Lady records an enchanting description of the view.

The descent gave them their first experience of a glissade; they got drenched in a storm but rode happily into Engelberg in time for dinner. The Lady reports that their 'carpet bags did not carry an extensive change of garments', but with the kindly aid of the innkeeper no one suffered any ill effects.

The holiday continued across a succession of passes, the Gries, the Albrun and finally the Rawyl to the village of Anderlenk. Here their mountaineering finished for the season and after a short stay at Les Diablerets they managed the journey from there to Chamonix in one day – the horses of 1859 must have been gallant creatures.

The next year, 1860, the family gathered at Sixt to meet up again with Couttet. They explored the district on foot and on horseback – not without incident as the Lady was badly thrown by her most unreliable animal.

The valley of Sixt was only the beginning of this holiday and after some days they set out to cross the Col de Croux to the Val d'Illiez and Champéry. The description makes one envious of their way of travelling; it was so leisurely. Today we might consider it unduly time-consuming if we were impatient to get to the next centre to climb the next peak of our choice. But the Lady and her party saw infinitely more of the mountain world than would those of us who thumb a lift down one valley and another up the next. She succeeds in convincing one that the best and most delightful way of approaching Champéry must surely be over the Col de Croux. They loved Champéry and the thirteen-year-old D- considered it far superior to the valley of Sixt.

The next resting place was the Hospice of the Grand St Bernard from which they had hoped to cross the Col de Fenêtre and the Col de Ferret to Courmayeur. Mist and rain put paid to this and they had to be content with a drive down to Aosta. Aosta seems to have been as unattractive then as it is now and the party soon decided on an extended excursion up the Cogne valley where they were rewarded with magnificent views of the Matterhorn, Monte Rosa, the Grand Combin and the Grivola. From Cogne they climbed the Pousset with Couttet, who told them that it had only once before been 'attained by a lady'.

Once more the party was *en route* – this time for Chatillon where they proposed to get horses to ride up the Val Tournanche to Breuil and then cross the Théodule Pass to Zermatt. At the inn at Breuil there was tremendous excitement; Professor Tyndall and Mr V. Hawkins had gone with their guide Bennen to attempt the Matterhorn. They failed to reach the summit but got higher than anyone had yet been; this, of course, was the highlight of the holiday for D-.

The Lady and her party left Breuil before dawn for the Théodule with Couttet and three porters— They found the rocks easy, the snow deep but dry and uncrevassed, the air exhilarating and the views quite beyond description. Zermatt welcomed them with muddy lanes after heavy rainfall, but at the Hotel Mont Cervin their rooms were ready with letters and newspapers from London awaiting them – in 1860!

The *pièce de résistance* at Zermatt was to be the ascent of the Cima di Jazzi for which they were to start from the Riffelhaus on the Riffelberg. Their hostess up there was horrified that anyone so young as D- should be taken on such an adventure, describing him, to his great indignation, as '*le pauvre petit*'.

The party that set out from the Riffelhaus soon after 4 o'clock one morning was larger than usual; a local guide had been engaged by Couttet and they were also joined by their friend Mr Hawkins and his companion. Everyone, including Couttet, wore gauze veils, these being considered essential on a snow climb of this kind; Couttet added a professional touch with a coil of rope slung across his shoulders.

On the Riffelberg it was a clear, cloudless day but a canopy of cloud hung between them and Zermatt down in the valley, 'as if the world had not yet drawn its curtains to admit the morning light', as the Lady picturesquely suggests. They marched down the Gadmen path to the Gorner Glacier and reached the seemingly limitless snowfield after many detours to avoid crevasses. They were in the midst of a wide, white world and the keen wind which whistles from around the Cima was beginning to make its presence felt. The climb up the final cone was hard work; the snow was deep and the bitter wind blew it about them in clouds. As usual 'D-

was first on the summit'; the sky was cloudless and they hoped
for a perfect view. But the usual fate awaited them. Looking
down the great couloir Italy was entirely concealed in a *mêlée* of
seething clouds. Has *anyone ever* seen Italy from the summit of
the Cima di Jazzi? But that was the only disappointment; the
view in every other direction was sublime – from the Tyrolese
mountains in the east to Mont Blanc in the west; to the Oberland
in the north and the whole range of the Pennine Alps close at
hand.

The wind, as it still does, cut short their pleasure; in all its
history no one has ever been able to stand on the summit of the
Cima di Jazzi for more than ten minutes. The party turned in its
tracks and *glissaded* at speed down the deep, dry snow. On the
glacier the snow had become soft and the snow bridges were
dangerously insecure. One broke under Couttet as he hurried
across and he went in up to his shoulders – an event which has
certainly recurred down the ages with many parties on their way
to or from the Cima. Couttet was soon hauled back to safety;
they reached the moraine where all danger was over and entered
the Riffelhaus at three o'clock 'after an expedition of great excitement and novelty'.

After so many expeditions and ascents no one could fail to
include The Lady in any list of women mountaineers; but she
has other claims to fame. Research reveals that she was Mrs Henry
Freshfield and D-, '*le pauvre petit*', was none other than the famous
Douglas Freshfield, later President of the Alpine Club, President
of the Royal Geographical Society and a member of many Everest
committees. To be the mother of one of the greatest of all British
mountaineers lends a very special importance to The Lady who
wrote this charming book. And Douglas Freshfield, perhaps, was
the first of a long line of climbers, well known and unknown and
extending to the present day, who owe their mountaineering
careers to wise and generous parents who have given them their
first chance in the Alps as keen and impressionable teenagers;
thus setting them on a course which has brought a lifetime of
happiness and satisfaction.

Every year in the early 1860s the pioneers, mainly British, reached the summit of one great peak after another; only the Matterhorn remained inviolate and became the focal point of alpine attention. Meanwhile the ladies, frequently but not always encouraged by their menfolk, became increasingly adventurous.

Mrs Stephen Winkworth was climbing with her husband in the Valais and in the Oberland. In 1863, with the guides J. J. Bennen and J. B. Croz they attempted the Rothorn from Zermatt. There was no Trift Inn and no Rothorn Hut at that time; climbers had to sleep out or make the ascent direct from the village. The Wink-worths decided on the latter course as the lesser of two evils; they left the Monte Rosa Hotel at 3.15 a.m. but they experienced a bad day and many difficulties and failed to reach the top. They were not unduly disappointed and recorded in the hotel register that they made a rapid descent, witnessed a wonderful sunset and were back in the hotel at 8 p.m.

In the Oberland they were more fortunate; with the same guides they climbed the Jungfrau. Mrs Winkworth had the satisfaction of being the first lady to do so.

As all the world knows, the Matterhorn was climbed at last in 1865 by Edward Whymper and his British party consisting of Charles Hudson, Lord Francis Douglas and Douglas Hadow, with the two Taugwalders from Zermatt and Michel Croz from Chamonix as guides. On the descent disaster occurred; there was a slip; the rope broke; Hudson, Hadow, Lord Francis Douglas and Michel Croz were all killed. The event shattered the climbing world of Europe and far beyond; newspaper reporters in every country told their stories and pronounced their verdicts regardless of whether they knew anything about the matter or not. For a year or two 'mountaineering' became almost a dirty word.

In 1867, while the battle over the cause of the tragedy was still raging, a group of Italians crept quietly out of the village of Breuil *en route* for the Italian ridge of the Matterhorn. They were J. J. and J. P. Maquinaz, Victor Maquinaz, Caesar Carrel and J. M. Carrel – these Carrels were not related to the famous Jean-Antoine Carrel, Whymper's rival in 1865. For some reason J. M. Carrel took with him his daughter Félicité: possibly, in spite of the opprobrium with which people still regarded the Matterhorn, she hoped to be the first woman to climb it. She very nearly succeeded. The party was only three hundred feet below the summit when a tremendous gale roared up. It blew Félicité's skirt over her head; unfortunately she was wearing a crinoline which made matters worse. Her father and his friends had the greatest difficulty in disentangling her; the wind continued unabated and the situation became so dangerous on account of Félicité's skirt that they had to abandon the climb. To make up for the disappointment they christened the spot they had reached on the Italian ridge *Col Félicité* and so it remains to this day. Thus the intrepid Félicité left her mark upon the Matterhorn in spite of her failure to achieve the summit.

Gradually the clouds hanging over mountaineering lifted; before the end of the decade they had dispersed and revealed a small but brilliant crowd of women climbers who had been quietly finding their feet in the Alps while the storms of controversy raged. The stage was set for a new era in mountaineering; the Golden Age of women mountaineers was about to begin.

Chapter 3

Petticoat Pioneers

It came as something of a shock to mid-Victorian minds to discover that, incredible as it might seem, lady mountaineers actually existed. People suddenly became aware of the fact; the exploits of the great male pioneers were known to all; their names were household words; but climbing by women was unheard of; such a thing was entirely out of keeping with the current idea of a well-bred young lady. At first Victorian drawing-rooms were horrified, but so demure and so unobtrusive were these adventurous young women that no public scandal ensued. The critics shrugged their shoulders and left it at that and slowly but surely women climbers were not only accepted but publicly applauded.

The very first woman, and still one of the most famous, to climb regularly in the Alps was Miss Lucy Walker. She arrived in 1858 with her father and brother, both already well known as alpinists. Lucy was twenty-two at the time; she had never previously engaged in any form of sport but she took to mountaineering at once – in a quiet, business like, self-assured way. She was rather a large young woman with dark ringlets and pronounced spectacles. History places her among the 'new' women the Victorian age produced. This was not at all how Lucy Walker regarded herself. She was not interested in the status of women, nor in their position with regard to sport. Apart from a little quiet croquet her only physical activity was mountaineering and she climbed because she liked it. It gave her insights into a world she hardly knew existed – a world of beauty and excitement where even danger had a part. Having seen the vision she was captivated; mountains henceforward became part of her life. But she climbed essentially as a woman; she never got round to wearing breeches;

throughout her long career she climbed always in voluminous skirts – usually in a white, print frock which was carefully refurbished after each ascent.

Every year the Walker family came to the Alps; moving from one mountain district to the next, from valley to valley, from centre to centre. Meanwhile the long-suffering wife and mother of them all pursued her family from place to place with clean clothes, mending materials and bundles of letters sent out from England. She it was who saw to it that they set out on each new adventure dry and well-shod, with adequate and suitable provisions in the rucksack carried by the guide. Not that Lucy's provisions caused much difficulty – all she required on the mountains was a diet of champagne and sponge cake.

Lucy Walker's introduction to high mountains took place in the Oberland. Staying with her family at the Schwarenbach Inn she announced that she wished to make the ascent of the Altels. Her father suggested Melchior Anderegg as a suitable guide. Melchior accepted the engagement, conducted the young lady up the mountain and returned her safely to the family circle. From that day Lucy never climbed with any other guide. In the course of twenty-one years they made ninety-eight expeditions together – never alone it must be clearly explained. Such indiscreet behaviour would have been quite unthinkable; Papa or brother Horace were always in attendance and Lucy preferred it that way. Nevertheless theirs was one of the first great guide–climber partnerships which are among the richest rewards that mountaineering brings. Once, when she was in middle life, someone asked Lucy why she had never married. The reply came back instantly, 'I love mountains and Melchior, and Melchior already has a wife.' The easy-going morals of the twentieth century had no part in her philosophy of life.

In 1862 Lucy did the Dufourspitze of Monte Rosa (15,002 feet) with her father and Melchior and followed this up with an ascent of the Finsteraarhorn. In 1864, again with her father, she was on the Rimpfischhorn and later in the season the Walkers, *en famille*, made the pioneer ascent of the Balmhorn; on all these trips Melchior Anderegg was of course the leading guide.

Already, therefore, before the boom in women's climbing began in the 1870s, Lucy Walker was a thoroughly experienced alpinist. But no one had ever heard of her – in those early days there was nothing to suggest that she would become the heroine of her generation whose legendary spirit still hovers benignly over the world of women's climbing a hundred years later. Suddenly all was changed. On 20th July 1871 Lucy climbed the Matterhorn, the first woman to do so, and that only six years after the success and subsequent tragedy of Edward Whymper's party.

The story goes that she began the ascent in a crinoline but discreetly removed it early in the climb, having heard of the unfortunate happenings caused by the crinoline of Félicité Carrel. It makes a good story – it might even be true – but everything we know about Lucy suggests that she wore her usual white print frock and suffered no apparent inconvenience. What she wore is of little importance compared with the fact that she had actually climbed the much-feared and ever-compelling Matterhorn. She became news at once; even those who had doubts about the propriety of such doings were filled with admiration.

On 26th August *Punch* published a poem in her honour entitled 'A Climbing Girl'. By this time news of her earlier exploits was being noised abroad, including the fact that she had been the first woman on the Weisshorn and the Lyskamm even before her success on the Matterhorn. Lucy rapidly became a striking figure in alpine circles; no gathering seemed quite complete without her – and this in spite of her quiet, unassuming disposition. In Whymper's famous picture, *The Clubroom at Zermatt*, she is the only woman in the group; standing behind her father in front of the door of the Monte Rosa Hotel.

In 1879, on her doctor's orders, she gave up long expeditions but she never forsook the mountains. She came every year to the Alps, meeting her old friends, calling on Melchior Anderegg and his family in their Oberland home and always spending a few days at the Monte Rosa at Zermatt, where she was received as a loved and honoured friend.

Lucy's glory never faded at home or abroad. In Liverpool,

where she eventually reigned over the family home, she led an active social life as a charming hostess and loyal friend. She was an expert needlewoman and an authority on the literature of many foreign countries. It was not necessary to be a mountaineer to be included in Lucy's wide circle of friends.

But it was among mountains and among climbers that her deepest loyalties lay and where her many gifts found their best expression. She was one of the first members of the Ladies' Alpine Club when it was founded in 1907, doing all she could to help it through the early precarious years. In 1912, at the age of seventy-six, she became its second President. To this office she brought the dignity, lack of ostentation and firm gentleness that had always characterised her. It was not easy to make the long journey from Liverpool for the annual dinner but she insisted on doing so, to the special delight of the younger members who still regarded her with immense admiration. She lived largely in the past but she had no jealousy or bitterness for the present or the future. Her speeches at the dinners were witty and racy; members looked eagerly for her broad smiling face and her straight smooth hair, neatly coiled in a bun at the back; her arrival was always something of a sensation.

In 1915 in the *Journal of the Ladies' Alpine Club* she paid her simply, glowing tribute to Melchior Anderegg who had died in December 1914 at the age of eighty-six.

'He is known to the present generation', she wrote, 'as the greatest Swiss guide of his own or any time. In addition he was one of the finest and most well-bred gentlemen I have ever known. He always thought of others, never of himself, and his courtesy to all was unfailing.'

In September of the next year, 1916, less than two years after the death of her beloved guide, Lucy Walker died peacefully in Liverpool.

While Lucy Walker was establishing her brilliant career with her father and brother two English sisters were building up a hardly less remarkable reputation for alpine exploits. The Misses Anna and Ellen Pigeon were members of a large family of daughters

living with their parents on Clapham Common. Like Lucy
Walker they were quiet, unspectacular women; they were already
in their mid-thirties before they undertook their biggest expeditions – an age at which, in those days, most spinsters having been
placed firmly on the shelf were occupying their spare time with
their tatting. This was not how Anna and Ellen Pigeon visualised
life. For something like ten years they travelled out to the Alps
every summer, engaged guides and porters and set out on a
climbing programme devised entirely by themselves. Their
adventures awakened considerable interest long after they had
given up active mountaineering and in 1885, in response to
repeated requests, they published a slim little volume called
Peaks and Passes, a diary account of their achievements between
1869 and 1876. Ellen Pigeon had evidently married by this time,
the authorship of the book is Anna Pigeon and Ellen Abbott.
More than twenty years later *Peaks and Passes* was presented to
the library of the Ladies' Alpine Club and is today one of its very
prized possessions.

Their list of achievements is impressive; in seven years they
climbed sixty-three peaks and crossed seventy-two passes. The
entries in the diary are always brief and succinct and sum up in a
few words exactly what these ladies thought about any particular
ascent. In the manner of the times in which they lived meticulous
attention is paid to detail. This in no way detracts from the book,
in fact it adds to the interest and amusement – if only because no
modern writer would ever dream of mentioning such things. For
example:

'Sunday – 6.0 a.m. church.'

'Stayed at the Riffel for Monte Rosa, could not go owing to
non-arrival of luggage.'

'After church walked up to the Bel Alp.'

'Could not start early enough on August 15th owing to Fête
Day so remained in the village.'

(Incidentally this experience could be repeated up to the present
day by those of us who climb with guides. 15th August is sacro-
sanct in the Roman Catholic valleys of Switzerland and no guide
leaves the village.)

Entries dealing solely with climbing are equally evocative.

'Failed on Aiguille Verte thanks to a Chamonix guide.'

'Tried Mont Collon with Jos. Gillioz who failed to find the way. Out 17½ hours and no peak.'

'After descending Bietschhorn to Rhône valley drove in hay cart to Visp.'

Anna and Ellen were tough and courageous; there are frequent references to sleeping out on alps, in hay chalets and in Swiss huts. Even when attempting the biggest and most difficult peaks they thought nothing of spending the preceding night in the open at a considerable height. 'Slept out for Gabelhorn', 'Slept out for Weisshorn' are only two of many occasions when most mountaineers would have thought that a reasonable night in an S.A.C. Hut was essential.

In 1873 they made a successful pioneer expedition – the first traverse of the Matterhorn from Breuil to Zermatt by women. The climb was made under very difficult conditions; they slept at the Italian Hut on the Matterhorn and during the night a fierce snowstorm occurred. Fresh snow on the Matterhorn usually means that the mountain is out of condition for a couple of days. But it took more than a snowstorm to deter Anna and Ellen; they were accompanied by three excellent guides – Jean-Antoine Carrel, K. Maquignaz and J. Martin from Breuil and between them it was decided that the mountain would 'go'. It did 'go' – entirely without incident and the ladies were not in the least aware of having achieved anything extraordinary.

One entry for 1874 has a truly feminine flavour. 'Tried the Aiguille Verte but got caught in a snowstorm together with Messrs Matthews and Morshead of the A.C. *Both* parties had to return.'

To be denied the Aiguille Verte on an earlier occasion because the guides failed to find the way was frustrating. To be turned back by weather conditions which also defeated two of the most experienced members of the Alpine Club was something entirely different.

Their most famous and dramatic mountain expedition took place in 1869 at the very beginning of their alpine careers. In the autumn of that year they crossed the Sesia Joch from Zermatt to Alagna. This pass had only once been crossed before – in 1862 by Messrs George and Moore of the Alpine Club – when it had been regarded as 'a most daring exploit', possibly a *tour de force* which should never be repeated.

Members of the Alpine Club were astounded to hear of the remarkable adventures of Anna and Ellen, especially as the latter part of the climb involved descending a very severe wall of rock. However, strict investigations were made of the facts, some notes were supplied by the Misses Pigeon themselves and the Alpine Club agreed unanimously that they had indeed crossed the pass by this very bold route.

The newspaper *Monte Rosa Gazetta delle Val Sesia* carried a highly coloured account of the expedition on 4th September 1869. This included a purple patch concerning the descent of the wall of rock where the climbers, their guide and their porter, according to the paper, were 'in the most imminent peril of rolling as shapeless corpses into the crevasses below'. The account concluded with a paragraph in which the view was expressed that the absence of fatal consequences was largely due 'to the masculine education, too little imitated by the Italians, which the English give their children'.

The modest account which Anna and Ellen sent on request to the Alpine Club gives a more credible and sober picture of the course of events. They explained quite frankly that it was partly due to them that the guide, Jean Martin of Anniviers, kept too far to the left and thus missed the Lysjoch – the pass they were intending to cross. They were translating to him passages from *Ball's Guide Book* which repeatedly exhorted travellers not to wander too far to the right. They mentioned that they were lucky in that fresh snow decreased the labour of step-cutting on the descent of the ice slope. They lost much time because the guide and porter so frequently had to leave them while they went off to reconnoitre. At 5 p.m. it seemed as if further descent was impossible; heavy mist made things worse; sunset was approaching when the guide at last found a way down onto the glacier. This they literally ran across in a desperate attempt to reach the comparative safety of the moraine before darkness finally fell. At 8.45 p.m., after nearly eighteen hours out in the mountains, nine of which had been spent on the descent, they found the welcome shelter of a shepherd's hut. No mention is made in the ladies' notes to the Alpine Club that the porter was so incompetent that one of them – whether Anna or Ellen is not known – was obliged to come down last on the rope for the whole of the descent. They merely state that the porter was of no use whatever except to carry the knapsack. The Alpine Club, however, was by this time well aware of the true facts and has recorded them for posterity in Volume V of the Alpine Journal.

We do not hear much about the later years of Ellen Pigeon after she married, but in a letter to W. A. B. Coolidge in 1892 she wrote, 'In days gone by many members of the Alpine Club would not speak to us.' The chief offender seems to have been Sir W. E. Davidson, at that time Permanent Legal Adviser to the Foreign Office. He held very strong opinions about women and mountains and was particularly offensive. This was only a passing phase; by 1911 Sir Edward Davidson was an honoured guest at the Ladies' Alpine Club dinner and the Misses Pigeon are still held in great regard by the Alpine Club.

Anne Pigeon remained active almost to the end of her life. She became a member of the Ladies' Alpine Club in 1908, was elected a Vice-President in 1910 and remained a keen member until her death in her Clapham Common home on 15th March 1917, at the age of eighty-four.

In September 1865, just two months after the Matterhorn disaster, there arrived in Zermatt an American lady, Miss Meta Brevoort, accompanied by her fifteen-year-old nephew – a rather short, fat boy, noted for picking up every disease that flesh is heir to. Miss Brevoort decided that the air of Europe, and particularly that of the Alps, was exactly what this unhealthy child needed. She loved the mountains herself and had every intention of inspiring her nephew with the same passion. She succeeded far better than she could possibly have hoped – the nephew was W. A. B. Coolidge who became one of the most famous and controversial figures in the alpine world and one of its best-known historians.

On this first occasion they climbed the Cima di Jazzi and crossed the Théodule Pass; Coolidge hero-worshipped his aunt and partly because of this was completely captivated by the mountains. In a sense he owed everything to her; without her encouragement he might never have taken to serious mountaineering.

Meta Brevoort was a mountaineer in her own right; like Lucy Walker she was one of the first women to engage in a regular programme of ascents season after season. She was not particularly strong and not in the least masculine; but she had tremendous vitality and an immense capacity for enjoying everything. She was a colourful personality and could make any event an exciting occasion. In the year that she first brought her nephew to Switzerland Meta Brevoort climbed Mont Blanc with Mme Sylvain Couttet, two guides and two porters. On the summit they drank champagne, after which she insisted that they should dance a quadrille in the snow and cap the performance with a spirited rendering of the *Marseillaise*.

Like her nephew Meta Brevoort did not look much like a climber; she was slow-moving and always much encumbered with heavy clothing. She never ceased experimenting with her clothes but never finally attained satisfaction. One imagines that she endured the flannelette drawers, heavily boned corsets and calico chemises in vogue at the time as more or less inevitable; something about which nothing could be done. But skirts were a different matter; she devised a scheme which included a cord run through a series of rings round the bottom of the skirt; by this means she hoped to haul the skirt up at least a few inches. The experiment proved to be entirely useless and she complained that her skirt was more sodden than ever and, as a result, she had to baste the hem. On at least one occasion she was driven to trousers; she must have been truly desperate; such behaviour was absolutely taboo in the code of etiquette of the day. However, none of these things affected her climbing; she was first-class and achieved many pioneer ascents.

Most of her climbing, although not all, was done with her

nephew Coolidge – usually accompanied by the dog Tschingel about whom we shall hear later. They were back in the Alps in 1867 and in 1868, and in that year they engaged Christian Almer as their guide and began their serious climbing career together. Meta Brevoort had two great ambitions. The first of these was to be the first woman to climb the Matterhorn. She attempted it in 1869 from the Italian side without success; in 1871, with all her plans carefully laid, she arrived in Zermatt only to find that Lucy Walker had made the ascent only a day or two earlier. She was bitterly disappointed but quite undaunted and within a few days, with her nephew and their guides, she made the first traverse by a woman, from Zermatt by the Hörnli ridge descending to Breuil by the Italian ridge.

In September of the same year they climbed the Bietschhorn; it was an exciting expedition as on the descent they were forced to bivouac in a cave on the edge of the glacier without food or blankets. It was dangerous to sleep as they might become frozen, and Christian Almer kept them awake by yodelling lustily throughout the night. Meta Brevoort wrote a paper, entitled 'A Day and a Night on the Bietschhorn' which she submitted to the Alpine Club under Coolidge's name – knowing that it would never be accepted under her own. It makes delightful reading and contains the nice little details and descriptions which women can do so well and which no man would ever think of mentioning.

Winter climbing had scarcely been heard of in those days (certainly nothing of any consequence had been done by a woman) but on 15th January 1874 Meta Brevoort successfully ascended the Wetterhorn with Coolidge and Christian Almer and three porters; she followed this up on 22nd January with the first winter ascent of the Jungfrau.

Meta Brevoort's second dearest wish, perhaps even dearer than her first, was to be the first woman to climb the Meije in the Dauphiné. In 1870 her party had made the first ascent of the Pic Central or Doigt de Dieu. This was quite an achievement but it did not satisfy her. The Meije became a ruling passion; they returned year after year always to be defeated by bad weather. At last in 1876 there seemed some hope that they might be lucky. But funds were beginning to run low; Meta always kept an eye on the expenses; there was not sufficient cash to support two climbers in the Dauphiné. With that selflessness which she always displayed where her nephew was concerned, she decided to remain in the Oberland so that he might do greater things in the Dauphiné. When they were separated in the Alps aunt and nephew corresponded daily; Meta Brevoort's letter from the Oberland showed how much the Meije meant to her. 'Give my love to all my dear old friends', she wrote, 'and especially to that glorious Meije and ask her to keep herself for me.'

Alas, it was not to be; only a few months later she contracted rheumatic fever; it affected her heart and in five days she was dead. Meta Brevoort's greatest wishes may not have been granted but by her unlimited courage and exuberant spirit she lighted up the alpine scene of those days for all time.

No apology need be made for including among the outstanding women mountaineers of this period a lady who climbed on all fours. This was Tschingel, the faithful bitch who for nine years accompanied Meta Brevoort and Coolidge on their adventures in the Alps, earning for the latter the description: 'The young American who climbs with his aunt and his dog'. She became as famous as any human climber of her time.

Tschingel was born in 1865 and was originally the dog of the Oberland guide Christian Almer. She was so named because, as a puppy, she made a successful crossing of the Tschingel Pass. She was at first thought to be a male but soon gave the lie to this belief by producing a litter of puppies. Meta Brevoort refused to recognise the puppies as any connection of Tschingel's and obstinately referred to her as 'he' to the end of her life.

In 1868, when Coolidge and Meta Brevoort engaged Christian Almer for a month, they successfully climbed the Wetterhorn but three days later failed on the Eiger owing to poor conditions. The teenage Coolidge, at that time somewhat spoiled and pampered, was inconsolable; Christian Almer sympathised with his disappointment and as they trudged sadly back to Grindelwald promised him Tschingel as a gift – explaining that Bella, one of her sons, was now suitable as a watchdog. Coolidge, who shared his aunt's love of animals, was delighted. The following day Tschingel was brought to the hotel and formally presented; she solaced her young master during a week of bad weather and on 18th July set out with the party for a successful ascent of the Blümisalphorn.

This season launched Tschingel on her remarkable career, if one regards her two earlier minor ascents in 1865 as a prelude. Between 1868 and 1876 she did sixty-six major peaks and about one hundred minor expeditions. She was involved in no less than three first ascents and three first traverses of passes. On the occasion when Coolidge and Meta Brevoort were forced to bivouac during the descent of the Bietschhorn, Tschingel had wisely decided to remain in the tent and welcomed them back with a friendly if somewhat 'I-told-you-so' bark. When they made their winter ascents of the Wetterhorn and Jungfrau she made it plain that she preferred the comparative comfort of the huts.

The account of her ascent of Mont Blanc in 1875 is slightly reminiscent of Henriette d'Angeville nearly forty years earlier. When Tschingel reached the summit a cannon was fired in her honour and Meta Brevoort, writing to her sister about the triumphant return to Chamonix, explained that Tschingel entered the village with her head held high and wagging her tail. The next day, prone on a sofa in the hotel drawing-room, she held court to several hundred people and all the guides.

Tschingel never climbed the Matterhorn; her master made all arrangements for her to do so but Meta Brevoort, who was not in Zermatt at the time, could not bear not to be included in the party and wrote begging that the expedition should be delayed until she could be present. Coolidge agreed and to everyone's sorrow the opportunity never occurred again.

With regard to her canine lineage it seems that Tschingel could hardly be described as an aristocrat. People had their own ideas about her breed and someone even spoke of her as a bloodhound. She was, in fact, a rather large beagle; she had a brown coat with a tidy white shirt-front and four white stockings; her large soulful brown eyes won all hearts. She looked and behaved like a perfect little lady whatever skeletons there may have been in the ancestral kennel.

Tschingel's climbing outfit consisted of a ring on her collar (her workaday collar, that is, she possessed a smarter one) through which the rope was looped. Coolidge had four special little leather boots made for her but these she despised as too human and promptly kicked them off. The party must have been an intriguing sight; the two men, Christian Almer and Coolidge, in front; the two ladies, Tschingel and Meta Brevoort, behind; all roped in good order making their way over glacier, snowfield, pass and peak. There was never an accident of any kind and, so far from being an encumbrance, Tschingel once, when the guide had lost the way, rediscovered the route and led the party home in triumph over the glacier.

Tschingel, of course, lived in England with her owner. She journeyed out to the Alps every year in a special travelling box and gave great pleasure to all by recognising Christian Almer almost as soon as she saw him. Her 'Sunday best' collar, as distinct from the 'workaday' model, was a handsome affair decorated with a host of little silver medallions recording her alpine achievements – it was never worn while climbing but was reserved for state occasions. Felicitas von Reznicek, in her book, *Von der Krinoline zum sechsten Grad* – a book about women mountaineers – describes how on one occasion when Tschingel was returning to England from the Alps with Coolidge and Meta Brevoort a reception committee met them at Victoria Station. Tschingel was arrayed in her best collar and was the centre of attention while her little medallions were examined with astonishment and congratulations were showered upon her.

When Meta Brevoort died so suddenly just before Christmas in 1876 Tschingel had made her last ascent in the previous summer – the first ascent of the second peak of the Fusshörner. Perhaps it was fitting that their climbing days should end together. By the next summer she was getting too blind to travel with her master, who found himself suddenly deprived of both his lady companions. She continued to live comfortably in Surrey in the old home of Miss Brevoort until the summer of 1879 when Coolidge realised that life held nothing more for her and made the hard decision that it was best that she should go. Mercifully he was spared the agony of implementing it – a kindly Providence intervened and on 16th June Tschingel died peacefully in her sleep in her basket in front of the kitchen fire. She was buried at Dorking, full of years and honours.

Coolidge carefully kept her 'Sunday best' collar; he retired at length to Grindelwald and forty years after Tschingel's death he showed a friend the well-loved little collar hanging behind the front door of his mountain home.

About this time Frances Ridley Havergal the hymn writer came out to Switzerland. She was a frail, delicate creature, even more prone to the vapours than most of her contemporaries. She had had a strictly orthodox evangelical upbringing but she was quite a scholar in a quiet way; she was an expert in Hebrew and Greek and was able to converse fluently in French and German.

The Alps opened up a totally new world to Frances; she fell in love with everything she found. Not only the mountains themselves but the streams and the flowers, the quiet, quaint villages and the mountain people. The great peaks she found strangely compelling; she was remarkably adventurous and had she enjoyed better opportunities she might have developed into a good climber. In the circumstances she never achieved any very great heights but the modest expeditions she undertook gave her immense pleasure and satisfaction and her ready pen made them live for others. Her book *Swiss Letters* is quite a Victorian treasure and is eagerly snapped up on the stalls of second-hand bookshops today.

For many mountaineers the alpine dawn is one of the best moments of any climb; Frances Ridley Havergal's description of meeting the dawn as her party ascended the Sparrenhorn is a gem of alpine literature. She speaks of the 'daffodil sky' which Tyndall had mentioned, the 'calm glory of expectant light', 'the valley dark and gravelike in contrast below'. She watched enthralled as the first rose flush struck the Mischabel and then the Weisshorn – 'it was rose *fire*, delicate yet intense'. We have all seen it; many of us have experienced the same emotions; not all of us could express them so vividly.

Frances had the greatest admiration for the guides as a race; only one disappointed her and he succeeded in spoiling her trip to the Grindelwald glacier. At Zermatt she longed to do the Cima di Jazzi but carefully explained in a letter home that unless a certain Miss Anstey arrived this would be impossible as of course she was 'not so demented as to go on a climb *alone* with a guide unless she had a lady companion as well'. Like all her generation she remained true to the strict standards demanded by the times in which she lived. Unfortunately Miss Anstey, the sister of an Alpine Club member, failed to turn up and the expedition had to be abandoned. Instead they engaged a guide for the traverse of the Théodule Pass from Zermatt to Breuil and on to Chatillon. This seems to have been a very satisfactory excursion and made up for other disappointments.

Frances Ridley Havergal visited most of the big alpine centres and Chamonix remained her favourite. Together with a friend she made endless excursions with and without guides; the final 'feather in their caps' – to use her own words – was the ascent to the Grands Mulets on Mont Blanc. It was June and this was *'la première ascension'* of the year and was rated in the guides' tariff book as being a *'course extraordinaire'*.

They left in the afternoon and slept at Pierre Pointue: the guides lit a bonfire of rhododendrons to show the Chamonix hotels how far they had reached. At three o'clock the next morning they were off via Pierre à l'Échelle. Here they roped up and to Frances' delight it was real alpine club rope with a red thread running through it. The snow was soft enough for them to sink in up to their knees and crevasses were so frequent that the guides were constantly exhorting them to *'Faîtes tendre la corde'!* (Stretch the rope). However, all went well and they reached the Grands Mulets at eight o'clock: their arrival was observed in Chamonix and they were rewarded with a salvo of four cannonades.

On the descent the next morning there seems to have been only one *contretemps*: Frances slipped on the steep snow and pulled the guide out of his tracks; their far too rapid descent was halted by the last man on the rope who flung himself on his back. When the time came to remove the rope the whole party indulged in a series of rapid *glissades* and eventually arrived back in Chamonix three hours earlier than they had been expected.

Once more Chamonix excelled itself in its welcome; '*la première ascension*' of 1873 was quite something and everyone was as frantic with excitement 'as if we had returned from the moon itself'. There was champagne all round and ecstactic congratulations. The *Journal de Genève* implored them to write a short article for the paper and Frances being accustomed to journalism at last agreed to do so. She found the whole incident uproariously amusing, especially as most of the excitement was caused by the fact that the first ascent of the season had been done by a lady – such a thing had never happened before!

Frances Ridley Havergal's climbing achievements are trifling compared even with those of her own generation but she was a mountaineer at heart and her books have an assured place in climbing literature.

In these early years, when mountaineering by women was getting into its stride, most of the ladies – apart from the Misses Pigeon – seem to have been quite content to be the only woman in a male party. But there were two who for a number of years invariably travelled about the Alps together.

Miss Emmeline Lewis Lloyd was Welsh, brought up in an enormous house in the middle of Wales where she became an expert with rod and line. This sport did not engage her vitality sufficiently and she decided to take to mountaineering. She was short and fat and thoroughly good-natured and ready for any-thing. She was full of self-confidence and nothing upset her equilibrium. The story is told that when returning from a solitary evening scramble above Gressoney she fell into conversation with a stranger whom she took to be a chamois hunter. He escorted her back to her hotel discussing mountaineering matters in perfect English. It did not occur to Miss Lewis-Lloyd to ask who he was until he had gone; she took quite calmly the news that her com-panion had in fact been King Victor Emmanuel of Italy.

Miss Isabella Straton was Emmeline Lewis-Lloyd's constant companion for many years. She first visited the Alps when she was twenty-three, but it was not until she was twenty-seven that climbing really got under her skin and she began her long association with Emmeline Lewis-Lloyd. Their similar approach to mountaineering was the real bond between them. They did not feel the compelling power of the mountains in the way in which many of their contemporaries did. They were really early exponents of Women's Lib who could see no reason why any sport – and particularly mountaineering – should be the preserve of men. They set to work to prove their case with great courage and determination and met with considerable success.

With two guides they made the first ascent of the Aiguille de Moine and the first ascent by women of Monte Viso. About 1873 Emmeline Lewis-Lloyd gave up serious climbing but Isabella Straton continued her remarkable career, climbing usually with Jean Charlet as guide. She made four ascents of Mont Blanc, including the first winter ascent; she did the Aiguille du Midi; the North Summit of the Aiguille de Blaitière and the first ascent of the Pointe Isabella; the Dents du Midi and the Dom, not to mention many ascents in the Pyrenees.

Isabella Straton was a wealthy woman, endowed with a private income of £4,000 a year, but this did not prevent her eventually marrying her guide, Jean Charlet. She had met him first when he worked for a short spell as a groom for Emmeline Lewis-Lloyd in Wales. In those days it was a little unusual, to say the least, for rich young women to marry grooms. But Isabella cared as little for convention as did her friend Emmeline. She settled down with Jean Charlet in a small house near Chamonix, continued to climb as Isabella Charlet-Straton, had two sons, one of whom climbed Mont Blanc at the age of thirteen and the other at eleven and a half, and appears to have lived happily ever after.

Shortly after Meta Brevoort disappeared from the alpine scene another remarkable lady took up the torch. She was Miss Kathleen Richardson, an Englishwoman, and an entirely different type from most of the women climbers of those days. She was *petite* and dainty and fragile-looking, with brown hair and grey-green eyes. Her appearance was deceptive; she was unusually tough and utterly tireless.

She was sixteen when she paid her first visit to Zermatt; the mountains immediately held her in thrall and she was discovered scrambling about on the rocks of the Hörnli. The next year she was in the Engadine and soon had two or three climbs to her credit. During the next eleven years Kathleen Richardson made 116 major ascents; six of them were pioneer first ascents and fourteen were first ascents by a woman – small wonder that the French christened her 'the immortal Miss Richardson'.

From Zermatt in one week, in the year 1882, she did the Zinal Rothorn, Weisshorn, Matterhorn and Monte Rosa. She must have travelled from peak to peak without any respite in the village. When one remembers that huts were primitive, and in many cases virtually non-existent, one marvels at the tremendous physical achievement.

One of Kathleen Richardson's most outstanding exploits was her pioneer ascent of the Aiguille de Bionnassay which included the traverse of the East Ridge and the Ice Ridge to the Dome du Goûter. After this success the *Morning Post* wrote, 'The honours of 1888 fall to a lady, Miss Richardson, who, with Emile Rey and J. J. Bich, ascended the Aiguille de Bionnassay and traversed the eastern arête to the Dome du Goûter, previously considered impossible!' For most women this might have been enough for a week or two but not so for Miss Richardson. She proceeded, within a few days, to traverse all five points of the Grand Charmoz – even her guides must have been hard put to it to keep up with her.

After the Grand Charmoz she set off rather precipitately for the Dauphiné; a rumour was circulating that an English woman, whom no one could identify, was planning to make the first ascent of the Meije. This did not suit Kathleen Richardson at all; she herself had very definite designs on the Meije. Demure and fragile as she might appear, if she got her teeth into anything she was not inclined to let go. She arrived with all speed in La Bérarde, only to find that it was her own reputation that had preceded her. She at once decided to turn rumour into unassailable fact and climbed the Meije straight from La Bérarde in one day.

'Katy' Richardson, as she became affectionately called by her friends, was the essence of feminity; she always climbed in a skirt and however strenuous the climb on which she was engaged she lived quite contentedly on bread and butter, with honey or jam, and tea. Nothing would persuade her that there was anything unusual about her mountaineering career; to the end of her life she refused to consider herself in any sense a 'famous' climber and seemed quite amazed if people remarked on her many pioneer ascents.

It is almost impossible to separate 'Katy' Richardson from Miss Mary Paillon, although they did not meet until 1888 when 'Katy' had already been climbing for a good many years. But their long and treasured friendship and the many great climbs they did in partnership have bound their names together inextricably – and they would not wish it to be otherwise.

Mary Paillon came from a French medical family and was a very different personality from 'Katy' Richardson. She inherited excellent health and immense energy from her mother – a remarkable woman who climbed Mont Blanc at the age of sixty. Mary grew up with a group of brothers and did all her training and most of her early climbs with them.

She met 'Katy' Richardson in 1888, two days after the latter's ascent of the Meije. They very soon formed a close friendship and 'Katy' came to live on the estate of the Paillon family at Oullins near Lyons; she remained there until she died in 1927.

Together, during several years, they established a number of records and their mountaineering programme each year was quite astonishing. In the severe winter of 1890–1 they made a traverse in snow shoes of the Belledonne group – the party included Mary Paillon's mother and her brother Maurice. In 1891 they set out for the Méridionale d'Arves; it proved to be a unique occasion. It was the first ascent of this mountain by women and it nearly ended in disaster. Mary Paillon's skirts which, unlike 'Katy' Richardson, she much disliked, swept away a stone which crashed down on 'Katy's' head. It might easily have killed her but fortunately very little harm was done. As they neared the summit 'Katy' drew back and urged Mary on ahead saying 'You go first. I have the Meije: you take the Aiguille d'Arves.'

In 1893 they made the third ascent by women of the Meije Orientale and each succeeding summer they were out in the mountains again, more often than not in the Dauphiné Alps. In 1897 they did the Pelvoux – one of the peaks of the Pelvoux *massif* has since been named the Pointe Richardson – but it proved to be the last big climb for both of them. On the descent Mary Paillon began to realise that her failing sight was becoming a danger to herself and her companions on the rope. She decided to give up climbing high peaks; it was a hard decision and an unselfish one. 'Katy' Richardson, ever mindful of her friend's feelings, loyally followed suit and forthwith was lost to major mountaineering.

But these two friends were mountain lovers as well as mountaineers; they continued to walk in the hills with ever-increasing enjoyment, getting even more happiness out of the lower ranges now that the great peaks were denied to them. 'Katy' made watercolour sketches of the mountains, Mary wrote articles and gave lectures about alpine subjects in general and her climbing contemporaries in particular.

Mary Paillon was an interesting, if slightly complicated, character. She had a great love of nature which found expression in her climbing; but she was a born feminist and the mountains were a useful outlet for this passion. She was most insistent that women ought to wear breeches rather than skirts for climbing, knowing full well that such an idea was still considered very fast and that she was certainly going too far in suggesting it. She was never, in fact, seen wearing breeches herself. Similarly, she was in the forefront of the campaign for votes for women, but when at last the battle was won she did not use her vote. It was the principle involved which engaged her energies; she had little interest in the concrete results.

For many years she continued her alpine writings until her blindness became too much of a handicap. She was saddened by the death of her favourite brother in 1938; an even greater blow was the loss of her nephew Hugues in the Second World War.

Nevertheless, Mary Paillon kept her faith and her courage to the end; like 'Katy' Richardson she was a member of the Ladies' Alpine Club and later was elected a Vice-President; this gave her great joy. She died in March 1946 at the age of ninety-eight having never wavered in her strict code of conduct, *'Faire face toujours, iusqu'à la fin'*.

One of the best-known woman mountaineers of her own, or any other generation was Mrs Aubrey Le Blond. She climbed in summer and winter and was also an excellent organiser. She it was who founded the Ladies' Alpine Club, which became and has remained the premier ladies' climbing club in the world. She was an entertaining speaker and writer and her many books, although most of them are definitely dated, still give immense pleasure to mountaineers of both sexes and all ages.

Few climbers can have had a less propitious start mountain-wise. She was born Elizabeth Hawkins-Whitshed, the delicate child of wealthy parents, and spent most of her early life in Ireland – a good deal of it in the whirl of social gaiety popular at that time. In 1879, at the age of eighteen, she married Fred Burnaby, a dashing Guards officer considerably older than herself. With him she became involved in what was known as the 'Prince of Wales' set – a way of life which she very soon found uncongenial. Her health deteriorated so much that she was sent out to Switzerland, to the Engadine, to recuperate. This brought mountains into her life in a big way; previously, in her own words, she 'knew nothing about mountains and cared less'. But almost overnight her outlook was revolutionised; she walked up the Diavolezza pass from Pontresina, armed with a long alpenstock, and the view thrilled her as much as the first sight of the Alps from the Weissenstein thrilled Hilaire Belloc. She decided there and then that mountains were for her, and her subsequent climbing career lasted for more than twenty years.

In 1881 she was at Chamonix and attempted Mont Blanc but was defeated by the weather. In 1882 her soldier husband was killed in Egypt, leading his men at the battle of Abu Klea. Elizabeth – always known as 'Lizzie' – returned to Chamonix and found solace in the mountains. She climbed Mont Blanc and the Grandes Jorasses; on the latter she managed to get benighted and admitted with glee that she had 'enjoyed herself immensely'. Meanwhile her family at home were horrified at her goings-on but believed that she would soon tire of it. She had not the slightest intention of doing so; her early Victorian great-aunt proclaimed in disgust, 'Stop her climbing mountains! She is scandalizing all London.' But Lizzie turned a deaf ear and later wrote that she owed 'a supreme debt of gratitude to the mountains for knocking from me the shackles of conventionality'. It was when she arrived for the first time to spend the night at a mountain hut that she realised that she had no lady's maid with her – never before had she removed her boots with her own hands!

Lizzie was a naturally adventurous spirit. The bicycle had only recently made its appearance in London; bicycling ladies had scarcely been heard of, much less seen, in the Engadine. This did not deter Lizzie; she adored Italy and decided that the best way to get there was by bicycle. She trundled her machine over the mountain passes and when the descent became too much for the primitive brakes she attached a small tree by a length of rope and trailed it behind her, so maintaining her equilibrium.

With regard to mountains she was insatiable; she made summer ascents of all the main peaks in the Alps and was one of the first women to attempt winter mountaineering. She made the first winter ascent of the Aiguille du Tour, the Col du Tacul, the Col du Chardonnet and the Col d'Argentière. When she did the Aiguille du Midi the people of Chamonix witnessed her arrival and the inevitable cannon was fired. She had scarcely finished her programme in the Chamonix area when she set off for Monte Rosa. It was March and conditions were not good; she met Vittorio Sella who had previously made the first winter ascent of the Matterhorn and they decided to join forces for Monte Rosa. They reached a height of 4,200 m. before the violence of the storm forced them down. Lizzie found the expedition well worth while.

In the course of all these adventures she met and married her second husband and became Mrs Main. They had some exciting journeys together to China but sadly she was widowed again within a few years. She finally married Mr Aubrey Le Blond, who survived her, and it is as Mrs Aubrey Le Blond that she takes her honoured place in the history of women's mountaineering.

In the Engadine Mrs Le Blond made a long series of winter ascents including Piz Palü, Piz Sella and Piz Zugö and also one of the longest expeditions ever attempted in winter – the Disgrazia. She had the distinction of being the only lady who had led a guide-less party in winter and in spring, and it is highly probable that her ascent of Piz Palü in 1900 with Lady Evelyn McDonnel was the very first 'women's rope'.

She climbed with Edouard Cupelin of Chamonix and with Emile Rey; at Zermatt her favourite guide was Joseph Imboden, often accompanied by his son Roman.

Mrs Le Blond was an outstanding character as well as a great mountaineer. As one used to mixing in the best society she at first thought it entirely suitable that she should be accompanied in the mountains by her lady's maid. She was the personification of elegance and no doubt found a maid a necessity; it has never been made clear if she insisted on climbing qualifications when she engaged the girl. However, she was a flexible type and after one of these treasures had eloped with a courier and another suffered from hysteria when she was only a few minutes late returning from a climb she decided to dispense with their services.

In spite of her bold approach to many matters Mrs Le Blond loyally obeyed Victorian standards of respectability. For many years she wore climbing breeches under her skirt. When the village had been left behind and the last cow had been passed she quietly removed the skirt and the guide carried it in his rucksack. This method resulted in an unfortunate situation on at least one occasion. With her guide and a porter she climbed the Rothorn from Zermatt, intending to make the traverse and descend to the Zinal valley. As they approached the first village the alarm was given – the skirt had been left on the summit! No compromise was possible; the party re-ascended, rescued the skirt and made a late return to Zermatt.

After 1895 Mrs Le Blond did very little climbing in the Alps. In that year Roman Imboden, the son of her guide Joseph, was killed on the Lyskamm and neither she nor Joseph seemed able to face the sad associations of the Swiss mountains. Instead they turned their attention to Norway where they met with considerable success; but the spell of the Alps had been broken and early in the present century Mrs Le Blond's climbing career came quietly to its end.

Her love for the mountains was in no way diminished – she was never happier than when she was talking or writing about them and visiting her old haunts and old friends. The formation of the Ladies' Alpine Club in 1907 was almost entirely due to her efforts; by the founding of the Club the future of women's mountaineering was assured; Mrs Le Blond became its first President and was re-elected for a second term in 1932. This event gave her great pleasure and she described it as 'one of the nicest things that has ever happened to me'. She died in 1934 while still in office, which is just what she would have wished.

Lizzie Le Blond was a talented and unusual woman, beloved by all; the debt that women climbers of all generations still owe her is incalculable.

Moving gracefully across the scene of this second generation of women mountaineers – the successors to Lucy Walker, the Misses Pigeon and Meta Brevoort – was Mrs E. P. Jackson, described to the Ladies' Alpine Club twenty-five years later by Mrs Le Blond as 'one of the greatest women climbers of her time'. This was high praise indeed, for Mrs Le Blond was famous for her sound judgement.

It is sad that so little is known of Mrs Jackson, who was undoubtedly one of the most attractive figures of the mountain world of those days. Unassuming, unsophisticated and quite unspoilt she never hit the headlines as did Lucy Walker and Lizzie Le Blond; but many of her achievements equalled theirs as they would be the first to admit.

As early as 1876 she made the first ascent of the east face of the Weissmies with her husband and Ferdinand Imseng as guide. Two years later she began her long association with Alois Pollinger of

St Niklaus which resulted in many years of happy and exciting adventure. In 1878 they pioneered the west ridge of the Dom, the highest mountain standing entirely on Swiss territory. In 1884 they did the Dent Blanche and made the first descent by the Ferpècle ridge. In 1886 they were on the Grand Dru, one of the stiffest of the Chamonix climbs, and 1887 found them celebrating on the summit of the Grand Charmoz.

Mrs Jackson's entries in the registers of the Monte Rosa Hotel at Zermatt give the key to her approach to mountaineering – and to her character. Her remarks are quite unacademic; she does not mention the severity of the route, the time taken or any such mundane trifles, the sheer exhilaration of the climb satisfied her; of the remarkable ascent of the west ridge of the Dom she wrote, 'The Dom – by a new way!', almost as if she was surprised to find that she had accomplished it.

Until that year, 1887, her climbing had been done in the summer but she was a regular visitor to the Alps in the winter and gradually became fascinated by the possibility of winter mountaineering.

Mrs Jackson arrived to spend Christmas 1887 at the Baer Hotel at Grindelwald; she had several ascents in mind but dominating all her thoughts was a secret desire to traverse the Jungfrau from the Bergli Hut to the Guggi and so down to Wengernalp. This is a difficult ice climb in summer; it demands almost superhuman endeavour in winter.

It was typical of Mrs Jackson's relaxed attitude and her keen enjoyment of all happy things that the gay Christmas festivities at Grindelwald temporarily took precedence over climbing; she found it quite unthinkable to take time off for the mountains until all the exciting parties were over. There was tobogganing every day and a series of lunchtime picnics to the Faulhorn Inn, where it was so bitterly cold that they had to dance eightsome reels to keep warm.

At last, however, the New Year of 1888 dawned, the social round slowed down and on 4th January she set off with Emil Boss, one of the four brothers who owned the Baer at Grindelwald; on this occasion the guides were Ulrich Almer and Johann Kaufmann – presumably she felt it was wiser to have Oberland men for an ascent of this grade. The guides appeared with their ropes and axes exactly as they did in summer and the party was accompanied by half the hotel visitors armed with cameras, plus a large assortment of dogs, who went with them as far as the Schwarzegg Hut. It was a glorious day, the presence of a large party introduced a festive note. Mrs Jackson felt truly inspired.

The next morning at 4.30 her party, consisting of Emil Boss and the two guides left the hut *en route* for the Strahlegg and Lauteraarhorn. In her own inimitable way she wrote later of the glacier 'glittering in the moonlight, as a fairy ballroom strewn with countless diamonds'. 'I wondered', she said, 'if rough mortals had any right to tread there.' It was a good climb, not too difficult, and as they reached the summit a cheer went up from their party, already making its way back from the hut to Grindelwald. The view from the summit was magnificent with the circle of Oberland peaks close at hand and the Matterhorn, Weisshorn and Mischabel guarding the horizon. They came down by a series of swift *glissades* and reached the hut before dark, content in the knowledge that they had made the first winter ascent of the mountain.

The next morning they were off again, not too early, as they were bound for the Kleine Viescherhorn, a pleasant little peak of no great difficulty. Once on the summit they had hoped to descend to the Bergli Hut, but the weather broke suddenly. It was well known that there was very little in the way of comfort at the Bergli; the only solution was to return to Grindelwald. They came down to the Zisenberg Hut, made tea and reached the Baer in time for dinner. The mountains were out for the next three days so once again there were tobogganing parties with all their attendant pleasures.

On 10th January the weather improved and they were *en route* again; the plan was to spend two nights at the Bergli, while all the time there were lurking hopes that the Jungfrau might be possible. The frailty of human nature put paid to that project; they slept late – much too late – and with the philosophy of the true mountaineer they made do with the Gross Viescherhorn. It was a perfect climbing day; every step of the ascent was pure joy and the view from the summit 'a dream of beauty and delight'. It was too good to leave; they stayed too long and did not reach the Bergli again until after dark.

In the morning there was much housework to be done in the hut before a start could be made – the usual lot of the mountaineer from that day to this. They started in high spirits but it was only too obvious that conditions had worsened since the previous day. The farther they went the more bitter and tempestuous the wind became. They had thirty-five steps to cut before they could reach rocks that were free from snow. They laboured for three hours but in the end the gale defeated them; their limbs were frozen and their clothes as stiff as boards. They made tea in an ice-grotto – 'was ever afternoon tea made in such a place', commented Mrs Jackson – and fought their way back to the Bergli in the dark. Back to Grindelwald again, bitterly disappointed; a black moment indeed and she could not rest – the Jungfrau was for ever in her mind.

A quick change for the better in the weather brought the party back to spend the night at the Bergli on 15th January. The morning brought perfect weather; all promised well and the steps they had cut so laboriously in that never-to-be-forgotten gale still remained intact. On the Roththal Sattel they halted for a second breakfast; delicious hot beefsteak was handed round with cups of tea to follow. The climbers of those days knew how to look after themselves and made a party of every *al fresco* meal.

The ascent to the summit proved to be less difficult than in summer; the final peak was a cone of solid ice from which they had superb views, especially of the Dent d'Herens, so often obscured by the Matterhorn. But they stayed only a few minutes; Ulrich Almer was taking no chances; it was the traverse that they were all so eager to complete – that was the main object of the exercise – and there was a sense of elation as they began the descent. They experienced few difficulties; ice axes were hardly needed until they reached the arête leading to the Silberlücke; the descent to the Giessen Glacier was easy. Once down on the glacier speed was esssential and they had a 'mild steeplechase' over its almost unbroken surface. There was no time to lose; the light was going;

there was still a steep wall of rock to descend and then the tortuous way must be found through the great ice-fall leading down on to the Guggi glacier.

For the first time on this epic expedition things began to go wrong for the party; the cornice on the Schneehorn gave them considerable trouble; the descent of the rock wall seemed endless. Darkness came suddenly and too soon; one lantern packed up, leaving them only one and a small torch to find their way through the ice-fall. This proved to be too much under such conditions; there is only one outlet and they failed to find it. A bivouac was the only course open to them; they found an ice cavern below the surface of the glacier and this, they decided, would have to suffice.

'Things might have been worse,' Mrs Jackson explained gratefully. They carpeted the cavern with rucksacks and used ice-axes as seats; they had an opossum rug and quite a collection of warm garments between them. Provisions, unfortunately, were running short; there was a little bread, a small piece of cheese, a few raisins, a little brandy, 'and let me not forget' said Mrs Jackson, 'I believe – one chicken bone'. They dined sumptuously on cheese and raisins, left the bread for breakfast and settled down for the night. One would hardly have thought that an ice cavern would have much to recommend it under such conditions but Mrs Jackson was enchanted with its ethereal beauty and never forgot to describe it when recounting her experiences afterwards. Even the longest night has an ending; in the first five minutes of daylight the guides found the chimney outlet only twenty paces distant. They were soon over the Guggi glacier and it was only a short time before their anxious friends welcomed them back to the warmth and comfort of the Baer.

The Alpine Club asked Mrs Jackson to write an account of this amazing first winter traverse for the *Alpine Journal*. She agreed and called it 'A Winter Quartette'. It is altogether charming and captures exactly the whole spirit of the enterprise. The only cloud for her was the sad death of Emil Boss before the year was ended; she could hardly believe that never again would she meet him at the Baer to re-live the great moments of their adventure. Her article, 'A Winter Quartette' and Douglas Freshfield's obituary of

Emil Boss appeared simultaneously in Volume XIV of the *Alpine Journal*.

It was quite in keeping with Mrs Jackson's sunny disposition that she never mentioned in her article that as a result of the night in the ice-cavern she suffered severe frostbite of the feet; this caused her much suffering and the eventual amputation of several toes, which brought to an end her magnificent climbing career.

This disaster made no difference to her deep love for the mountains or her enjoyment in them. She had paid a high price perhaps for her happiness, but to her it was worth it; she never lamented or complained. She went back to her old haunts and revelled in the beauty around her. In vain did Alois Pollinger, her grand old guide, try to persuade her to do just one more simple climb. His great desire was to take her up the Wellenkuppe; but there was no Rothorn Hut and not even the Trift Inn in those days and the long haul from the village would have been beyond her. She remained adamant but was greatly touched by Alois' devotion.

Her pain and her lameness did not detract from Mrs Jackson's graceful bearing or embitter her in any way. She loved to hear of the adventures of those who climbed where she could no longer follow; every winter on the Wednesday after the Alpine Club dinner she gave a dinner party at her home for a group of climbing friends so that together they could share the joys that were a common bond between them. She was a charming, dedicated and deeply sincere mountaineer – a kind of snow queen whom everyone loved.

In the late 1880s A. F. Mummery, already well established as a redoubtable climber, brought his bride out from England to have her first introduction to the mountains. Perhaps an agreement on these lines had been privately included in their marriage vows; whether or not that was the case the arrangement delighted young Mrs Mummery. She was athletic and anxious for adventure and approached any problem in a carefree, light-hearted manner that must have made her an ideal climbing companion. Her husband introduced her to his guide, Alexander Burgener from Saas Fee, and outlined what must have seemed a rather ambitious programme for a young lady in her first season; it included the Jung-frau, the Obergabelhorn and, of course, the Matterhorn.

Mrs Mummery's climbing abilities made a considerable impres-sion on the guide; Burgener was a man who believed in ghosts and other strange phenomena, but he also believed quite firmly that women could climb. By the middle of July in this first season Mummery and Burgener were planning to make the first ascent of the Teufelsgrat on the Taeschhorn. Burgener announced that Mrs Mummery must 'go up the Teufelsgrat'. She was delighted at the compliment and they solemnly shook hands, her husband fortunately being in full agreement.

On 15th July 1887 they set out from Zermatt to sleep in the highest chalet on the Taeschalp – there not being the luxury of the little inn at that time. They were joined by some friends who had come up to witness the sunrise; the whole party was in great spirits. As a prelude to adventures yet to come the chalet was attacked during the afternoon by an irate bull. Everyone was obliged to take refuge on the roof and the animal was eventually driven off by a concerted attack with ice-axes. They watched the *Alpenglüh* on the incomparable Weisshorn until the last hint of sunset had faded; then they lit their candles and converted the chalet into a ballroom. It was only twelve feet square and the beams were low but Mrs Mummery reports that the dance was 'brilliant'; there were songs from the guides and porters and dance music was provided by Andenmatten, the second guide, on a weird and wonderful musical instrument. They wound up the evening with a discussion about the weather – such a discussion being *de rigueur* before any big climb – and retired early, only to be disturbed by a second attack by the bull; he was dealt with as before and retired into the darkness to re-think his strategy.

At 1.30 a.m. they set off, leaving their friends sleeping peace-fully. Burgener led, followed by Mrs Mummery, then Anden-matten; A. F. Mummery brought up the rear. Burgener, as soon as the real climbing began, kept up a running commentary of warnings concerning the criminal negligence and dire results of sending down stones on other members of the rope; the recurring theme being, 'You kill your man, you not like that.' Mrs Mummery took the hint and did not kill her man; her whole attention was riveted on the route; she was fascinated by the convenience of the handholds and the intricacies of the rock ridges.

At one point an unprecedented event occurred when the second guide came off the mountain and swung suspended on the rope fifteen feet below her. Fortunately everyone, including Mrs Mummery, was prepared for emergencies and the situation was saved. Andenmatten, the second guide, was completely demoralised and lay sobbing at their feet on the rocks. Wine was produced and worked miracles; meanwhile Mrs Mummery rendered first aid, mainly of a psychological nature! Another near-disaster happened when her ice-axe was swept away into space; but she was quite undeterred and was inclined to treat the matter as a joke, if only as a means of cheering up the unfortunate Andenmatten. Her good-humoured reactions when the climbing was proving difficult went a long way towards re-establishing his self-confidence.

Since this was a first ascent the route had to be pioneered; frequently the way forward proved to be impossible and new routes had to be found. Again and again a traverse had to be made, greatly adding to the fatigue, but everything was accepted as part of the pattern. When at last a narrow cleft in the rock proved to be just big enough for them all to squeeze through, so that an awkward obstruction in the shape of a great tower could be turned, a chorus of Swiss yodels and British cheers rent the air.

Difficulties and disappointments were endless; at one point Burgener, after a reconnaisance ahead, returned to announce, 'Herr Mommery, it is quite impossible.' 'Herr Mommery' was not prepared to accept this decision as final and suggested that an attempt should be made up a wall of loose, broken rock. The danger of falling stones was agonisingly apparent. Burgener shrieked incessantly, 'You will kill your man if you not more careful are.' Mrs Mummery said later that her own impression was that she would not only kill her man but would bring down the whole party and most of the mountain onto the glacier below.

At last, after prolonged struggles, there came the joyful, all-important announcement, *'Herr Mommery, das geht'*.

For a short period this news spurred them on to greater efforts but then, as is nearly always the case on the mountains, more difficulties emerged. The snow, which had been in fairly good condition, gradually became black ice and every step had to be hacked out. The cold increased and deepened their depression but they laboured on; surely after the next rock ridge the worst would be over and the summit in sight! Alas, it was no more than a pipe-dream; there was no sign of the summit; it was already 1.30 p.m. and they had been climbing for nearly twelve hours; fatigue, cold and hunger were beginning to make inroads on their reserves of strength. At one point Mrs Mummery was obliged to stand for three quarters of an hour on a tiny rock ledge, while splinters of ice rained down from above. Only the occasional cheery assurance from her husband, and the knowledge that the alternative to her precarious position was a fall of some thousands of feet, kept her steady.

As if to give them a momentary chance to recover their breath the next pitch was easy, but the relief was short-lived. Worse difficulties lay ahead; a rock cornice had broken away and made further progress impossible by that route. Chill horror seized them; to return was out of the question, advance seemed impossible. It was a desperate situation, so desperate that common sense told them that a solution simply had to be found.

'After a few moments', Mrs Mummery wrote in her account, 'we began to recover from the mental shock caused by this most dramatic break in the ridge, and proceeded to reduce its tremendous appearance to the dull and narrow limits of actual fact.'

This approach proved to be their salvation, but not many mountaineers in their first season, in a position of such peril, would have responded quite so calmly.

By carefully climbing down and then up again the difficulties were gradually overcome. Suddenly they found themselves on the snow ridge and the summit was only half an hour away. The cold was so cruel and Mrs Mummery was so frozen that Burgener had to wrap her in his coat and gloves. At 5.30 p.m. they stood on the summit – but only for a moment. A thunderstorm was threatening and Burgener was determined to get them off the ridge. He hurried

Mrs Mummery along the arête; thunder grumbled and clouds enveloped them. 'You must go on,' implored Burgener, 'I could a cow hold here,' and on they went, helter-skelter down the ridge to safety.

Their joy was immense; to a greater or lesser degree this kind of satisfaction is one of the great rewards of mountaineering that can be shared by all climbers. Thunder, falling snow, sinking in up to their knees, tired, frozen, bruised – they cared little for any of these things! The Teufelsgrat was theirs – nothing else mattered.

At 8 p.m. as they plodded wearily up the moraine, they realised that they had not eaten since 10 a.m. Under the shelter of a rock they sat down for a meal; their hands were numbed and their clothes – what remained of them – wet through. Large parts of their garments were still decorating the rock ridges of the Teufelsgrat but even that seemed of small importance. They were obliged to spend the night out above the tree line, but somehow survived. When daylight came they dragged themselves down through the forest and reached the little inn at Randa at 5.30 a.m. The astonished, but hospitable, landlord lit a blazing fire and prepared an enormous breakfast. A couple of hours later they drove triumphantly up to Zermatt in a little cart, euphemistically described as a '*char-à-banc*'.

The Mummerys' ascent of the Teufelsgrat is still considered one of the greatest husband and wife exploits ever undertaken in the mountains. '*Erst Besteigung des Täschorns über den Teufelsgrat*', rejoiced Burgener, '*und eine Frau war dabei.*' And eighty years later Felicitas von Reznicheck put it even more pithily, '*Mrs Mummery ist eine Britin. Sie hat kein Angst.*'

Mrs Mummery must have been an endearing person; her famous husband was a rather complex character – in her simple, happy way she was the perfect foil for him; she understood him and she adored him, as he adored her. In his great book *My Climbs in the Alps and Caucasus*, still known almost by heart by modern mountaineers, he saw to it that she wrote the chapter on their ascent on the Teufelsgrat – a graceful tribute to her courage and cheerful companionship.

A. F. Mummery was killed on Nanga Parbet in the Himalayas. His wife then wrote the introduction to *My Climbs in the Alps and Caucasus*. It is a vivid, sensitive piece of writing, describing his career up to the moment of his death; the final sentence is moving in its quiet dignity – 'On August 24th, 1895 my husband and the two Gurkas were seen for the last time.'

During the 1890s an intrepid lady made history as the only woman included on a rope of famous members of the Alpine Club. This was Miss Lily Bristow, who made many major ascents with and without guides. In 1892 with A. F. Mummery and Ellis Carr she made a guideless north–south traverse of the Grand Charmoz; on this occasion she had a lady companion – a Miss Pasteur. The next year she did the north ridge of the Zinal Rothorn guideless with A. F. Mummery and followed this with yet another guideless expedition – the Italian ridge of the Matterhorn, making the descent by the same route, on a rope with Mummery, Collie and Hastings. This was a great year for Miss Bristow; with Mummery, Hastings, Slingsby and Collie she did the Petit Dru guideless – a climb which she led as far as the foot of the gendarme; one of the earliest recorded instances of a woman leading on a rope composed of men.

In 1894, with the guides Matthias Zurbriggen and Josef Pollinger, she made the first descent of the Z'mutt ridge on the Matterhorn and then in 1895 there came the climb which capped her career and brought her undying fame – the second traverse of the Gré-pon, guideless with Mummery, Hastings, Slingsby, Collie and Brodie from a bivouac on the Rognon. A. F. Mummery gives a delightful account of this great adventure in his book. They slept in a tent on the Rognon; 'wrapped in sleeping bags we sat sipping hot tea until the stars were awake'. At 5.0 a.m. they had breakfast of hot bacon, rolls and tea with fresh milk. At this point Messrs Slingsby, Collie and Brodie arrived and the serious climbing began. Miss Bristow sometimes scorned the use of the rope altogether in order to be able to take photos with her tripod camera. Conditions were poor; the rocks were glazed; the rope became snow-covered and frozen and the cold was 'positively excruciating'. However Mummery declared that Miss Bristow 'showed the representatives of the Alpine Club the way in which steep rocks should be climbed' and earned the honour of being the first lady to stand on the summit of the Grépon. In spite of the weather there seems to have been quite a festive repast when they reached the top; even the cooking stove having been carried up. But it was hardly a relaxed meal; wind, rain and snow chased them off the mountain.

It was Miss Bristow's ascent of the Grépon that gave rise to Mummery's famous remark that all mountains appear to pass through three stages – an inaccessible peak, the most difficult ascent in the Alps, an easy day for a lady. However, it is still agreed by most climbers that, more than sixty years after Miss Bristow first stood on its summit, the Grépon has not yet reached the third stage.

There remains one more lady to be introduced before this period of women's mountaineering is complete. Margherita, the wife of the famous Oberland guide Christian Almer, made no claims to be a climber. She had brought up their children, cooked and kept house for her spouse and experienced the anxieties that are inseparable from being the wife of a famous guide. But in 1896 the Almers were to celebrate their Golden Wedding; in Victorian times the men made most of the decisions and Christian Almer was no exception. He had an abiding affection for the Wetterhorn and he proposed to celebrate his Golden Wedding on the summit. Obviously it was essential that both bride and groom should be present on this important occasion and Margherita, faithful to the end, agreed to make the attempt. She was seventy-one and her husband was seventy!

On 20th June 1896 quite a large party set out from Grindel-wald; Christian and Margherita accompanied by their eldest daughter and two of the younger sons, plus a friend, Dr Huber, from the village. They spent the first night and the whole of the next day at the Gleckstein Hut; soon after midnight on 22nd they left the hut and six hours later they were rejoicing on the summit. A high wind prevented a long sojourn but the party toasted the happy pair and excellent photographs were obtained. Without further incident they returned safely and in triumph to Grindelwald and, rather late in life, Margherita discovered herself to be a climber. It was a loyal and plucky decision to make and no one ever grudged her the little bit of fame it brought her.

The nineteenth century, momentous turning-point in so many fields of modern history, was moving to its close. In the glittering cavalcade of great events and brilliant personalities the little galaxy of outstanding women mountaineers glows with its own special radiance.

Chapter 4
Gallant Successors

The name of Gertrude Bell appears in many books, on many subjects; she was a remarkable, gifted and brilliant woman. Her stepmother, Lady Bell, who edited the three published volumes of her letters, described her thus: 'scholar, poet, historian, archaeologist, art critic, mountaineer, explorer, gardener, naturalist, distinguished servant of the State; all of these and recognised by experts as an expert in them all'.

Such an extraordinary woman might easily have been something of a dragon; an inhuman creature inclined to terrorise lesser mortals. Nothing could have been further from the truth in the case of Gertrude Bell; she was a natural, unsophisticated young woman who enjoyed the things that loom large in the life of any girl – dancing, shopping, acting, clothes. Indeed it was said of her that she had 'Paris frock, Mayfair manners'. She loved almost any sport and, above all, mountaineering. In her earlier years, before she became so deeply involved in her work among the Arabs, climbing was probably her greatest thrill and relaxation.

Gertrude Bell was born in 1868 and paid a few visits to the Alps in the mid-1890s. But, like so many women mountaineers of that time, she was in her thirties before she began any serious climbing and 1899 was her first big year. And what a season she had! Two years previously she had come under the spell of the Meije, had fallen hopelessly in love with it and immediately determined that she must climb it.

Towards the end of August she arrived at La Grave in the Dauphiné on her way home from the Middle East and straightway set about fulfilling the promise she had made to herself concerning the Meije. Her letter home describing the ascent gives a perfect picture of a first big mountaineering experience. None of her family were climbers but the bond between them was so close that she knew without any doubt that they would want to share every moment with her. She began by explaining how she had sent a wire 'Meije traversée' and would now give them the story. 'Well, I'll tell you', she wrote, 'it's awful. I think if I had known what was before me I should not have faced it.'

Small wonder that the Meije seemed daunting; as she points out she had hardly ever been on rock before and was almost a complete novice. But this did not deter her; her tremendous enthusiasm and natural ability carried her along and she was careful not to let the guides know how little experience she had. When the day was done Gertrude Bell had made the traverse of the Pic Central of the Meije and was almost certainly the first British woman to do so.

Her account of this great achievement is packed with humour and interesting sidelights. There were places on the descent which she thought to be impossible until she found herself in action, and it was 'with thankfulness' that she put on her skirt again on the Glacier du Tabuchet. They did not unrope until 5.30 p.m., but late in the evening they came safely back to La Grave, where they found all the guests assembled on the steps of the hotel and the proprietor letting off crackers. Inspired by her success on the Meije she stayed long enough at La Grave to get in an enjoyable ascent of the Ecrins and got back to England in September well pleased with her climbing progress.

Most of the next year Gertrude spent in and around Jerusalem exploring the deserts of the Middle East, but she somehow managed to squeeze in a climb in the Chamonix area; this was nothing less than the traverse from the Grand to the Petit Dru with the guides Ulrich Fuhrer and Ernest Simon; it widened her mountain experience considerably.

In 1901 she was back in the Alps again, this time at Grindelwald. She arrived in the late summer and in her letters confessed to enjoying herself madly. She began with the Schreckhorn; she admitted to having some bad moments but nevertheless thoroughly enjoyed the climb.

At the back of their minds Gertrude and her guides had designs on the virgin arête on the Finsteraarhorn, which had been attempted three times unsuccessfully, but they were keeping their plans a deadly secret. This was just as well as the weather broke, a heavy snowfall occurred and the mountains were out for several days. Instead she walked over the Scheidegg to Rosenlaui where she fell in with a family of English climbing friends. Since the mountains would not go they turned their attention, in truly English style, to cricket with fir-tree branches for stumps and large butterfly nets handy to fish the ball out of the river when anyone hit a six.

The weather treated Gertrude badly that year but she had a grand time on the Engelhörner and at the end of the holiday was able to report that the fortnight's bag was two old peaks, seven new peaks and one new saddle traverse. 'That's not bad going, is it?' she asked with pardonable pride.

The next year, 1902, must surely be regarded as Gertrude's greatest alpine year – albeit one that nearly ended in disaster. Her first plan with Ulrich Fuhrer was the Wellhorn arête. The weather defeated their first attempt but their luck was in on the second occasion. She wrote, 'We have done the first of the impossibles, the Wellhorn arête, and are much elated.' She went on to give a detailed description of the ascent and finished her letter with the news that 'if the weather holds, I shall go over the Grimsel, for our second impossible is now on our minds and we want to set about it as soon as we can'.

Before they got to grips with the 'second impossible' they had designs on a new ascent of the Wetterhorn but they seem to have given up that idea. There was a long gap before her next letter reached home; when at last she was able to write again it was from her bed in her hotel at Meiringen where she was nursing frost-bitten toes. She begged the family not to be alarmed, but admitted that she was lucky to be alive. There then followed one of the most dramatic and colourful letters that any mountaineer can ever have written home.

Their 'second impossible' was the N.E. face of the Finsteraarhorn – at that time unclimbed. This adventure made alpine history

PLATE V

Denise Morin (Evans), who has become one of Britain's leading women climbers, on the summit of Les Écrins, her first 4,000-metre peak
Photo by permission of Eyre and Spottiswoode Ltd

Anna Roelfsema, the famous Dutch climber, on the summit of the Matterhorn with Bernard Biner
Photo by permission of Anna Roelfsema

Janet Roberts (Adam Smith) on the Glacier du Mulinet
Photo by permission of J. M. Dent and Sons Ltd

Joan Busby on the platform just below the summit during her ascent of the South Face of the Obergabelhorn
Photo by permission of Joan Busby

PLATE VI

Countess Dorothea Gravina,
leader of the Women's
Jagdula Expedition, 1962
Photo by permission of Countess
Dorothea Gravina

Claude Kogan,
leader of the women's
expedition to
Cho Oyu, who
lost her life on the
mountain
Photo by permission of
Eyre and Spottiswoode
Ltd

and was described by Captain Farrar of the Alpine Club as one of the greatest expeditions in the Alps. The party set out on 31st July and did not return until 2nd August. The weather turned bad on them only a few hours after leaving the Pavillion Dolfuss and grew worse with every hour. They were beset by almost continuous thunderstorms, interspersed with driving snow and freezing temperatures. Once the rope was almost cut through by a falling stone; during one thunderstorm their ice-axes became veritable lightning conductors and they had to find shelter in a rock chimney. They were forced to bivouac in appalling conditions on two successive nights and during one of these a tremendous blizzard raged incessantly. They were out for fifty-seven hours, of which fifty-three were spent on the rope. They eventually arrived back at 10.0 o'clock on the morning of 2nd August to the great relief of the whole village.

Everyone was full of praise for Gertrude. Ulrich Fuhrer said that few could equal her technical skill and she had no equal in coolness, bravery and judgement. But for her courage and determination he was convinced that the whole party must have perished and all the honours of the climb went to her.

Fuhrer's personal written tribute to Gertrude was moving. 'When the freezing wind beats you almost to the ground, when the blizzard almost blinds you, half paralysing your senses, when the cold is so intense that snow freezes on you as it falls, clothing you in a sheet of ice, till life becomes insupportable – then indeed is Miss Bell pre-eminent.'

The whole climbing world was agreed that safe retreat under such conditions was a tremendous performance doing credit to all; the occasion was a defeat deserving more credit than many a victory.

After a gap of two years, during which she made a second world tour, Gertrude arrived in Zermatt for the first time. The village was thrilled and the old porter at the Monte Rosa took it upon himself to tell her how gratified they all were that she was going to climb in the district. At the Riffelberg she met Geoffrey Winthrop Young, who gave her much useful advice and a good general introduction to all the surrounding mountains.

Gertrude had a good time in Zermatt; she traversed the Matterhorn from Breuil back to Zermatt and managed to include all the other peaks she had planned – the Lyskamm, Monte Rosa and the Dent Blanche. A touch of real romance brought a truly happy ending to her visit. Lucy Walker, now rather old and frail, was paying her annual visit to the Monte Rosa Hotel. They met on Gertrude's return from the Dent Blanche and talked mountains over tea as only dedicated climbers can. Gertrude, in her letter home, marvelled at what Lucy had achieved under most difficult conditions; Lucy, for her part, must have rejoiced to discover a woman mountaineer with such a tremendous record.

Little was heard of Gertrude Bell in the Alps after this time. She made her home in Baghdad, where she became famous as political secretary to the High Commissioner there. She died rather suddenly in 1926. Among all her manifold activities some may have thought that mountains had a very subsidiary place in her affections; but mountaineers know better and still remember her to this day as one of the great women climbers of her time.

The Himalayas have been the focal point of mountaineering expeditions during the middle-years of the present century; it is not easy to realise that they were already being opened up by leading British alpinists like Martin Conway and A. F. Mummery before the end of the last century. Even more surprising is the fact that a woman was in the forefront of these pioneer explorations. Fanny Bullock Workman was an intrepid traveller who graduated to mountaineering in early middle-life. As a personality she stood alone; she could not be assessed as other people were assessed; she was just – Fanny Bullock Workman. Even her name stands out like a sore thumb; it seems to suggest a tough, aggressive, rather ruthless character; this exactly describes the most important side of Fanny – she was nothing if not a go-getter.

Fanny was American and immensely rich; she was married to Dr William Hunter Workman; it would, in fact be more correct to say that he was married to her; she was certainly the dominant partner. They never described themselves as Dr and Mrs Workman; it was always Fanny Bullock Workman and Dr William Hunter Workman. Fanny liked it that way and her 'mild husband' – as Geoffrey Winthrop Young described him – did not argue the point.

In their early married years they travelled extensively in all directions, almost always by bicycle. This gave Fanny the emotional and intellectual outlet she needed. She was, *par excellence*, the New Woman of the late-Victorian era; she did not propose to emulate the male-dominated, house-bound female of earlier decades; it was impossible to throw off the shackles at home but awheel in foreign parts, with her husband coasting along behind her, she had unbounded freedom of action and the world was her oyster.

Fanny's outfit was cumbersome beyond belief and her appearance was not improved by the ostentatious topee she was never without. The bicycles of both were festooned with luggage and on Fanny's handlebars there was always securely perched, no one knows how, the tea-kettle without which she refused to travel.

In 1898 the Workmans – Fanny would turn in her grave to hear them so described – pedalled their way to the Karakoram; she was forty and he was fifty-two at the time. The Himalayas made a vast impression on Fanny; the mountains gripped her immediately; thereafter they dominated her life and she had little time for anything else. Dr Workman, it goes without saying, acquiesced. Between 1898 and 1912 they visited the Karakoram eight times.

In 1899, after a cycling tour of Java, they arrived in Srinagar, the capital of Kashmir, to climb with the famous Swiss guide Matthias Zurbriggen, who had already made many ascents in the area with Martin Conway. There was a time when it was fashionable to suggest that the Workmans were inclined to exaggerate the heights they achieved. This could be so, but no one seems to dispute the fact that in their first year all the peaks they climbed were in the 18,000 to 21,000 feet range.

There were plenty of excitements and perilous adventures, particularly where Fanny was concerned. She had the misfortune to fall into a crevasse; she was a heavily-built woman and Matthias Zurbriggen needed all his strength and considerable patience to haul her out. A little later her topee was blown away; Fanny, however, was prepared for all such emergencies; underneath the topee she had a face mask and a cap with flaps; the incident only served to highlight her forethought.

In 1903, with her husband and three guides, she made the ascent of Pyramid Peak in the Karakoram. This is one of those events over which certain people were disposed to argue as to whether or not the summit was actually reached; at this stage in history it seems kinder to give Fanny the benefit of the doubt.

In 1906 she covered herself with glory by making the first ascent of Pinnacle Peak, 22,000 feet, in Kashmir; no one has attempted to disprove this fact. Fanny was ambitious; it may be that her success went to her head a little. She was also a fanatic for detail; everything that was done and said was of paramount importance, especially where mountains were concerned. She was convinced that the American climber, Miss Annie Peck – who, incidentally, made the first ascent of the North summit of Huascaran in the Andes – had grossly overstated the height of a peak she claimed to have climbed in Peru. Fanny was determined to have exact details about this matter and, there being no other way of finding out for certain, she despatched a party to Peru to measure the controversial peak. When the party returned with the welcome news that the mountain in question was quite definitely lower than the heights she herself had already scaled in the Himalayas, she made no effort whatever to conceal her delight.

In 1911 Fanny visited the Masherbrum Glacier from Hushe; this was a notable and quite unchallenged achievement – so much so that the 1938 British party to Masherbrum named one of the peaks 'Fanny' in her honour. In the following year the Workmans capped their long series of adventures in the Karakoram by making the first exploration of the Rose Glacier. All these great climbs were of course achieved without the assistance of carried oxygen.

Fanny was a staunch contender for Women's Rights – the current Women's Lib would have loved her. Even among the mountains this matter was often uppermost in her mind; before she left the Himalayas she stood proudly on a pass, which she christened The Silver Throne, brandishing a banner bearing the device 'Votes for Women'. Just what she thought this solo demo in aid of women's suffrage would achieve in the Himalayas it is difficult to imagine. She did, however, manage to get herself photographed and perhaps this brought hope and renewed zeal to those leading the crusade at home.

The outbreak of war in 1914 brought Fanny's climbing career to a close; before it was over she was already seriously ill and she endured much suffering before her death eight years later.

Those who at one time were tempted to think of Fanny as a figure of fun misjudged her. She *was* unusual – the kind of person around whom amusing incidents, true and untrue, invariably gather. She was never a ravishing beauty at the best of times; but photographs failed to do her justice and accentuated peculiarities which were meat and drink to cartoonists.

Fanny had her weaknesses and her eccentricities but fundamentally her intentions were good. She became a member of the Ladies' Alpine Club in 1908 and was elected as its Vice-President for America in 1912. Later generations owe much to Fanny who, decked out in topee and veil and vigorously flourishing her ice-axe, was, even in those faraway days, blazing the trail which the great Himalayan women climbers of today have followed so successfully. For all her peculiarities she was a grand person and a real mountaineer who truly loved the hills.

It might have been thought that living such a hectic existence the Workmans would not have had time for such trifles as raising a family. They did, however, have an only child, Rachel. She was in no way sacrificed to her parent's dramatic way of living. They sent her to Cheltenham; from there she went on to London University to read geology and graduated as a B.Sc. Rachel married and she must have inherited her mother's spirit and determination. In the Second World War she came into her own as the courageous Lady MacRobert whose three sons were all killed serving with the R.A.F. To commemorate their deaths she gave a Spitfire fighter to the Royal Air Force and christened it 'MacRobert's Reply'. Fanny Bullock Workman would have been proud of her daughter; and glad that the old spirit still burned like a living flame.

Alexander Burgener of Saas Fee must have had a special *flair* for detecting promising young women climbers. If it had not been for his persuasion Mrs Mummery might never have climbed the Teufelsgrat; and, humanly speaking, if there had been no Burgener there would have been no Eleonore Hassenclever.

Eleonore was German; a spritely young teenager, growing up at the time when the Mummerys were performing their great feats with Burgener. She came with her parents to the Alps and the mountains kindled her adolescent enthusiasm; with all the abandon of youth she flung herself into her new-found passion. Daily she implored her parents to let her make a beginning. Somehow an introduction to Alexander Burgener was arranged; with an unerring instinct of an experienced guide he discerned a mountain lover and a potential mountaineer.

Eleonore was enchanted; this was her opportunity; she seized it instantly. She hero-worshipped Burgener and put herself in his hands with complete confidence. She was an apt and attractive pupil; Burgener gave of his best, starting her off on the rudiments of mountain walking, step cutting and easy rock pitches; soon they were climbing their first snow peaks together. Each generation has produced its quota of teenage climbing enthusiasts who have had the good fortune to come under the influence of a great guide; they have learned their mountain lore as it can only be learned from such a man and as the years have gone by they have reaped rich rewards.

With Burgener, Eleonore climbed in all parts of the Alps; no mountain seemed too much for her; she thrived on the experience and was ever seeking new adventures. As was the case with many other women mountaineers she was not only a climber; she developed into a beautiful woman and a quite famous hostess, well known in European social circles. She married, became Eleonore Noll-Hassenclever and the mother of a delightful family. Her friends like to say that she was a great climber and, at the same time, '*une grande dame*' with all that that implies.

But Eleonore's passion lay deep within her; she was always striving for greater heights. Guideless climbing, still only in its infancy among men, was hardly to be thought of where women were concerned. Nevertheless it gradually became part of Eleonore's scheme of things – much as she loved climbing with Burgener. He had taught her so much, so well, that she had the confidence and the mountain know-how to wish to attempt guideless ascents with a party of her own choice. She began in a small way, very successfully; by 1911 she was already well known as a guideless climber and in that year she made the first guideless traverse of the Petit to the Grand Dru.

The First World War intervened, but at the earliest opportunity she was back in the Alps and with a little group of companions descended the Marinelli Couloir of Monte Rosa. In 1923 when she was forty-three she made a two-day traverse of the Matterhorn and the Dent d'Herens with two men friends. She chose difficult climbs but her experience by this time was immense; she was a careful climber and she enjoyed every moment she spent on the mountains.

In the summer of 1925 Eleonore was in Zermatt with her husband and two children. She was never happier than when she was there; she knew everybody, everybody knew her. She had a special place in the affections of the guides and the village people. The holiday drew to its close; her husband took the children back to Frankfurt, leaving Eleonore to do one last, much-desired climb with two friends. On a lovely summer evening they went up to the Weisshorn Hut; the next day they set out. That afternoon Leo Gentinetta, now the famous Zermatt doctor but then a guide, rushed into the Confiserie Seiler where the visitors were having tea. His face was pale from shock; he gave the news that Eleonore and one of her party were lying on the Bies Glacier; the survivor had sent for help. Every available guide volunteered for the *Colonne des Secours*, but each knew in his heart that there was little to hope for. When they reached the scene it was clear what had happened; a snow avalanche had broken away on the Bieshorn and had swept them down to the glacier below.

There has seldom been a greater demonstration in Zermatt over the death of a tourist; Eleonore had been known and loved for so long and was so highly respected as a climber. Every guide in Zermatt attended her funeral and the village turned out *en masse*. It was not so long after the ending of the First World War and some bitter memories still remained among the British concerning the Germans; only a few weeks previously German climbers had not been invited to the official dedication of the Whymper plaque on the wall of the Monte Rosa Hotel. But at Eleonore's death all bitterness was forgotten. The village church of Zermatt is Roman Catholic; Eleonore was a Protestant. So the English offered their little church, the parish church of the Alpine Club, and the offer was gratefully accepted. An unforgettable service was held. Eleonore was borne to her grave in the village cemetery, her coffin massed with alpine flowers; they buried her under the shadow of the Matterhorn. She was the first famous woman mountaineer to die in the mountains – perhaps she would have chosen that way.

Staying at the Monte Rosa Hotel at the time of Eleonore's death was a fifteen-year-old English girl, Eileen Jackson. She climbed with her father and brother; this was their fourth season in the Alps and her short mountain history was curiously like that of Eleonore thirty years earlier. In Zermatt they had already made several ascents with Alois Biner and were waiting impatiently for the Matterhorn, which was temporarily out of condition. On the day of the funeral the party had planned a day on the Riffelhorn with Alois; the start had to be delayed so that he might be present at the cemetery. When eventually they left on the train for Roten Boden they looked down on the crowds still gathered in the cemetery and Alois told them the details of the disaster and of Eleonore's unique place in the mountain world. The story made a deep impression on Eileen; she never forgot it. Two years later she published her school-girl mountaineering book *Switzerland Calling* in which she described the incident of Eleonore's funeral with great feeling. Eileen knew nothing of her early climbing years but in some telepathic way she seemed to have recognised a kindred spirit. We shall hear more of Eileen Jackson in the next chapter.

A small incident, but a significant one, told by Sir Martin Conway at the end of his great book *Mountain Memories*, seems worthy of a place in the story of women mountaineers. In 1898 Sir Martin decided that the time had come to bring his mountaineering career to a close. He climbed no more in the meantime but it was not until 19th August 1901 that he took formal leave of the snow mountains by going again to the summit of the Breithorn. This had been his very first climb as a schoolboy on the same date in 1872. Now, twenty-nine years later, he was accompanied by his schoolgirl daughter; it was to be her first climb as it had been his, and she was exactly the same age as he had been. On the summit he saluted for the last time all the great peaks which for so long had been his friends. But he had no regrets; they had given him health, joy, beauty, friends and rich memories. They were still his and infinitely precious – he was well satisfied to hand them on to his daughter.

Among the women who were making climbing history at the turn of the century was one who would never have described herself as more than a very modest mountaineer but to whom many of a later generation came to owe much.

This was Miss Edith Baring-Gould. She was brought to Zermatt by her parents at the age of twelve in 1883; by the next year the Riffelalp Hotel had been built and the Baring-Goulds established themselves there among a clientèle which included men famous in church and state and an ever-increasing number of first-class climbers. Before the First World War there can scarcely have been a famous alpinist who did not at some time sojourn at the Riffelalp. Edith Baring-Gould loved her annual six weeks in the mountains; excursions thrilled her; she adored meeting the great climbers and hearing their stories and she almost worshipped the Riffelalp itself. She made quite a number of ascents (Alphubel, Allalinhorn, Breithorn, etc.) and went on glacier trips with anyone who was willing to take her. She never had any great climbing ambitions – indeed, she never imagined she had the ability – but she enjoyed to the full everything that made up the alpine world of that time and carved for herself a permanent niche within it.

The family visits to the Riffelalp were unbroken until 1914. Edith was back again in 1920 and, except for the years of the Second World War, continued her visits until 1959. She was regarded by the Seiler family as part of the establishment ;she always left her climbing gear at the Riffelalp, not to mention her tin bath and her tea-making apparatus. She was the most forward-looking and liberal-minded woman one could wish to meet – in everything except clothes. In this respect she was a period piece; she continued to climb in her tweed skirt, norfolk jacket, felt hat and black stockings until her climbing days were done. Thereafter she sat in an easy chair and held court on the terrace or in the lounge, dressed in exactly the same outfit and nobody minded a bit – in fact, it would have been regarded as a disaster if she had made any change.

She had a host of young friends and to the climbers among them, who grew up between the wars, she was most generous. There would be invitations to spend a short spell at her expense at the Riffelalp; she gave her guests complete freedom to fix up with their guides and go off in the mountains whenever they wished to; in return they were expected to dress for dinner and give a detailed account of their adventures. She would sometimes announce that she would lead a glacier excursion and there are photos today in many mountaineers' albums of Edith dressed *circa* 1897 perched precariously among the seracs of the Lower Gorner Glacier, with a rope of bright young things of the late 1930s spreadeagled around her and a guide lurking in the background to prevent final disaster.

In the winter in London she would give dinners at her flat for her young climbing friends and one or two alpine celebrities would be invited to add interest to the occasion. She always had an invitation to the Alpine Club Reception in December and never failed to take a bevy of mountain-mad girls along with her. She gave many of us our *entrée* into the alpine world, for which we never cease to be grateful.

For her last few visits to the Riffelalp an invalid chair had to be provided for her; but with her usual adaptability she regarded this as just one more record she had established. She was thrilled to be present at the Centenary Meet of the Alpine Club and propelled herself in her chair to the open air *raclette* party, where all her mountain friends waited on her.

On 18th January 1961 a select gathering attended her ninetieth birthday party in her London flat; there was a bouquet of alpine flowers from Zermatt, an iced birthday cake representing the Matterhorn, and telegrams galore. Everyone had a marvellous evening – not least the heroine of the occasion.

Exactly a month later the Riffelalp Hotel was burnt to the ground; sadly this sounded Edith Baring-Gould's death knell. At ninety even her resilience was not equal to such a blow. Quietly during the next few months her strength failed and she grew weaker; she died peacefully on July 1st. A member of the Alpine Club took her funeral service and the climbers she had sponsored for so many years all gathered to do homage to a dear friend and a great mountain lover.

Another woman mountaineer particularly active in the early 1900s was Mrs C. W. Nettleton, looked up to by her contemporaries as one of the really great climbers of her day. She did the traverse of Monte Rosa in 1900; the Cinque Torri and Kleine Zinne in 1901; the Aiguille de Blaitière in 1903; the Weisshorn in 1904 and the traverse of the Matterhorn in 1906. Perhaps her greatest achievement in her early years was the traverse of the Grépon which she led in 1903 with her husband and a porter. Rock climbing was really her *métier* and she excelled at it in her home country as well as in the Alps; she led on Kern Knotts Crack in the Lake District only a year after Owen Glynne Jones had climbed it for the first time; indeed, some reports claim that she actually led this famous climber himself on Kern Knotts. Mrs Nettleton became President of the Ladies' Alpine Club in 1920 and even after she gave up climbing she continued with many other athletic pursuits, especially that of archery. Before she died at the age of eighty she had been English Champion, World Champion and, just a short time before her death, European Champion.

While women were becoming increasingly adventurous in the Alps in the first decade of the present century great things were happening in the Southern Hemisphere. A climbing centre had been established at The Hermitage in the Mount Cook area in New Zealand. It was under the direction of Peter Graham, the leading New Zealand guide of that time. It attracted climbers in considerable numbers and a good many of them came from Australia. In 1906 a party arrived from Sydney and with them came Miss Freda du Faur. She had not come originally with the intention of climbing, but she found the atmosphere of The Hermitage and the sight of the surrounding mountains so compelling that she went home with her mind made up to return.

In the winter of 1908–9 she was back again, determined this time to undertake some serious climbing. She made a good beginning; Peter Graham was impressed by her performance and agreed to take her in hand. Freda du Faur just could not stay away from the mountains; in December 1909 she came hurrying back to The Hermitage, from which she climbed Mount Kinsey and Mount Wakefield. By this time she had established herself as a competent mountaineer and Peter Graham offered to take her up Mount Sealy – a long expedition which necessitated a camp. Freda was delighted and accepted at once. Unfortunately she had reckoned without the prejudice and convention which was still rife among non-climbing visitors to The Hermitage. Deeply distressed she came back to Peter Graham to report that the old ladies ensconced in the sitting-room had informed her with one voice and in no uncertain terms that if she went alone with a guide to a camp she would most certainly lose her reputation. Graham was understanding but was as determined as she was that the climb was not going to be spoilt. Eventually a porter was engaged – this cost her a pound, which she found infuriating – but it was the only solution, and eventually the climb was successfully and respectably achieved. It was a good season; they added several more climbs to their list, including Mount Malte Brun which was quite an exciting affair.

Freda du Faur at first much preferred rock to snow; she found the latter rather boring and a little too slow for her impetuous taste. Peter Graham, who took her training seriously, would have none of this nonsense; he belonged to the old school and believed that a mountaineer should be expert in all aspects of the craft. Nor would he have the programme rushed; he made Freda take her peaks slowly; in his view the mountains had to be treated with respect and a prize such as Mount Cook was not to be seized at once, but earned by experience and hard work.

This philosophy cannot have been easy for Freda to follow at first; but she had immense respect for Graham, as he had for her, and events proved his advice to be sound. On 3rd December 1910 Freda climbed Mount Cook with Peter and his brother Alex in the remarkably short time of six hours – a very satisfactory result for all concerned.

With Mount Cook safely accomplished they set out for the Silberhorn, with Mount Tasman as their main objective; Mount Tasman was regarded as the most difficult ice-climb in the Southern Alps. They were making good progress when the weather broke and in the end defeated them when they were only 400 feet from the summit. It was a cruel climax to a hard sixteen-hour day.

Freda returned from Australia in February 1912 with many projects in view. They did one of the peaks of the Main Divide near the Copeland Pass and Graham was so proud of her that he christened the peak 'du Faur'. This was a good season for Freda; they went on to make the first ascent of Mount Dampier and then they were off once more to Mount Tasman. Conditions were terrible, even worse than before; the cold was intense; the snow never ceased falling and they both suffered from frostbite. But they had no intention of being defeated again; their determination carried them through and Mount Tasman was theirs at last.

The season that proved to be Freda's greatest was 1913–14, and her last recorded one. With Peter Graham and Dave Thomas she made the first traverse of the three peaks of Mount Cook. This was tremendous – a blue-riband achievement; they called it the 'Grand Traverse' and the name was no exaggeration. They had no crampons; the enormous amount of step-cutting demanded remarkable endurance and for almost the whole climb Freda was suffering considerable pain from swollen lips. But they succeeded, and the climb is still regarded as one of the finest feats in the history of the Southern Alps.

Another great traverse was Sefton and Freda had set her heart on climbing it. Peter Graham described her as 'a go-er' – you had only to suggest something and she would be with you! They engaged a second guide and had the great satisfaction of achieving their aim. The ascent was less arduous than the descent, which was made wearisome by mist and bad weather. They were much delayed and when they eventually reached The Hermitage they were greeted by the news, long delayed in coming, that tragedy had overtaken Captain Scott at the South Pole and he and his party were lost. It saddened their memories of Sefton, which never quite took its right place among their galaxy of great climbs. Perhaps if the 1914 war had not put an end to all mountaineering for six years even more would have been heard of Freda du Faur, but in spite of this early cessation of her activities she is still regarded as one of the greatest women climbers of the Southern Alps.

The year 1906 must have been a period when the star of women mountaineers was in the ascendant. Miss Beatrice McAndrew, a rather fragile little person, only four feet ten inches in height, had come with her family party to the Alps for a year or two and had been introduced to a number of climbers. At first they seemed to her to be a people apart, engaged in a pastime that was not for ordinary mortals. By 1906 she had come to realise that this was far from the truth and that people like herself could, and did, climb. She saw no reason why she should not make a beginning in this exciting new venture; her family was not so sure; she was thought not to be strong and they would have liked to discourage her. But Miss McAndrew was by then thirty-five years of age and had a mind of her own; she engaged a guide and a porter and set out on her first ascent. By the end of the season it was obvious that she was a born mountaineer and everyone had to agree that her health had never been so good. And so began a long life of devotion to the mountains, which became a never-ending source of joy. Miss McAndrew was a prudent person who was careful never to offend against codes of etiquette or take undue risks on the mountains that would bring women climbers into disrepute. She usually climbed with her cousin Freda and their guide was Theodor Baumann of Saas Fee. Zermatt and Saas Fee were their favourite centres and until 1914 they never missed a season.

In 1910 they were staying at the Little Bricolla Hotel when a group of Alpine Club members arrived. The ladies quickly sensed that their presence was slightly resented and tactfully kept out of the way. This must have touched the hard hearts of the A.C. men; they became more genial and enquired if they knew about the Ladies' Alpine Club which had recently been formed. The address of the Club was supplied and Miss McAndrew wrote at once to the secretary. She and her cousin were soon elected as members and this led to the many, many long years of service which Miss McAndrew gave to the Ladies' Alpine Club. She became its Honorary Secretary in 1913 and carried on for twenty years; her work was invaluable and she was always seeking new young members to introduce to the Club. Many of those who joined before and after the Second World War can testify to her unfailing kindness, the warm welcome she gave to everyone and the care she took over each new member.

In the 1920s and early 1930s Miss McAndrew had a strenuous programme arranged for each alpine holiday; when she was not climbing she was painting or sketching and she became well known as a water-colour artist in alpine subjects. In 1939, with Theodor Baumann, she climbed her last peak – the Allalinhorn. When she returned to the Alps in 1946 she was quite reconciled to the fact that the great mountains were now beyond her, but she and Theodor Baumann went off on a long alpine walk just to assure themselves that the old magic was not lost.

Miss McAndrew continued to travel out to the Alps every year and revelled in all that the mountains still had to offer – the flowers, the forests, the streams and most of all the young climbers striding off to the peaks which had given her so much pleasure. In 1957, when she was eighty-six, she enjoyed her last alpine holiday, but her enthusiasm was as great as ever; she came regularly to the meetings of the Ladies' Alpine Club and was a well-loved figure at the annual Dinner until 1968. One of her last big thrills was when her great-niece Jane Gamble was elected a member of the Club. She died in 1970 in her hundredth year. She is irreplaceable.

For later generations Miss McAndrew was the one last link with the heroic past. She symbolised that intrepid generation of women who broke through the barriers of social convention and, at the same time, mollified masculine prejudice and helped to open up the limitless joys of mountaineering to women. We looked up to her as one who had known our Club almost since its beginning and had talked with the great pioneers; she made Lucy Walker, Anna Pigeon, Katy Richardson, Mary Paillon and Mrs Aubrey Le Blond come alive for us. We shall not look upon her like again.

Towards the end of the first decade of the twentieth century women mountaineers were establishing themselves as a force to be reckoned with. They were getting together in groups and clubs and were kindly regarded by the giants of the Alpine Club.

Claude Benson, scholar, writer and keen climber, wrote a book which he entitled *British Mountaineers*, and so far had women advanced in public estimation that he felt it necessary to write a special chapter on 'Mountaineering for Ladies'. He paid great attention to their outfit. The hat, he suggested, should be a tam-o'shanter or soft motoring hat. If very hot a small sailor hat could be substituted, but it *must* (the italics are his) be securely fastened. Cotton or flannel was recommended for the shirt, with a nice neat collar and tie. A norfolk jacket worn over it would 'look work-manlike' and perhaps a golf jersey would be handy for rock climbing. A covert coat he considered to be essential in case of weather changes, pointing out that it might 'save many a cold and chill'. On the subject of skirts he was emphatic. The garment must be quite *short* – at *least* five or six inches from the ground. A good serge would be a suitable choice of material; but it must not be too heavy; navy blue or pepper and salt would be useful colours to consider. It must be cut without any superfluous fullness because in all cases it must be put into the rucksack at the foot of the climb. To climb in a skirt was *utterly insane*. One wonders if Claude Benson got his knuckles rapped by outraged Edwardian

PLATE VII

Margaret Darvall, Alwine Walford and Dorothy Lee on the last hundred feet of the North Face of Erciyas in Turkey
Photo by permission of Frank Solari

PLATE
VIII

Members of the Ladies' Alpine Club ... ... of ... J. M. .. R. ... ... T. J. M., A. L. F., M...

mammas or perhaps a gentle reprimand from the great Lucy Walker.

Naturally the question of knickerbockers loomed up next. These should be in dark blue linen, well-cut and very loose. The mind boggles at what those who followed his advice must have looked – and felt – like on a steep snow slope with a blizzard blowing and sopping linen bloomers flapping like wet sails around their knees. And why change from serge to summer linen on what was almost certain to be the coldest and most windy part of the adventure?

Puttees must be taken on expeditions involving snow mountains or snow-covered glaciers; also loose woollen gloves and a silk handkerchief, or scarf or muffler which might ward off a cold. For the personal impedimenta inseparable from ladies a small school satchel would meet the need and would not be cumbersome.

A little psychological advice rounded off the section on kit. 'Finally my dear lady please, please do remember that because you are doing something which foolish people consider unconventional, it is wholly unnecessary to make a guy of yourself. Some men do!'

Claude Benson sought to encourage his women readers and the advice he gave is as true today as it was then. 'Women are usually successful. They have a good sense of balance, less weight than men and all their strength is in the right place. It is in arm strength that they are weakest.'

Finally, a sound suggestion to those who might have reached the end of their tether – and who has not at some time? 'Not only admit that you are tired – also *declare* it.' And a word for the male companions in true Edwardian style, 'And you, O men, leave the ladies to set the pace and never hurry them.'

Well, perhaps it all sounds paternalist and maybe a little condescending; probably only the most naïve beginner would swallow the whole chapter without a pinch of salt. But it was well meant; Claude Benson's heart was in the right place; his book marked a new stage in the development of women's mountaineering; it is clear that he wished them well and saw a future for them.

. . . . . .

G

The Alpine Club was founded in 1857; it was the first climbing club and, for many years, the only one. From its inception it built up a tremendous reputation and during the 115 years of its existence its position as the greatest mountaineering club in the world has never been challenged. It is, of course, for men only and the standard required for membership is unequalled anywhere.

Probably the most important step in the history of women's mountaineering was the founding of the Ladies' Alpine Club in 1907 just fifty years after the Alpine Club. It began in an unassuming way as a section of the Lyceum Club with Mrs Aubrey Le Blond as its first President. Within a couple of years it had already become too large and too active to remain a subsidiary club and the committee was fortunate in finding rooms in the Great Central Hotel at Marylebone, where the Club quickly established a home of its own. Queen Margherita of Italy consented to become Honorary President and filled the office until her death in 1926. She was the only mountaineer among the royal ladies of Europe; she had a great love for the hills and was a keen climber. Queen Margherita had many peaks to her credit and early in the present century she ascended the Signalkuppe on Monte Rosa to inaugurate the Cabane Margherita, spending the night there with her lady-in-waiting.

The qualifications for membership of the Ladies' Alpine Club were set high from the beginning and have remained so throughout the years. It is this high standard, combined with the international outlook which soon developed, that maintains the position of the club as the premier women's climbing club of the world. Mrs Le Blond, whose drive and vision were invaluable in the early days, laid down some fundamental principles.

'A Club such as ours', she wrote, 'must grow and expand in a natural and healthy manner. It cannot be spasmodically galvanised into renewed life from time to time by artificial means. It must be nourished by the unceasing labour of the members and, above all, its high standard must be maintained so that, as membership carries with it a guarantee of efficiency, it may ever be an honour to belong to it.' The Club has adhered to these principles and, in spite of two World Wars, has prospered exceedingly during the last sixty-five years.

Most of the great pioneers still alive at the time joined the Ladies' Alpine Club: Lucy Walker, Anna Pigeon, 'Katy' Richardson, Mary Paillon and, of course, the invincible Mrs Bullock Workman, who became a Vice-President in 1912. Quite a number of climbers who qualified between 1908 and 1910 lived on for many years – Miss McAndrew, Lady Pattinson, Miss Margaret Osborne, Miss Jean Parker of Canada, as well as the two Miss Westerns, survived until long after the Second World War and forged much-valued links with the early days.

The Alpine Club became a very good friend to the ladies, after overcoming its earlier misgivings. Clinton Dent presented a number of alpine books which had belonged to Mrs E. P. Jackson; this formed the nucleus of the library which the club continued to build up in a big way and which is now one of its greatest treasures. No labour was spared by its founders in making the Club the very best that it could be. They were bursting with enterprise and enthusiasm; they were willing to do anything to ensure its success and they were particularly anxious that it should be a real link between climbers of different nationalities and a help and inspiration to the younger generation. In those early days almost everything the members did was a record for *women* and this helped to enhance the public image – a matter which had to be studied carefully at that time.

Mrs Le Blond remained President until 1913, when she was succeeded by Miss Lucy Walker. By this time the Club was indeed becoming truly international. In her Presidential report Lucy Walker announced members from Austria, France, Germany, Holland, Italy and Switzerland as well as from Australia, Canada, India and Japan. 'A proof', she said, 'that distance is no barrier to the brotherhood of the mountains or the comradeship of those who love the hills.'

The Ladies' Alpine Club has always been a sociable affair; its reputation for hospitality developed early in its career and has continued unabated. There were monthly lectures and 'At Homes', and in those more leisurely days there was nothing members

enjoyed more than to meet for tea. It was not an extravagance –
tea, bread and butter and cake and the pleasure of a coal fire cost
9d! Those were the days indeed.

The first Year Book was published in 1913 and the first published climbing lists recorded climbs in the Japanese Alps, two
peaks of 21,000 feet in the Karakoram and fine achievements in
the Alps. Outstanding among these were the many ascents of
Margaret Osborne, an Irishwoman who always climbed with her
brother, Judge Osborne, who was a member of the Alpine Club. By
1913 she had done all the great traverses in the Alps and the guides
used to say that they never reckoned her among women climbers
but counted her among the men.

The annual Club Dinners, which have become increasingly
famous in mountaineering circles, began in 1909 and continued
regularly until 1913. They were unable to be held again until
1920 but have continued since without cessation except from
1940–5, when luncheons were held instead.

In the early years many famous names appeared among the lists
of guests – Sir Claud Schuster, Sir Edward Davidson, Sir Martin
Conway, Geoffrey Winthrop Young. Equally well-known names
are included today, but in those far-off times it was considered a
particular triumph to have secured their presence. The Club
owed much to the active interest of these great mountaineers.

In 1914, of course, mountaineering came to an end for all British
climbers. According to the Year Book for 1916 ice-axes had been
converted into knitting needles and ropes into bandages! All
women were playing their part in any way open to them and the
members of the Ladies' Alpine Club were no exception. They
served as nurses, munition workers, and in the V.A.D. Some,
including Mrs Le Blond, went overseas. In 1916 the Great Central
Hotel was taken over by the government and with it went the
Ladies' Alpine Club rooms. Everything had to be stored until
the property was handed back to the Club in 1920. Meanwhile
the Club lost two of its most famous and well-loved members –
Lucy Walker and Anna Pigeon, both of whom were in their
eighties.

When Lucy Walker died in 1916 she had just completed her

three years of office as President; Miss Maud Meyer was elected to succeed her. Maud Meyer was a Resident Lecturer in Mathematics at Girton and later became Director of Studies. It might be thought strange that the society hostess Mrs Le Blond and the quiet home-loving Lucy Walker should be followed by a blue stocking. First-class women mathematicians were few and far between in those days and had a reputation for a stern, unrelenting attitude to life. Maud Meyer was exactly the opposite of all these things; her brilliance belied her. She had the flame-like spirit of the aesthete; she loved the mountains and, above all, the glory of them; she could spend hours just drinking in the beauty spread out around her.

She was a fearless climber, with immense staying power and a remarkable turn of speed when necessary. She tackled all the biggest climbs, including the Taeschhorn by the Teufelsgrat. More than anything else she loved the Meije – as so many women have done before and since. Like Mrs Le Blond she quietly freed herself from the shackles of her late-Victorian past, made the most of the greater liberty of the Edwardian age and, with others of her generation, saw the Ladies' Alpine Club successfully through its initial stages. The last years of the First War were not the easiest in which to be President, but Maud Meyer kept the flag flying and succeeded in keeping the members together and the spirit of the Club unimpaired. When better days dawned full advantage could be taken of them. She was killed in a bicycle accident in London in 1924; the Club lost a good friend and a popular President.

Shortly before the founding of the Ladies' Alpine Club, the Fell and Rock Club came into existence – in 1906. It filled a much-felt need for British week-end climbers who seldom visited the Alps but were mountain lovers, rock climbers and/or fell walkers. It was open from the first to men and women and is still one of the most popular climbing clubs in the country, and most adequately fulfils its *raison d'être*, namely to provide one centre where friends and relatives of both sexes can meet and climb together.

That there were a number of women members from the club's beginning and that they were very active is made clear in an amusing note at the end of the section entitled 'Club Meets', 1907, in the first number of the Journal, for which I am indebted to Lady Chorley. It reads thus:

'*A Ladies' Week at Wasdale.*'

A man hates a 'mannish' woman; but when a slight girl equals him at his favourite sport and yet retains her womanliness, he readily admits her claim to a place 'on the rope' and admires her greatly in consequence. It was with unbiased feelings of admiration, perhaps occasionally tinged with a little envy, that a privileged few watched the daughters of our worthy V.P., and the ease with which they recently waltzed up some of the stiffest climbs around Wasdale. It is no little feat, and I should say, rarely equalled by a lady, for the Misses Annie and Evelyn Seatree to have bagged during a ten day stay in the dale such climbs as: Moss Ghyll, North Climb Pillar Rock, Scawfell Pinnacle by Steep Ghyll and Slingsby's Chimney; Kern Knotts Chimney; Oblique Chimney; Doctor's Chimney; Pillar Rock by Right and Left Jordan and Pisgah Direct.

What a delightful period piece; the Misses Seatree were worthy predecessors of the notable climbers who followed them in the 1920s – Pat Kelly and Dorothy Pilley-Richards being among them.

In 1908 came the Ladies' Scottish Climbing Club – just one year younger than the Ladies' Alpine Club. It all came about in a delightfully informal way. Three Scottish ladies, Mrs Inglis Clark, her daughter Mrs Jeffrey, and Miss Lucy Smith, on their way back from a climb were sheltering in a mist behind a boulder on the High Road near Crianlarich. To pass the time they discussed women's mountaineering and decided, there and then, to form a Climbing Club, a club for women which would hold meets among their own Scottish hills and give them a chance to climb just as women.

The idea of guideless climbing with only women in the party

was new in 1908, indeed it was regarded as quite revolutionary; many Scottish women were a little doubtful and the number of members at first was few. Qualifications in 1908 were four mountains of 3,000 feet and two snow climbs – by no means easy to acquire. But there were some good women climbers about and in a few months the membership was fourteen.

There was still some lingering criticism of women climbers to contend with, which meant that the Club did not get off to an easy start. However, the founders were shrewd and experienced women with a wide vision and the precepts of the Club were drawn up with a view to disarming criticism from any side. These are some of them: 'The spirit of rivalry should never enter into mountaineering expeditions.' 'Always climb deliberately, slowly and carefully; a slip, even when harmless, is something to be ashamed of.' 'Remember above all that each member has the reputation of the Club to make and uphold, and that even the slightest mishap would immediately bring the Club into disrepute.'

Such rules may seem somewhat over-cautious today, but in 1908 they put the Club on its feet, the membership increased continually and today the Ladies' Scottish Climbing Club is still one of the most highly regarded mountaineering societies.

It seems rather strange that so little was heard of Swiss women climbers in the days when the pioneers were striving so nobly to establish mountaineering for women. It was not until the years of the First World War that Swiss women took the matter seriously. Then, cut off as they were from the rest of the world, they turned their attention to the Alps – in fact it seems as if, in their isolation, they discovered their own mountains. Climbing among women increased rapidly and in 1918 the *Schweizerische Frauen Alpen Club* was born. There have never been any qualifications for membership; it came into being to bring women mountaineers together and to assist them in the mountains in every way. Foreign members were welcomed at once and today large numbers of women climbers from all over the world belong to the Club. Members have reduced rates in the Swiss Alpine Club huts and on mountain

railways and teleferiques. The Club has its own chalet – a delightful place where members and their guests can stay quite inexpen-
sively. It is a pleasant Club and its attractive badge is admired
throughout the Alps.

The Swiss Women's Alpine Club now has a membership of
several thousand; this being so it is sometimes asked why it is
that Swiss women do not seem to have so many outstanding
achievements to their credit, and are not quite so well known
outside their own country. There are exceptions, of course, Loulou Boulaz and Yvette Vaucher are internationally famous.
Marta Daeniker, whose husband was for many years the Swiss
Ambassador in London, and who is herself a member of the
Ladies' Alpine Club and the Swiss Women's Alpine Club, once
gave a helpful interpretation of the situation. She pointed out
that in a country where climbing is so popular and is within such
easy reach, something that was once a hair-raising adventure has
become a week-end pursuit. Just because it is so usual and so close
at hand it is no longer regarded as an achievement. But this in no
way diminishes the Swiss women's love of their mountains or
their joy in climbing them; indeed, one has only to climb with the
Swiss to realise that mountains are part of their very being and if
they have to leave them for any length of time they feel strangely
deprived.

When the war ended in 1918 the world was a different place and
the position of women had been entirely revolutionised. They
emerged from the conflict as people who had proved themselves
and had acquired a new status in society. Their position was
recognised and applauded on all sides; no longer need they
struggle for their freedom; that contest had been fought and
won.

Women mountaineers were ready for this changed situation
and eager to take advantage of it. Throughout the fifty or so
years during which women had been climbing they had always
moved circumspectly; they had never sought to draw attention to
themselves and they had done homage to convention almost
ad nauseam. But it had paid off in the end; the reputation of women

mountaineers stood high; the Ladies' Alpine Club, the Ladies
Scottish Climbing Club, the Swiss Women's Alpine Club and the
Fell and Rock were all thriving; women stood poised to take off
into the great new era awaiting the world. They did so with confidence in themselves and in the world around them – the rewards
proved to be worth the winning.

Chapter 5

Ladies Only

By 1920 mountaineering had got into its stride again in all parts of the world and climbers were compiling their programmes with renewed zest. The enforced hiatus of six years had supplied a fresh impetus; there was a sudden flowering of mountain enthusiasm which widened horizons and tapped new sources of supply for would-be mountaineers. This was true of women as well as of men. In the past, like their male counterparts, women climbers had been recruited mainly from the families of the learned professions. They were gifted, highly educated ladies of leisure; many were artists, writers or linguists; often they gave unsparingly of their time and considerable financial help to voluntary, philanthropic activities and the war had proved what they could do in other ways if it was demanded of them. Maud Meyer, the Cambridge don, was one of the very few women mountaineers employed in a full-time occupation.

In the 1920s career girls, students, housewives, mothers and schoolgirls were added to the ranks of active mountaineers; they were enthusiastically received by the established climbers; there was little talk of the 'generation gap' or any nonsense of that kind. The mountains were the common denominator and the climbing world was a happy and usually united fraternity.

The year 1921 saw the emergence of the Pinnacle Club – the first rock-climbing club founded by women for women. It was the brain-child of Pat Kelly and was greatly encouraged by Geoffrey Winthrop Young; it was in no sense a feminist gesture. Many young women who had taken to mountaineering in such free time as they had during the war had been obliged to concentrate on Wales and the Lake District. This had brought rock-climbing to the fore, at any rate temporarily. They had come to feel that a rock-climbing club for women only would provide training in the responsibilities of leadership and in mountaineering in general and they felt very strongly that this could only be gained if they climbed by themselves.

The Inaugural Meeting of the Pinnacle Club took place on 20th March 1921, at Pen-y-Gwryd in North Wales. The first Honorary Secretary was Pat Kelly and the first President was Len Winthrop Young, wife of the famous Geoffrey. The qualification for full membership was the ability to lead an ordinary difficult climb. The club prospered slowly but surely; it established its own Cwm Dyli hut in Gwynant (it was the first women's club to own a hut) and among its earlier leaders were such brilliant climbers as Brenda Ritchie and Evelyn Lowe (Leech), to mention only two.

Within a year of the founding of the Pinnacle Club yet another association of climbers had sprung up; this was the M.A.M. (the Midland Association of Mountaineers) which from the first offered membership to women on equal terms with men. Women were numbered among the original members, of which there were forty-two, and they have always been very active participants. For some time the M.A.M. remained as an association of climbers who often belonged to other clubs but were not able to take full advantage of their membership in London or in the north. They were thus grateful for an organisation which met in their own area. Very soon, however, it was developing so quickly that it became obvious that it would have to become a quite independent club. Many famous climbers had close links with the M.A.M.: General Bruce, the Winthrop Youngs, W. P. Hasket Smith and L. S. Amery who became President in 1927–9. Time went by and in 1951 Miss Ailsa Jacques was elected President; she was the first woman to hold that office and proved to be an excellent choice.

Probably the outstanding woman mountaineer of the early 1920s – and for many years after – was Dorothy Pilley, now Dorothy Pilley-Richards, who was a founder member of the Pinnacle Club and later Editor of the *Pinnacle Journal*. She began as a rock climber, but once the Alps were opened up again there was no stopping her. She had only to see a major peak to be filled with an insatiable longing to climb it; and the more difficult the route the more alluring she found it.

But Dorothy Pilley-Richards was, and is, a mountain lover as well as a mountaineer: her mountains are not merely for climbing, they are for enjoying to the full, for providing an answer to the meaning of life, for emphasising the little as well as the great things of the natural world. For all these things she is grateful and she regards the mountains with reverence.

Dorothy became a member of the Ladies' Alpine Club in 1920 and was rather overwhelmed by the honour. She stood in great awe of the older members with their long experience and spectacular achievements; she loved the club-room and the library and the cosy teas which could be ordered and eaten against a décor of portraits, mountain pictures, famous books and 'emblematic ice-axes'. If Dorothy admired the club, the club soon came to admire her and regard her as a virtuoso, with her annual list of exciting ascents.

In her first alpine season she did the traverse of the Charmoz, the Grépon, the traverse of the Drus, the Dent du Géant and the Petit Clocher de Planereuse; this astonishing curtain-raiser set the pace for the rest of her fabulous climbing career. In her next season, 1921, Dorothy decided to investigate with two friends, Lilian Bray and Annie Wells, the possibilities of women climbing 'sans hommes'. They had success on the Mittaghorn-Egginer and survived a violent thunderstorm on the Portjengrat. It was a short experiment but a useful one and established the truth of the fact they had set out to prove. Dorothy went over to Zermatt – her first visit and so a great event – and climbed the Z'mutt ridge of the Matterhorn. A few days later she arrived at Ferpècle to join a group of friends; it was an historic occasion, for here she met Professor I. A. Richards, destined to be not only her life-long climbing companion but also her husband. After several ascents together from Ferpècle they came down from the Douves Blanches to the Bertol Hut and here another fateful meeting took place. Chatting with the *gardien* of the hut was a gay young guide with bright blue eyes – none other than Joseph Georges, *le skieur* who became their friend and guide until serious illness and death brought his career to an end in 1960.

The stage was now set for great events and for the next three years Dorothy, I. A. R. (as he is always known) and Joseph Georges tackled the biggest peaks they could find in Spain, in Italy, in the Mont Blanc chain, in the Oberland and Valais. Times change and mountaineering standards change with them, as Dorothy Pilley-Richards is the first to point out in the second edition of her alpine classic *Climbing Days*. Routes thought to be next to impossible in her early days are sometimes dismissed as mere scrambles in the present era. Nevertheless, for ordinary run-of-the-mill mountaineers it is quietly satisfying to read in her description of the Wellenkuppe-Obergabelhorn-Arbengrat traverse that a Swiss enthusiast described it as *'la course la plus chic de la région'*. Some simple souls still regard it as such!

For two years after this Dorothy was breaking new ground in the United States and Canada – a prelude to the many years she was later to spend there – and finally came home to marry I.A.R. As a delayed honeymoon trip they decided in 1928, in collaboration with Joseph Georges and his brother Antoine, to try the first ascent of the great North Ridge of the Dent Blanche. They had been disappointed on this some years before and had never lost the desire to try again.

Whatever may be said about rising standards of difficulty this pioneer climb is still spoken of as one of the great mountaineering achievements of the century. After incredible adventures they reached the summit successfully; Dorothy never forgets how shortly before the final pitch Joseph Georges peeped down over an enormous rock bulge, found Dorothy and I.A.R. clinging desperately to one joint handhold and remarked with a twinkle, *'Ah, les amoureux'*! Of such events are the golden days of climbing composed.

The Richards have always described 1928 as 'the Great Year'. When it was over they left the Alps to travel far and wide and climb in many distant mountain regions in the process. For years they lived in the United States, but whenever possible they stole away to the Alps in the summer. As the years have gone by their ascents have inevitably become less spectacular, but they enjoy them with the same enthusiasm. A few years ago, as they were wandering slowly down from the Breithorn to the Plateau Rosa, one of the great Zermatt guides was watching them through binoculars from Testa Grigia. 'There you see', he said admiringly, 'British climbers of the old school: they have never been bettered, and seldom equalled.'

Some of the leading women explorers and travellers of this century have had more than a passing interest in mountaineering. Freya Stark (Mrs Perowne) is no exception. Soon after the First War she made a few expeditions from her home in Dronero in Northern Italy; the Alps gripped her at that time and drew her back year after year. She did the Breithorn and was captivated by the view of Monte Rosa and the Matterhorn. After many doubts had been expressed by the guides on account of her fragile appearance, Freya got her own way and traversed the Matterhorn from Zermatt to Breuil. She did this with so little apparent effort and with so much obvious ability that the guides assured her that they would be willing to take her on any or all of the biggest climbs in the Alps. It was tempting, but her time was limited; there were not many opportunities for mountaineering and Monte Rosa still remained her lode-star.

In 1924 Freya was staying, as she often did, at Macugnaga; from there the Marinelli Couloir of Monte Rosa beckoned incessantly. A close intimacy was created between the mountain and the climber; the call of that couloir was a call that could not be denied – the more so since it had never yet been done by a woman.

At last the day came when her guide Topfi pronounced the weather to be suitable and they set out with a porter, and a young Belgian companion to share expenses, for the Marinelli Hut. While Topfi cooked their supper they spent the evening watching the great convoys of avalanches crashing down the couloir. Monta Rosa by this route is a long climb but the greatest danger – the crossing of the Marinelli Couloir – is of comparatively short duration. There is a sheet of wide, smooth ice; it can only be crossed soon after midnight, when frost grips the mountain in iron hands, and it has to be accomplished with all possible speed.

Freya's party crossed quickly and safely; from there they had an ascent of twelve hours to the summit, entailing five hours of step-cutting up the face of the Loccie glacier, which falls in a steep cascade of tumbled ice. They reached the summit in exactly twelve hours and made their way under the brow of Monte Rosa to the Cabane Margherita to spend the night. At 3 a.m. they began the return journey, descending via the Turbo Pass, and were back in Macugnaga in time for tea.

It was a great climb and Freya Stark describes it as the only really big ascent of her life. Illness, sadly, put an end to her climbing not long after this, to her great disappointment. 'I have regretted the loss of mountaineering more than most things,' she wrote, 'it was the key of a world a little above the human world and beyond it, where one could always find a refuge from friction and time.'

Another name to conjure with in those days was that of the Dutch woman climber Rini Deelen-Jurgens. Small and wiry, possessed of immense energy and perseverance and, above all, a deep love of the mountains, her favourite centres were the Dolomites and Zermatt, with occasional visits to Chamonix. When she was at the height of her powers her lists of ascents included Spigolo del Velo of the Cima della Madonna; the North Face of the Breithorn; the Nadelhorn-Lenzspitze-Dom traverse; the Bieshorn-Weisshorn traverse, up the North ridge and down the Schalligrat with a bivouac on the Schallijoch; the Dent Blanche by the Viereselgrat; the traverse of the Matterhorn by the Zmutt ridge; the Younggrat on the Breithorn; the Grépon and Mont Blanc by the Brenva ridge. In spite of her origin in a country almost devoid of hills Rini Deelen-Jurgens was one of the outstanding women climbers of her time and Holland had a very special pride in her achievements.

Non-climbers tend to associate mountaineering with the large, tough, he-man type of woman; it is hard to persuade them that most, although not all, women mountaineers are light and slimly built. Dorothy Thompson who, from the mid-1920s until after the Second World War, was one of the really great British women climbers was a neat, unobtrusive little figure, scarcely known outside mountaineering circles until her book *Climbing with Joseph Georges* was published posthumously. Indeed she was so quiet and unassuming that younger climbers, meeting her after her heyday, seldom realised what a tigress she had been.

'Tommy', as she was affectionately known to all her friends, began her climbing career in 1922 when Dorothy and Ivor Richards introduced her to Joseph Georges *le skieur*. Tommy and Joseph Georges proved to be perfectly suited as climbing partners. For the next six years they concentrated on the great standard routes in Savoy, the Valais, the Graians, and the Dauphiné, where their programme included the Aiguille d'Arve and the Meije. Somehow she managed also to fit in a short, guideless spell in the Tarentaise with two fellow members of the Ladies' Alpine Club, Dorothy Pilkington and Molly FitzGibbon.

In 1929 Tommy was attracted to the great ridges of Mont Blanc; during the next few years she reached, in all senses, the peak of her climbing career. In that first year, with Joseph Georges and Marcel Meyseiller, she did Mont Blanc from the Quintino Sella Hut by the Emil Rey Couloir and the Brouillard Ridge. As they sat enjoying a meal between the Italian and French summits Joseph Georges remarked, 'Do you know, Mlle, that you have made climbing history today as the first woman to climb the Brouillard Arête – the first woman to climb one of the Val Veni ridges'?

Tommy wrote later that she just sat and stared at them, unable to believe that they were speaking the truth.

'*Bien sur*', said Marcel decisively, '*jamais aucune dame.*' They descended to the Grands Mulets for the night and the next day strolled down in leisurely fashion to the Montanvers, where the long day ended in the best possible way – with an evening spent with members of the Groupe de Haute Montagne, recounting experiences and singing French songs.

The greatest and most satisfying of all Dorothy Thompson's achievements was the traverse of Mont Blanc from the Refuge Durier over the Aiguille Bionnassay with the first-ever descent by a woman of the Peuteret Ridge to the Gamba Hut. The Peuteret Ridge is regarded as the finest, longest and most difficult ridge in the Alps – something to which all great climbers aspire but few achieve. With Joseph Georges and Marcel Tommy did it in thirty-four hours; almost a record in itself.

From 1933 onwards ski-mountaineering became a new delight for Tommy and in 1939, just before the curtains of war closed on the Alps which she loved so much, she did Piz Kesch, Piz Flinna, the Signalhorn, the Fluela Weisshorn, the traverse of the Pischahorn and many more.

Dorothy Thompson died in 1961 at the age of seventy-three after a long illness which she faced with the same courage and gaiety that she had always shown in the mountains. Her book, intended as a tribute to her beloved guide Joseph Georges, has, in the eyes of her friends, become her own memorial.

Before 1920 comparatively few schoolgirls were taken on mountaineering expeditions in the Alps, in fact teenagers were seldom heard of in the climbing world; it was usual to embark on such adventures rather later in life. The post-war period changed all that as it changed so much else; if girls wanted to climb, parents were prepared to give them the opportunity.

Eileen Jackson, the only daughter of a climbing family, commenced her career at twelve years of age by doing the Mittaghorn and the Allalinhorn during a holiday at Saas Fee. The following year the family were in the Engadine where she did the Piz Morteratsch, the Drei Schwestern and the Piz Albris. After a rather frustrating visit to the Tyrol in 1924, when the mountains were out of condition for almost the whole of August, they arrived at Trient in 1925 to get in training for the Zermatt mountains, which were the real objective that year. The Aiguille du Tour. with her father and a guideless scramble on the little Mont Arpille

H

with her brother were a good prelude to greater things and Eileen arrived in Zermatt with her heart set on the Matterhorn.

Alois Biner had been engaged as their guide and planned a programme which was to culminate with the Matterhorn – weather permitting! Eileen was endowed with all the enthusiasm of the women mountaineers of earlier days; everything connected with the mountains was full of interest. The medallion portrait of Edward Whymper had just been inserted in the wall of the Monte Rosa Hotel; Charles Hudson's daughter was present in the English church for the dedication of the altar rails given in memory of her father; the old guide in charge of the Alpine Museum proved to be the very one who had accompanied the American woman climber Annie Peck on the first ascent of the north summit of Huascaran in the Andes; two members of the Ladies' Alpine Club introduced themselves in the Monte Rosa and admitted to having climbed the Matterhorn no less than three times – it was all a great thrill for a keen, talented young climber. And there was, of course, the sad occasion of the funeral of Eleonore Noll-Hassenclever, mentioned in the previous chapter, which Eileen found so moving.

Alois Biner, one of the kindest and most understanding of guides, entered into the spirit of everything. He took them on all the various Riffelhorn routes; they went to the Gandegg Hut for the Breithorn, only to be driven home by a foot of snow. But on the next fine day the whole family went over the Furggjoch to Breuil and climbed the Breithorn from there. The Wellenkuppe followed for Eileen and her father with Alois and then, at last, the weather became suitable for the Matterhorn.

Nothing was left to chance; Alois engaged three more guides, one of whom was his son Bernard, so that there should be two guides for each climber. On a sunny day they walked up to spend the night at the Belvedere; everything seemed to be perfect, and then the unbelievable happened. Alois became unwell in the night and at 2 a.m. he knew that he would be too unfit to risk the climb. He came to Mr Jackson to break the news.

'I am very sorry sir,' he said, 'I shall not be able to climb this morning; but if you can trust your daughter with my son, I can trust my son with your daughter.'

And so it came about that Eileen, aged fifteen, climbed the Matterhorn with Bernard Biner – with whom she had never climbed before – and made the descent in one hour forty minutes, at that time the fastest descent on record. Years afterwards, when Bernard was Chief Guide of Zermatt and one of the most famous guides in Switzerland, he told us, 'That child was the fastest climber I have ever had on my rope.'

As might be expected, Eileen went on to greater things with Bernard; in the following year she did the Rothorngrat and the Matterhorn couloir on the Riffelhorn; by the time she was eighteen she had added the Dent Blanche and the Wellenkuppe-Obergabelhorn-Arbengrat traverse. When she was at the university she was leading 'severes' in the Lake District and making even more exciting ascents in the Alps; to many it seemed that another 'Katy' Richardson had appeared on the scene. But it was not to be; in her early twenties Eileen was struck down by a rare and serious illness. In the course of years modern medicine and her indomitable courage have triumphed; she has never again been able to climb, but in 1969 she was in the high mountains again, pony trekking in the Himalayas – a just reward indeed.

By the 1920s women had become such an integral part of the climbing world that they were always personally involved in any major mountaineering enterprise. Thus when in 1922 the first British Expedition was ready to set out for Mount Everest the Ladies' Alpine Club gave a dinner in London in honour of the members of the expedition.

It took place on 17th March on the eve of their departure for India and all the members of the expedition accepted the invitation. It was a convivial evening and such occasions seem to have had a more romantic atmosphere about them than might be the case today. One member of the expedition made a speech in which he reminded the assembled company that in earlier days, in the Age of Chivalry, when knights set out in search of adventure each carried with him an embroidered banner – a token of esteem and good wishes from the ladies they had left behind them. The Ladies'

Alpine Club took the hint but decided, with down-to-earth commonsense, that an embroidered banner might prove an embarrassing gift in the Himalayan context. Instead an L.A.C. badge was presented to each member; it was received with gratitude and each recipient promised faithfully to carry it with him to the highest point he reached on the mountain. Those in the keeping of George Leigh Mallory and Sandy Irvine must presumably have been taken to at least 27,000 feet, the height at which these two climbers were last seen alive. Whether or not the L.A.C. badge has in fact reached the highest summit in the world is one of those mysteries which must for ever remain unsolved.

In France, soon after the First World War, a very exclusive climbing club was born. Three young Frenchmen, Jacques de Lépiney, Paul Chevalier and Henry de Ségogne, while bivouacking on the Peuteret Ridge of Mont Blanc decided to found the Groupe de Haute Montagne – as a section of the French Alpine Club. The club was open to men and women; its members must be able to lead on severe climbs and to climb without guides. The standard of difficulty was very high and so ensured great alpine efficiency among the members.

The response was encouraging; the club flourished; it produced a new type of climber – a kind of professional amateur endowed with much of the climbing ability and know-how of the great professional guides. To be elected to the G.H.M. – as it has always been known – became the ambition of many of the young 'tigers' of all nations, and not least of a good many women mountaineers. Some of those mentioned hereafter in this chapter achieved membership during their climbing careers.

By 1930 outstanding first ascents by women in the Alps, and farther afield, were making news in each succeeding season.

Una Cameron, later to become a President of the Ladies' Alpine Club, had great success in the Mont Blanc range with the guides Edouard Bareux and Elisée Croux. She did the Sentinelle Ridge, the Innominata Ridge, the Route Major and the Brenva Ridge. Then with the same companions she joined forces with another future President of the Ladies' Alpine Club; this was Dora de Beer, who climbed with the guides Mario Rey and Mario Cosson. This combined party climbed the Peuteret Ridge of Mont Blanc in 1935 and Una and Dora became the first British women to make this famous ascent. Una then turned her attention to Africa; accompanied once more by her same guides she did the Nelion and Batian peaks of Mount Kenya in 1938 and was the first woman to climb both peaks.

Incidentally, Mount Kenya seems to have been particularly popular in 1938; a guideless ascent was made by a woman climber, Geraldine Sladen, with her brother and this was almost certainly the first time this famous mountain had been climbed without guides.

Flashback from Africa to the Alps brings to mind Mollie FitzGibbon who climbed, like so many more, with Joseph Georges, *le skieur*. Together they did the East Ridge of the Aiguille du Plan and the first traverse of the Eiger-Hornli. And there was Hermione Blandy (de Freitas Martins), so chic and so gentle, who, with her guide, made the first ascent – '*Direttissime*' – of the South Wall of Pomagagnon and the first ascent by a woman of the North Ridge of Badile, and who always managed to return from any climb, however severe, looking as if she was just about to set out!

To the delight of all climbers, and especially to the devotees of Zermatt, this decade brought to the Alps Ethel Whymper, the only child of her famous father. She visited Zermatt for the first time in 1929 and during the next few years did the Dom, the Rothorngrat, the Younggrat of the Breithorn, the Brenva Ridge of Mont Blanc and, to her great satisfaction, traversed the Matterhorn from Zermatt down to Breuil. In 1937 Ethel married Edward Blandy, a member of the Alpine Club. Later chapters of this book will reveal that in due time a member of the next generation has followed in the footsteps of her renowned grandfather.

In 1933 Mrs Odell, wife of the Everest climber Noel Odell the last man to see Mallory and Irvine alive) made an extensive tour

of Greenland with her husband and later accompanied him to New
Zealand where they continued their explorations.

From New Zealand also there came in 1933 the epic story of
the courage and resource of another British woman climber. Wren
Corry (Robinson) set out in January with her guide Mark Lysons
for some major ascents among the peaks at the head of the Franz
Josef glacier in New Zealand. All went well until they were descending Mount Goldsmith; here Mark Lysons attempted to jump
a bergschrund, slipped and broke his leg. There was no other
party in sight at the time and distances in the Southern Alps are
enormous. Wren improvised a splint from a split ski, which she
bound on with puttees and a leather belt. With the injured limb
relatively secure they decided to try to get back to the Almer,
realising that there was little chance of a search party finding them.
Wren led down the peak an inch at a time; when they reached the
glacier Mark was able to use their ice-axes as crutches; slowly and
painfully they crossed the glacier. After nearly twelve hours
darkness forced them to bivouac until dawn. Provisions were
running short and they were existing on a diet of gingernuts,
raisins and chocolate. In the cold light of a mountain morning
they set out once more. The accident had occurred at midday on a
Tuesday; they reached the hut at 8 a.m. on the next day, Wren
having brought the guide down quite alone during a wearisome
period of twenty hours. She expected no laurel wreath and did not
seem to regard her performance as in any way exceptional. Her
real reward was that her guide made an excellent recovery and was
able to climb again.

Many British women were building up great reputations during
the unsettled years of the 1930s, among them two sisters, Dr Maud
Cairney and Mrs Murray. They had started in the Alps way back
in the 1920s. Dr Cairney made the first winter ascent of the
Obergabelhorn in 1927 – having skied from Ayez to the Mountet
hut – and in 1928 she made the first ascent of the N.E. face of the
Dent Blanche with the guides Théophile and Hilaire Theytaz of
Zinal. During the next ten years the two sisters tackled peaks of
every difficulty in almost every mountain range in the world. They

said very little about their achievements but their names are never forgotten when the great events of that period are discussed.

This was the great era too of the guide–climber partnerships inaugurated fifty years before by Lucy Walker and Melchior Anderegg. Joseph Georges with the two Richards, Dorothy Thompson and his many other friends; Théophile Theytaz who led Dr Cairney and her sister; Othon Bron the trusted leader of Michael and Janet (Adam Smith) Roberts. There were many, many more, not least Bernard Biner of Zermatt to whose *Führerbuch* so many contributed their paeans of praise and gratitude in later years. A glance through Bernard's *Führerbuch* spells out a long story of mountain adventure; the messages from his male clients are succinct, grateful and to the point and were valuable recommendations for any guide. Those from his lady climbers are infinitely more interesting and more revealing. Miss Edna Joslin, for example, a frail little lady who, at the age of sixty-eight, was still prepared to tackle the North Face of the Breithorn with Bernard, wrote year after year of his 'charming companionship', how difficulties vanished under his selfless leadership, and how at the end of the season she was already longing for the next. And Christine Reid from America who embellished her contributions with microscopic water-colour sketches and paid tribute in verse to their ascents of the North East Face of Monte Rosa and the Marinelli Couloir; the Younggrat on the Breithorn even produced a few bars of music!

It was a far cry from the days of Lucy Walker and Melchior Anderegg and Meta Brevoort and Christian Almer, but the *rapport* between guide and climber was almost identical in spite of the lapse of sixty years.

It was by no means only British women who were setting the pace in the years leading up to the Second World War. Mrs Don Mundy, a Canadian, made many pioneers ascents with her husband in British Columbia, often with her little daughter in a rucksack on her back. A French woman, Mme Paul Dalmais, with her husband and the Charlet guides made the first ascent of the

Col du Pain de Sucre from the North East – a particularly mag-
nificent ice-climb. Away in the Himalayas Frau Dyrenfurth with
her husband and two guides pioneered the ascent of Queen Mary
Peak in the Karakoram – the first woman to follow Mrs Bullock
Workman. Elizabeth Cowles (Partridge), a charming and intrepid
American from Colorado Springs, climbed the East Ridge of the
Grand Teton and reached a height of nearly 19,000 feet in the
Sierra Nevada. And during these years, too, the Swiss woman
explorer Ella Maillart, who travels and climbs and lives in fearless
and happy solitude, travelled east from Moscow to the mountains
on the eastern frontier of Russian Turkestan and from the summit
of her first climb of 17,000 feet saw a vision of China to which,
henceforward, her life was orientated.

Nearer home a young Dutch girl was beginning a great climbing career which is by no means finished yet. The lack of hills
in their own country has never prevented the Dutch from climbing. The Netherlands Alpine Club – since its jubilee known as the
Royal Netherlands Alpine Club – has always had its quota of
great climbers. Not least among these was the Roelfsema family;
first the father, then Roeli the son, and finally the daughter Anna.
In the 1930s Anna climbed with her brother and their Zermatt
guide Bernard Biner, and occasionally she and her brother climbed
guideless. Probably their greatest climb, and the one which gave
them the most pleasure was the guideless ascent of the Younggrat
in 1936; it was the first ever guideless ascent with a woman in the
party. In 1928 four French climbers had attempted the Younggrat
without guides; the day ended in disaster and all were lost. This
sombre story was unknown to Anna, and Roeli decided not to
enlighten her until their own adventure was safely over.

In 1936 tradition was not scorned as it so often is today.
Roeli and Anna were young – Anna was still in her twenties –
but they found real delight in the things which had been hallowed
by previous generations of climbers. They dined at the Monte
Rosa in Zermatt, mecca of all mountaineers; they slept at the
Riffelberg, just because in earlier days it had been the starting-
point for Monte Rosa and the Breithorn. They left at midnight
under a full moon with the mountain world glittering around

them. Five hours later the slow dawn found them just below their snow ridge; they sat down for a second breakfast, taking no thought of time, 'only of the beauty of this moonlight night, the tension and excitement of the climb', wrote Roeli, using language understood by every true mountaineer. They mounted the snow ridge, 'thin as a blade and impressively steep'. Looking up they saw the final face, more or less overhanging, barring direct approach to the top. At the spot where the four French climbers had failed Roeli had to find a way out. Relying on a sixty metre rope he traversed thirty metres to the right and climbed up through a chimney of iced rock; every step had to be cut in black ice. After a further ten metres there was a good place to belay and Anna came up to join her brother. More iced rock and steep snow; then suddenly a warm welcome blaze of sunshine; the traverse, which is the clue to the climb, had taken them an hour.

The next hour, to quote Roeli again, was 'pure bliss'. At 11.30 a.m. they took a final look from the summit down the great North Face then, grateful and content, they began the descent.

It was Roeli's last guideless ascent; he was killed in the war. Anna continued to climb with Bernard Biner and, later, with Bernard Perren, but by 1965 both these fine guides had died. In 1969, thirty-three years after that unforgettable first ascent, a great urge overcame her to experience once more the fascination of the Younggrat. With Gottlieb Perren, twin brother of Bernard, she set out to re-live the glories of that day 'yesterday, many years ago'. She was not disappointed; all her most splendid memories were fulfilled.

With so many remarkable ascents being performed by women climbers all over the world it is hardly surprising that Mrs Herbert Dawson should write in the editorial columns of the Ladies' Alpine Club Journal during the 1930s: *'Can we hope that the day is not far distant when our achievements will be judged on their own merits, rather than over-praised because we are women.'*

This pious hope was speedily fulfilled; women began climbing not only guideless with husbands and brothers, but *sans hommes*. This turn of events set the seal on the honoured position they had already attained. Now, as it were, they had 'arrived'; in future they took their place among the climbing fraternity as mountaineers rather than as women who happened to be climbers.

In the years immediately preceding the Second World War there were a good many women who were involved in climbing *sans hommes* but there were three leading exponents whose names will always be especially associated with this brave new venture: Miriam Underhill, an American; Loulou Boulaz, a Swiss from Canton Vaud; and last, but not least, our own British Nea Morin.

Miriam Underhill (or O'Brien as she was in her earlier days before she married) is a colourful character who paid her first visit to the Alps just before the First World War and is still part of the mountain scene in the 1970s. Miriam was brought up in New England so the mountains of that part of the United States were always at hand to influence her development. In her fascinating autobiography *Give Me the Hills* she writes that even as a small child she spurned dolls as presents or playthings and was always looking for something to climb.

In 1914 her mother took her and her seven-year-old brother to Europe. From Chamonix they walked up the 5,000 feet to the top of the Brévent and looked out on Mont Blanc and the rocky spires of the Chamonix Aiguilles. They had hardly returned from this first ascent when they discovered that war had been declared. There appeared to be no trains to the coast for civilians so the family decided to take a look at Zermatt – just to fill in the time. They went up to the Gornergrat and gazed spellbound at the view spread out before them; it never occurred to Miriam then that one day she would not only ski down Monte Rosa but would also tread the summits of most of the mountains she could see. At the end of August a train across France was organised for the transport of stranded Americans and Miriam, with her mother and brother, left Europe for the comparative calm of America.

In 1920 they were back in Switzerland again; in 1921 Miriam did the Breithorn. Looking back it seems a tardy beginning for one so dedicated to the hills and Miriam still says that she cannot understand why she was so slow in getting started. In 1924, however, things took a turn for the better. She had returned from the Pointe de Zinal to the Schönbühl Hut, where she met George Finch, of Everest fame; he sensed an embryo mountaineer immediately and advised her not to waste her time on small things but to tackle 'Some real stuff'. Miriam took his tip, proceeded to do the Matterhorn Couloir on the Riffelhorn, followed by the Wellenkuppe-Obergabelhorn-Arbengrat traverse; her climbing career had begun at last.

During the next two years Miriam built up her experience in New England and later in the Dolomites, where she had the good fortune to meet the Dimai guides – Antonio and his sons Angelo and Guiseppe. They judged her to be a coming climber and encouraged her to attempt more and more adventurous ascents. In 1927 she was again at Cortina; Antonio disentangled her from her group of climbing friends and explained that he had a new route for her on the Torre Grande, one of the most difficult in the whole Dolomite region; she would be the first tourist to make the ascent and he proposed to call the route the 'Via Miriam'. What enthusiastic young women would not be thrilled at such a suggestion! Miriam accepted at once with pride and pleasure. On 7th July 1927 with Margaret Helburn, another distinguished American climber, and the guides Angelo and Antonia Dimai and Angelo Dibona, Miriam did the 'Via Miriam', a magnificent climb, and one still highly rated. More than twenty-five years later she found it quite exciting to hear the 'Via Miriam' still being discussed eagerly by the young Cortina climbers.

Fresh from this success Miriam went on to Chamonix where, with Alfred Couttet and Vital Garny, she made the first ascent of the Aiguille de Roc from the Montanvers. Another good year was 1928. Accompanied by Georges Cachat she led the traverse of the Grépon – the first feminine lead – and with the same guide she also made the first feminine lead of the Meije as far as the Brêche Zsigmondy, where, owing to an injured finger she had to hand over to the guide. In that year, too, with Robert Underhill, her future husband, and the guides Armand Charlet and Georges Cachat she succeeded in making the first complete traverse of the Aiguille du Diable.

In 1929 Miriam turned her attention to the Oberland, where she met the young guide Adolf Rubi who was to remain a lifelong guide and friend. They climbed well together and during the next year crowned their many triumphs by making, with Fritz Rubi as second guide, the third ascent of the North-East Face of the Finsteraarhorn. This was the great climb attempted by Gertrude Bell nearly thirty years before; Miriam was the first woman to follow her and Gertrude Bell, had she lived, would surely have been delighted that a woman had at last succeeded where she herself had failed so magnificently.

By this time Miriam's record was fantastic, but she still quested for greater adventures, above all to climb *sans homme* – without guides or male companions of any kind. This was partly because she was interested in the intellectual aspect of mountaineering; she wanted to test her judgement, to learn to make wise and proper decisions regarding the weather, the route, the amount of danger involved; she wanted to taste the thrill of carrying the final responsibility and, particularly, to learn the limits of her own capabilities.

Henry de Ségogne (of the Groupe de Haute Montagne) was convinced that a woman could never lead a climb and took infinite pains to explain to Miriam just why this was so. She found his arguments unconvincing, especially since she had already led several big climbs, albeit with a man in the party. She looked around among her circle of climbing friends and found some who were more than willing to back her up.

On 14th August 1929, with Winifred Marples (always known as Jo), a British woman climber of considerable experience, Miriam achieved her first manless climb. It was the Aiguille du Peigne, a very suitable first choice. They spent the night at the little chalet of Plan de l'Aiguille and during the evening they carefully prospected the route. This is something the amateur generally leaves to the guide and Miriam was determined not to be caught out on the very first precaution; there are climbs where it is possible to get lost leaving the hut, an ignominious situation indeed for women planning a manless ascent.

Miriam and Jo Marples found the Peigne an encouraging

experience, so much so that three days later they set off with Alice Damesme, a French woman climber, for the first manless traverse of the Grépon. This was a much bigger assignment and caused great excitement among those they met *en route*. Everyone wanted them to start first on the climb, in order, as they knew only too well, to get a good view of what happened. There was a lot of mist and route-finding proved difficult; however, they manifested a good show of confidence for the ever-growing audience below. They found their way, sometimes by slightly unorthodox routes, to the Mummery Crack, still one of the most famous of all climbing problems. As Miriam explains in *Give Me the Hills*, no leader has ever fallen out of the Mummery Crack near the top and lived! It was a long job, longer than they had expected, but cheerful greetings called across from friends engaged in traversing the Charmoz helped them on. When at last they reached the top of the Crack there was a well-deserved outburst of cheering. For the next two or three strenuous pitches they met a high wind, bitter cold, and a brief but suffocating blizzard; they struggled on and at last emerged on the large flat rock that forms the summit of the Grépon. Their luck improved. The snow stopped, the sun shone and they enjoyed a festive lunch, watched through the telescope in Chamonix by Miriam's mother and Alice's little daughter. The manless traverse of the Grépon has been successfully accomplished. It brought a glow of pardonable pride.

Naturally now nothing could satisfy Miriam but the Matterhorn; but, as so often happens with that elusive peak, it was a matter of years rather than weeks before final success was theirs. Perhaps it is this very quality of aloofness that makes the Matterhorn yesterday, today and for ever the symbol *par excellence* of alpine mountaineering.

In 1931 Miriam, with Alice Damesme and an American friend, Jessie Whitehead, arrived in Zermatt full of plans and enthusiasm. They had done several manless ascents in the Dolomites and around Courmayeur – all in aid of the Matterhorn. Miriam also did the Jungfrau and the south-west ridge of the Mönch with the brilliant French woman climber Micheline Morin. It was a grand experience, but all the time she had an eye on the great compelling peak stabbing the distance away in the south. The rest of the season was spent in trying to get up the Matterhorn, defeated on each occasion by the weather. They took to hiring mules to take them up to the Hörnli Hut; Jessie Whitehead claimed that every mule in Zermatt knew her personally! On two occasions they actually reached the Solvay Hut, but in common with all the other parties on the mountain, they still had to turn back.

In 1932 Jessie Whitehead was unable to come over to Europe, but Miriam and Alice were once again in Zermatt after a visit to Chamonix. July had been a wretched month for weather but in August things improved. On 12th August they went up to the Hörnli Hut to spend the night. The next day was perfect; there was a lot of snow but no insurmountable difficulties; after all the endless frustrations and disappointments the final successful ascent was comparatively easy. They sat on the summit blissfully content. Sixty-seven years after Whymper's first ascent, sixty-one years after Lucy Walker's epic success, the Matterhorn had been climbed by women alone.

Strangely, this proved to be Miriam's last manless ascent. Instead of going over to Chamonix where the G.H.M. had prepared a gigantic reception for the intrepid ladies she joined Robert Underhill in the Eastern Alps for some guideless, but not manless, climbing. After this her constant companion on every climb and for all her life was Robert. As she so rightly says manless climbing had been fun for a while but the new arrangement was infinitely better.

Miriam and Robert were married in the autumn; Bernard Biner in sending his congratulations wrote that he 'hoped that mother blessings would not prevent a return to the mountains'. They did not. In years to come the Underhills arrived once more in Zermatt, this time with two enthusiastic sons eager to follow in their parents' footsteps.

Loulou Boulaz – now an Honorary Member of the Ladies' Alpine Club – began her climbing career in the 1930s and is still one of Switzerland's most distinguished women mountaineers. Her achievements in the Alps must be almost unique. They include,

to mention only some, the first ascent of the North Face of the
Zinal Rothorn; the third ascent of Mont Blanc by the Pear route;
the third ascent of the Grandes Jorasses by the Central Spur; the
second ascent of the North Face of the Petit Dru and the North
Face of the Aiguille Verte. All these were done with guides, either
Pierre Bonnant or Raymond Lambert; but 'women's ropes' were
the talk of the day and with so many brilliant achievements to
her credit Loulou Boulaz naturally had an interest in these matters.
With Luly Durand she did a number of climbs *sans hommes* in the
Chamonix district. The most outstanding were the Requin; the
traverse of the Grand Charmoz from left to right by the South
West Face and North West Ridge and the South West Face of
the Dent du Géant; on all these they were the first feminine
party.

A little later she made even more notable ascents with guides.
It was she who, in 1937, made one of the very first attempts on the
North Face of the Eiger before it was ever climbed. After the war,
with a large party she did the North Face of the Grandes Jorasses
by the Walker Spur, which included no less than three bivouacs;
and about the same time, with Pierre Bonnant, she made what was
probably the first femine ascent of the Furggen ridge of the
Matterhorn. In 1962 she made yet another attempt on the North
Face of the Eiger; the party got as far as the Ramp before they
had to retreat in atrocious weather conditions; it was a magnificent
performance – some say even more magnificent than Fräulein
Voog's successful ascent in good conditions. Loulou Boulaz is
undoubtedly one of the great women mountaineers of her time
and a shining example to others.

Each generation seems to produce its quota of great climbers and
the active life of many of them covers a longer span of years than
is the case in other forms of sport. Certainly Nea Morin, who
began her career in 1925 as Nea Barnard, is one of the most
brilliant of all British women mountaineers and more than forty
years later she is still making a great contribution to the climbing
world.

Nea had a lucky start as a child; her father was a member of the

Alpine Club; the family home was at Tunbridge Wells and she and her brothers began their early scrambles on the rocky outcrops in the surrounding district. At the age of fourteen she seriously damaged a knee and this remained a slight handicap throughout the years, but by the time she was sixteen she was sufficiently recovered to be fitted up with her first climbing gear and introduced to a guide for proper instruction. The climbing centre chosen was St Anton am Arlberg; the guide was no less a person than Hannes Schneider, hero of many mountaineers and skiers and founder of the Arlberg Ski School.

For their first ascent Hannes chose the Fasul Nadel, a short but quite severe climb. Nea found it exhilarating and, to her delight, it all seemed to come quite naturally to her; height and exposure held no terrors. Hannes guessed he had a potential genius in his charge; he took her on a dozen climbs and taught her to *abseil* and to *glissade*. Nea knew instinctively that she had found the answer to the problems her damaged knee had posed; in skiing and in any kind of game it would always be something of a disability, but when climbing she could forget it; here was something she could do really well. In her own words, 'That first alpine season was heaven.'

It was not long before Nea set out on an independent climbing holiday with a girl-friend. They chose La Bérarde in the heart of the Dauphiné Alps, engaged Casimir Rodier as their guide and climbed Les Écrins (13,123 feet) as Nea's first '*Viertausender*'. There is magic in this word for all mountaineers; no one really claims to be a climber, in the alpine sense, until the first peak of 4,000 metres has been achieved. Their next objective was the Meije; but the Meije, like the Matterhorn, is not easily wooed and they were chased off the mountain by thunder and lightning. Nea was desperate; her resources would not run to a second attempt and she was relying on the Meije to produce the necessary qualifications to make her a full member of the Ladies' Alpine Club, being so far only a Graduating Member. How many members of the Club, before and since, have struggled in exactly the same way? At the time it seems hard and sometimes frustrating; in retrospect one is glad and proud that the high standards have been maintained. When at last full membership is granted everyone knows that it has been worth the effort.

However, the failure on the Meije was not an unmitigated disaster. Casimir Rodier recommended the Tour Carrée de Roche Méane (quite a hard climb) and on the way over the Col du Clot des Cavales he discussed with Nea the *Groupe de Haute Montagne*, the G.H.M., with its exclusive rules and very high entrance qualifications. Nea made up her mind immediately that one day she would become a member of the G.H.M. – she succeeded, of course, with the same effortless ease with which she was elected to the Ladies' Alpine Club and the Pinnacle Club. For her there was a *mystique* about the letters G.H.M. and in years to come they were to influence her life in ways undreamed of when she heard them first on the Col du Clot des Cavales.

The next year at Wasdale Head, in the Lake District, Nea met Jo Marples, a member of the Ladies' Alpine Club who later climbed *sans hommes* with Miriam Underhill. They fixed up to go to Chamonix, the home ground of the magical G.H.M. They stayed at the Montenvers Hotel, 3,000 feet above Chamonix; it was swarming with mountaineers and was an ideal spot for keen young climbers. There Nea met for the first time Miriam Underhill (at that time still O'Brien) and her delightful mother who, in her sixtieth year, had just made an ascent of the Grépon.

Nea and Jo had a fine season which proved to be the beginning of a long and rewarding friendship between them. With the guide Anatole Bozon they did the Requin, the traverse of the Grand Charmoz, the traverse of the Grépon and the Aiguille d'Argentière. Miriam Underhill 'lent' them her guide Alfred Couttet for the traverse of the delightful and difficult Mummery and Ravanel Aiguilles; after this they returned to the Requin Hut to climb the Dent du Requin again by the Voie des Plaques. They stayed a second night at the hut and there they met a young Frenchman in his early thirties, Jean Morin, wearing the coveted G.H.M. badge. He and his English companion turned out to be short of food; Nea nobly offered a share of her own – any hunger pangs would be easily allayed by the proximity of the G.H.M.!

The next day Nea and Jo finished the holiday with the Dent

du Géant and came down that night to the Montenvers. Who should be staying there but Jean Morin and a crowd of his G.H.M. friends – the climbing season ended in a riotous dinner and a blaze of reflected glory.

The next season, 1927, was a rapturous affair in every sense; Jean Morin invited Nea and Jo to climb with him from the Montenvers; as usual it was full of famous climbers and they met Frank Smythe and Professor Graham Brown, who were engaged in a series of remarkable first ascents.

Jean Morin had his eye on the first ascent of the Aiguille de Roc on the Mer de Glace face of the Grépon. Miriam Underhill and her guide Alfred Couttet also had plans well advanced on the same peak. In the end it was they who made the first ascent; Jean Morin was disappointed but was partly consoled when only a few days later he and his party made the first *guideless* ascent – Jean and a friend climbing with Nea and Jo Marples, with two more G.H.M. friends on another rope. It was a long climb with a large party and they were late in reaching the summit. However, they cared little about that since they had secured their record. On the descent thick mist developed and Jean Morin decided that the only course was to bivouac. They had little equipment but the mist soon lifted to give a clear night with a full moon and incomparable views of the Géant, Grandes Jorasses, Verte and Drus.

Back in Paris at the end of the climbing season Jean and Nea became engaged; gradually it dawned on Nea that Jean had always intended that they should bivouac on the descent from the Aiguille de Roc – a bivouac was something he loved greatly himself and he wanted to be the first to introduce her to this rare experience. Perhaps also he hoped that it would ensure the right answer to the vital question he was to ask when the season ended!

It was an ideal partnership; Nea was marrying into a family devoted to two of the loveliest things in this world – mountains and music. Micheline, her future sister-in-law, was a first-class climber and a brilliant pianist; Jean was a composer as well as a performer – Nea was happy indeed. Throughout the autumn there was much coming and going between Paris and Tunbridge Wells; for Jean to explore Nea's beloved Harrison's Rocks; for

Nea to climb at Fontainebleau and meet the G.H.M. friends. Soon they were married and disappeared to the Pyrenees for their honeymoon.

It was fortunate that Jean and Nea were such a well-suited couple; the economic conditions caused by the disastrous depression of that time made things difficult for young marrieds. Life was a struggle for them and by the time things improved financially the shadow of the Second World War was spreading across the horizon at an alarming pace. The young of that period – and particularly, perhaps, the young mountaineers – had a desperate sense of urgency; every minute must be seized for the Alps before they were deprived of them.

Nea and Jean could not afford to get to the Alps every year but they were living in Paris and not far away were the rocks of Fontainebleau, the week-end hunting ground of the G.H.M. who christened the addicts 'Bleausards'. Here there flourished a spirit of close comradeship; the group was small and intimate and climbs of every degree of severity were the order of the day; one such was christened the Rocher de Nea and has remained thus named to this day.

During the course of the next few years Jean and Nea became the proud possessors of a daughter, Denise, and a son, Ian. To a certain extent this set limits to their alpine ambitions; the responsibility of a family meant that guideless climbing together had to be rationed for the sake of the climbers-to-be in the pram and the cradle. But they still allowed themselves a few climbs alone; they had found it over the years a profound and satisfying experience with which they could not entirely do without.

If the Morins as parents felt it right to have some reservations climbing *en famille* there seemed no reason why Nea should not sometimes climb *en cordée féminine*. At least Jean would not be involved and the climbing would not be prejudiced by a natural anxiety for each other's safety. Not that it was easy for women climbers to persuade their mountaineering husbands to let them loose on their own on big ascents. Dedicated alpinists as the husbands were, they were almost too well aware of the risks involved to agree without argument to the pleadings of the wives.

In 1933 Nea had plans for traversing the Meije with Micheline Morin and Alice Damesme, who had climbed the Matterhorn with Miriam Underhill in the previous year. They knew that the climb, if successful, would be the first 'ladies only' traverse of the Meije. The situation was not improved by two fatal accidents – one involving a personal friend – in the near vicinity. However, male permission was at last secured and Nea, Micheline and Alice set out for La Bérarde. Here more bad news awaited them; the death of another friend on the Meije itself. Their morale, already shaky, sank to an all-time low. Feminine honour would not allow them to turn back and they trudged on up to the Promontoire Hut. For once bad weather proved a welcome respite; a storm blew up in the night; climbing was out of the question and they returned thankfully to La Bérarde. Here they met Maurice Damesme, Alice's husband, who just could not keep away under the circumstances. Things took a turn for the better; the weather improved and the morale of the *cordée féminine* improved with it. But now there was a new difficulty – Maurice wanted to come along too. This did not suit the ladies and they said so plainly. Maurice retorted by saying that they could not expect to have the mountain to themselves and he proposed to traverse the Meije with three friends. There seemed no reasonable answer to this; good humour was restored and both parties set off once more for the Promontoire Hut.

This time all went well; the weather was perfect; the mountain in good condition. Nea, Micheline and Alice had their *cordée féminine* without male interference and shared the lead between them. It seemed they could do nothing wrong, not even on the difficult ice-coated north face. Up and down they climbed along that rippling crest to a final *rappel* and at last down to the Aigle Hut and, because they had no food left, down finally to comfortable beds at La Grave and the dreamless sleep that comes to those who have safely achieved a set purpose and enjoyed a great climb.

The next year was a true, feminine triumph. Alone at last, and with no men anywhere within sight or sound, the same trio made their way to the Aiguille de Blaitière. There are three summits to this mountain; Meta Brevoort had been the first woman to climb the Central Summit with Ulrich Almer in 1875; Isabella Straton did the North Summit with Jean Charlet in the same year. Nea and her party hoped to climb all three summits by the Rocher de la Corde, thus making another women's record.

On the terrace of the Montenvers they had bid Good-bye and Good Luck to the male friends and relations and endeavoured to pack them off to the Requin Hut; this they found quite the hardest part of the whole venture. It was not at all how the men had intended it to be. Throughout the season they had all been climbing together; true, the women had from time to time been on a rope on their own, but always with the ubiquitous males hovering close at hand. It seemed well-nigh impossible to shake them off and then right at the end of the season, the men had the temerity to suggest a fairly big expedition with a *cordée féminine* following them! This was too much for Micheline Morin, at that time the only unmarried member of the party. One sometimes has fewer inhibitions in standing up to a brother than to a husband; after all, the process probably starts in the pram! Micheline pulled out all the stops and announced to Jean, with a sidelong glance at Alice's husband, that the girls were starting there and then for the Blaitière and nothing they could say would alter that decision. Nea and Alice sat tight, hoping for the best; Micheline eventually won the day. The parties separated amicably, even if there was an atmosphere of armed truce about the whole affair.

Very early the next morning Nea, Micheline and Alice started with Micheline leading. When it came to putting on their crampons it was discovered that Alice had one of her own and one of her husband's; with a little ingenuity she managed to make the necessary adjustments but it was agreed among the party that it was probably just as well that they were out of earshot of male comments away on the Plan-Midi arête. All went well until it was found that on a short cut they were hoping to make the fresh snow was not adhering to the established layer; there was nothing for it but to take the longer route; it was only a setback, not an insurmountable disaster. On the crest of the arête of the Rocher de la Corde Alice's ice-axe slipped from her frozen fingers and clattered down on to the glacier below. This event was treated light-heartedly; Alice was at ease in the mountains with, or without, her axe; it was a cause for rejoicing, however, that there were no men around.

It was a glorious day; there was no need to hurry, they were making no bids for speed records; they rested when and where they wished and were utterly content. They climbed the Pointe de Chamonix first; raced up the final rocks which were easy; stayed long enough on the summit to congratulate themselves and came down to try their luck on the Pointe-Centrale. Here the last pitch is the most difficult – a chimney forming a kind of letterbox through which the climber has virtually to post herself. It was not easy; there were some amusing struggles but at last even Alice, the largest of the three, was eventually posted! The final summit, the Pointe-Sud, is the stiffest and was made worse on this occasion by *verglas* – black ice on rocks. It took nearly an hour but they made it and looked out triumphantly beyond the Charmoz-Grépon to the serene and smiling Aiguille Verte, which had spitefully defeated them with snow and a thunderstorm a few days earlier. The descent presented a few difficulties, but none of them beyond their powers and they arrived safely and in excellent time at the Montenvers. Here they refreshed themselves with endless cups of tea while waiting with ill-concealed superiority for the return of their menfolk. They too had had a satisfying trip and it was a happy party that travelled down to Chamonix in the last train. It was the last climb of the season – and the best.

In 1938 they were all in Chamonix again; this time the goal was the traverse of the Mummery and Ravanel Aiguilles. For Nea it could not be a *cordée féminine* – that had to be left to Micheline and Alice, who succeeded in making the first feminine party. Jean Morin was not well on the appointed day (an unknown tragedy as it turned out, they were never to climb together at Chamonix again) so Nea did the Mummery and Ravanel with Maurice Damesme. It proved to be a complicated expedition but Nea led the rope and thereby established the first feminine lead on this really first-class climb.

The sands were running out; war was at hand; in 1939 Jean and Nea failed to reach the Alps before hostilities began. It was

nearly ten years before Nea saw the Alps again; when she did so
Jean was not with her. In 1943 the military transport plane in
which he was returning from a special mission crashed into the
sea off Gibraltar; the pilot was the only survivor.

The year 1939 brought the end of an era just as 1914 had done.
Between the wars women mountaineers had made tremendous
progress. In the Alps such battles as needed to be fought for
independence had been won unobtrusively and with good
humour. Women climbed when, where and how they liked; their
position in the climbing world was assured and unassailable. The
Ladies' Alpine Club, the Pinnacle Club, the Scottish Ladies'
Climbing Club, the Swiss Ladies' Alpine Club and many others
were flourishing. In the course of those twenty years inevitably
some great women climbers had passed from the scene: Miss
'Katy' Richardson, Mrs Bullock Workman, Miss Maud Meyer,
Dr Cairney and, most notable of them all perhaps, Mrs Aubrey
Le Blond, who died in 1934 while in her second term of office as
President of the Ladies' Alpine Club. Some of the stalwart,
original members of this club were still climbing in 1939; the
war put an end to their activities and when peace came they were
too old to start again. They remained valued and respected
members and during the war, just because they were past the age
for active service for their country, they did much to keep the
club alive for younger members.

Two of these gallant ladies, while not ranking perhaps among
the greatest climbers, will nevertheless be remembered with special
affection and gratitude, not only by the Ladies' Alpine Club but
by most of the mountain fraternity. They were Miss Higgins and
Miss Dolling – known everywhere affectionately, if slightly
impolitely, as the Higgins and the Dolling. Miss Higgins was a
famous Principal of Holloway College, Miss Dolling her devoted
secretary. They became involved in alpine activities soon after
the First World War and they took the matter, as they had always
taken everything else, extremely seriously. They were to be found
at most alpine gatherings and parties and the young climbers of
those days owed a lot to them.

Miss Higgins looked terrifying, especially as she always dressed like a man, merely substituting a skirt for trousers. For evening occasions she invariably appeared in a dinner jacket and some of the more frivolous among us were continually trying to discover if she arrived at these functions wearing an opera hat! But beneath that rugged exterior was a heart of gold, a great wealth of kindness and immense courage. She did not qualify for the Ladies' Alpine Club until she was well on in years but she was a great mountain lover and a true mountaineer at heart. In the late 1940s, only a year before her death, she was to be seen struggling gallantly, but painfully slowly, up the forest path from Zermatt to the Riffelalp to have one last look at her favourite view, still spurning the mountain railway which most people of her age would have thought more convenient.

Miss Dolling did a lot of climbing; she seldom missed a season in the Alps and worked tirelessly for the Ladies' Alpine Club. Many of us were accepted as Graduating Members while she was secretary; she was so insistent on high standards that one felt one's chances of being elected a Full Member were infinitesimal; but she was kindness itself to all her young protégées and no one, however insignificant mountainwise, was ever allowed to feel anything but thoroughly welcome within the precincts of the club. When war came she temporarily took on the duties of treasurer as well as those of secretary and kept the club going. It was a sad day when Miss Higgins and Miss Dolling were bombed out of their London flat and retired, rather surprisingly, to Edinburgh.

Nea Morin has a lovely story about the Higgins and Dolling which perhaps gives the key to their characters and explains why we all regarded them with affectionate respect. On the day on which Denise Morin was born in 1931 the Higgins and Dolling were passing through Paris on their way to their annual climbing holiday. They were not ladies prone to changing their plans easily but, knowing the birth was imminent, they broke their journey to call on Nea, whom they naturally regarded as one of the most coming climbers of the day. Denise was already a few hours' old and they were permitted to peep at her. They peered at the little bundle with some embarrassment while Nea, the proud Mum, waited for their comments. There was a short silence, then the Higgins turned to the Dolling and remarked gruffly, 'She will be much more interesting in eighteen years' time.'

Fortunately for the future of women's mountaineering most of the young tigresses of the twenties and thirties were still in their prime at the outbreak of war and were there to carry the torch for many years to come when climbing in the Alps became possible again. What Bernard Biner described as 'manless, guideless, women's climbing' went on from where it had left off in 1939 – there was only a temporary break and not a breakdown in the programme. Dorothy Pilley-Richards, Micheline Morin, Nea Morin, Anna Roelfsema and many more were out on the mountains the moment the recall to the Alps was sounded.

On the battle-torn continent of Europe mountaineering had continued during the war years in attenuated form. In Occupied France people were able to move about at times and Micheline Morin and her G.H.M. husband Gerard Blachère continued to do some notable climbs in the Chamonix and Dauphiné districts. In Switzerland, so isolated from the rest of the world, more and more women became keen climbers and were there to welcome back, with every kindness imaginable, those who for so long had been cut off from the mountains.

Meanwhile in America mountaineers seized what climbing they could while there was still time; many people were convinced that it could not be long before the United States was involved in Europe and that would mean the end of mountaineering for a long time to come.

In 1941 two well-known American women climbers decided to join forces for an expedition to the Sierra Nevada de Santa Marta of Colombia, 'the highest coast range in the world'. These two ladies were Betsy Cowles (later Mrs Partridge) from Colorado and Elizabeth Knowlton from Boston. They had both been attracted for some time to the Sierra Nevada de Santa Marta; Elizabeth Knowlton described its snows as 'floating in the upper sky above the Caribbean coast, at the northern end of the Andean chain, just across from Florida' – a description which suggests at once the compelling nature of these mountains. It was quite new ground to them; indeed, no one had heard of women climbing there before. They took with them as guides Paul Petzold of the Tetons of Wyoming and a young Swiss named Max Eberli.

After long journeyings by plane and train they arrived at San Sebastian, the last outpost of civilization in those parts, and made ready to set out on the expedition. Their caravan consisted of eight bulls and two riding mules, on which they took turns. On the third day from San Sebastian they established Base Camp at a spot rejoicing in the uninviting name of 'Gloomy Gulch'. However, it proved to be a most enjoyable Camp, ideal for relaxing after strenuous trips. They slept out under the stars and sprawled on warm rocks by the lake reading aloud to each other from the *Oxford Book of English Verse*.

They planned as their main climbing objective two peaks in the eastern part of the range and eventually left 'Gloomy Gulch' with supplies for two weeks' climbing and exploration. Their next resting place was Sunset Camp at over 14,000 feet, and it was here that Betsy and Elizabeth decided to christen their two peaks – 'Pico Ujueta' was the rock one and the snowy dome became 'La Reina'.

After Sunset Camp they bivouacked for one night and then established 'Condor's Nest Camp' high on the side of La Reina. La Reina, 18,160 feet, proved to be disappointingly easy – just a long snow walk – but it had to be done in blistering heat under a tropical sun. The view, fortunately, proved to be all that they could have wished for and the day was voted a success. On the next day Pico Ujueta, the rock peak 18,010 feet, did not present many difficulties, but there was at least some rock climbing and some step cutting; once again the view from the summit was superb.

Back at Base Camp they loaded up the bulls and renewed their acquaintance with the mules; it had been a most worth-while trip into virgin country which was far more beautiful than they had ever imagined. When they reached civilization again at Fundación they were greeted with the news that the United States had that day passed the Lease-Lend Bill – it seemed a fitting climax to their hastily snatched adventure.

In Great Britain climbing was still sometimes possible for those who could find the time for it. The monthly meetings of the Ladies' Alpine Club, held spasmodically on Saturday afternoons because of the Blitz and the blackout, produced a kaleidoscope of colour. Two thirds of us were in uniform, and the A.T.S., W.R.N.S., W.A.A.F., Transport Corps and Red Cross were all represented. We came when we could and when Nea Morin, who by then had become President, organised a climbing meet in Wales in 1944 and in the Lake District in 1945 some of us almost perjured our souls to get week-end leave to snatch a couple of days on the hills away from the deadly drone of the doodle bugs and the earsplitting crashes of the V2s. It will never be known how much the mountains helped those who loved them to struggle through the war years with a secret, high-hearted happiness. However bad things were, however terrifying some moments might be, there was always the thought at the back of the mind that, if one was lucky enough to survive, the mountains would still be there. As Bernard Biner said to me at the station at Zermatt when we left for home two days before war broke out, 'No dictatorship can destroy the Matterhorn and, remember, you have forty more years to climb.'

Chapter 6

Like Mother, Like Daughter

In 1946 foreign travel, which for seven years had been virtually at a standstill all over the world, was at last possible again. The nations were exhausted, their cities lay in ruins and vast areas of Europe were devastated; the Alps, however, remained – untouched and eternal. War-weary climbers came flooding back seeking restoration and peace among the hills. There were great, glaring gaps in their ranks: Jean Morin, Roeli Roelfsema brother of Anna, Graham Jackson brother of Eileen, Hugues Paillon nephew of the famous Mary Paillon and countless others were all gone. Many women climbers returned to the mountains poignantly aware that for them climbing would never be quite the same again. Perhaps this had something to do with the rapid development of mother and daughter, mother and son ropes; whatever the cause, this was one of the important new movements of the post-war climbing world and as such deserves a short chapter to itself.

In the past climbing *en famille* had been much more popular among continental than among British mountaineers. Second World War British parents, who had served their apprenticeship in the Alps in the 1930s, saw to it that their children, by this time approaching their teens, should be introduced without delay to this most rewarding way of life. Well-known climbing personalities like the Chorleys, the Bicknells and the Longlands arrived in the Alps with rope loads of youngsters; needless to say, among the keenest and most prominent were Nea Morin and Miriam Underhill.

Nea, knowing full well that her children would never share the delight of climbing with their father, took Denise and Ian to the

Tyrol in 1946 for their first vision of the snow mountains. Conditions in Austria were bad; food was scarce and regulations of all kinds abounded. Nevertheless it was a beginning; they had a trip to see the Kaisergebirge and another up the lovely, lonely Oetztal for the children to have their first glacier excursion. They slept at the Schönweiss Hut and proudly set out the next morning up the Gurgl glacier. Before they left the Tyrol Nea inaugurated what was probably the first mother and daughter rope by taking Denise up one of the easier routes of the Totenkirchl. It was only a mini-mountaineering season but it was a suitable sequel to the preliminary rock scrambles the family had undertaken in North Wales and certainly set the feet of Denise and Ian firmly on the mountains, as subsequent events have proved.

The next summer Nea climbed *en famille* with her sister-in-law Micheline Morin, and in spite of the long years of absence from the Alps, they made the first *cordée féminine* of the Chapeau à Cornes of the Requin and established a similar record on the south-west ridge of the Auguille du Moine. Lack of training and the tragedies and deprivations of the war years had not robbed them of their earlier form.

The year 1947 was the first real alpine holiday for the Morin family; the first time, that is, when a climbing programme was properly scheduled. They were based on Les Contamines; Nea took Denise up Mont Tondu, her first 3,000 feet peak and quite a group of Morin cousins, aunts and nephews did the Aiguille de l'M led by Denise. After this there was no family mountaineering in the Alps for some time but every winter they were skiing above Briançon and in the spring they continued their climbing education in the Lake District.

By the summer of 1950 they were back again at Briançon and Nea took her son and daughter up the Pic Nord des Cavales; she brought them down to cross the dreary desert of the Clot des Cavales where, so many years ago, she had first heard the magic mention of the G.M.H. from the lips of her guide. Later in the season there was a happy family party up the Glacier Blanc to the Col des Écrins and a feminine family trio consisting of Nea, Micheline and Denise on the traverse of the Cinéastes. Last, but

not least, Denise with her mother, her aunt and her uncle achieved
the traverse of Les Écrins – her first '*Viertausender*', as it had been
her mother's twenty-five years earlier. Just to add a final touch
of romance, on the summit they met Nea's guide of that occasion,
Casimir Rodier, silver-haired now and getting on in years, but
still active. To Nea's unfeigned delight he recognised her!

Denise Morin was by now thoroughly dedicated to the mountains and was fast becoming an excellent climber. In the Oberland
she did the Mönch and the Jungfrau with her mother; with a group
of French friends she did a series of climbs in the Dauphiné,
including the traverse of the Meije.

In 1953 mother and daughter set out for the Dolomites – new
ground for Denise. They climbed the Vajolet, the Winkler, the
Stabeler and the Delago – just as a prelude. By their traverse of
these three peaks they established a record for the first feminine
party. They followed this with the first *cordée féminine* on the
Nordwand of Cima Piccola di Lavaredo. Well content with their
Dolomites 'bag' they went on to Saas Fee where, with a male
friend, E. H. Marriott, they traversed the north ridge of the
Weissmies which Nea led, being the first woman to do so.

After Saas Fee Denise had to leave and Nea went on to Zermatt
to climb with her son Ian. Their record-making ascent of the
Matterhorn will be the finale to this chapter but mention must be
made now of their expedition on the Rothorngrat. This was very
much a mother and son affair; in fact the party consisted of two
mothers and two sons, plus another sixteen-year-old boy and the
Zermatt guide Bernard Perren.

It was a somewhat unique occasion. The 'other mother' was
Janet Roberts (Adam Smith); her husband Michael Roberts,
famous as mountaineer, poet and critic had died tragically in 1948
leaving her with a family of four, the youngest of whom was only
a year old. It was an exacting responsibility but Janet shouldered
it nobly. She became Literary Editor of the *New Statesman* and
then found time to introduce her children to the mountains.
Born of mountaineering stock and a climber of no mean repute
herself she was determined to give the family a chance on the
mountains. Thus it was that Janet arrived in Zermatt with her

fifteen-year-old son Andrew and John Scott, aged sixteen, a mutual school-friend of Andrew and Ian Morin. To Nea and Janet it was quite obvious that here was a heaven-sent opportunity for a climbing party. They toyed with the idea of taking all the boys guideless up the Rothorn by the ordinary route. This meant inevitably that there would have to be three on one rope, not an ideal situation for a party consisting mainly of novices. They had another think; decided to call in a guide and to do the Rothorn by the much more exciting Rothorngrat.

The guide chosen was Bernard Perren – young, enthusiastic, always a favourite with women climbers and happy to find himself part of a family expedition. They climbed on three ropes; Janet handed her son Andrew over to Bernard and climbed herself with John Scott; Nea climbed with Ian. All went without a hitch of any kind; all the boys climbed confidently and competently; Bernard Perren, going ahead with Andrew, called out directions when handholds were difficult to locate and all three parties arrived on the summit unscathed and much elated. This was the first time the boys had been on a summit surrounded on all sides by great mountains; for the mothers it was a moving experience to see them responding as they themselves had responded in those far-off halcyon days. There was only one small disappointment; on the east side of the ridge there is an overhanging corner, the kind of pitch on which any expert woman climbing guideless would particularly enjoy trying out her strength and techniques. Bernard Perren, with the best of intentions, insisted on dropping a rope to both Nea and Janet; secretly they felt outraged but they had engaged a guide and a particularly good one; it was not for them to question his wisdom.

In 1955 Nea and Denise were together again in the French Alps; in the intervening period they had been performing feats of every grade of difficulty in North Wales; Denise was now not only an experienced and first-class climber but also a competent leader, sharing the lead with her mother on most of their important adventures. This year they began with some small but entertaining climbs followed by a good day on the Dent du Géant. Their *pièce de résistance*, however, was to be something much more exciting – nothing less, in fact, than the Mer de Glace face of the Grépon, the peak that draws dedicated climbers to it with the force of a magnet.

In the event this long-planned and much-hoped-for expedition was almost too exciting; indeed, to quote Nea's own words, 'I have never come quite so close to annihilation.' Janet Roberts had agreed to climb ahead with a guide, thus providing a kind of remote companionship should Nea and Denise need it. Unfortunately the guide proved to be far from first-class; during the night it transpired that he had never before been on the Mer de Glace face of the Grépon. This did not make for a happy start and throughout the climb they seemed to be dogged by bad luck. Denise was hit on the thigh by a stone dislodged by the guide and only a miracle saved Nea from a huge block of rock swept out into space by his rope. At one time Janet and the guide were far ahead and out of sight – not an unmitigated disaster in the opinion of Nea and Denise. These two had to spend time hauling their rucksacks up chimneys and stiff pitches; one of the chief difficulties which *cordées féminines* have to face is the fact that women climbers, however expert they may be, find it almost impossible to lead severe pitches while carrying a heavy rucksack. Consequently these impedimenta have to be dragged up separately and valuable time gets used up.

At last, and after several more unfortunate *contretemps*, both parties arrived on the summit; even this pleasure was slightly marred by mist and falling snow. Bad weather was obviously setting in and the sooner they were off the mountain the better. As soon as they reached the dangerous Nantillons glacier on the descent the guide whisked Janet away and they were lost to sight in the mist. Nea and Denise ended the day, by being caught in an avalanche from which they only managed to extricate themselves with difficulty.

In retrospect, of course, most of these hazards and near-disasters were forgotten – it is always so in mountaineering. They had achieved their ambition to climb the Mer de Glace face of the Grépon together and theirs proved to be the first ever *cordée féminine* on that face. The game had been worth the candle.

Events crowd in apace in the lives of the young; when next Denise joined her mother in the Alps, in 1958, she had become the wife of Charles Evans, a member of the successful Everest team of 1953, and their honeymoon had been spent in the Himalayas. This was a match that delighted all mountaineers; it seemed exactly right that the daughter who had followed so successfully in the steps of a brilliant father and mother should find her life partner in one of Britain's foremost mountaineers.

With Micheline Morin, Nea and Denise sought new worlds to conquer in the Dolomites, which had always had such a fascination for them. They camped in the fields near San Martino di Castrozza; they had designs on nearly every peak they could see but the weather decided to be utterly unco-operative; they got involved in an alarming thunderstorm on the Sass Maor; by sheer determination they succeeded in making the first all-woman ascent of the Dente de Cimon by the Langes route but the whole climb had to be done in thick mist and was less rewarding than it should have been.

Every day from their camp they had been watching the Spigolo del Velo ridge of the Cima della Madonna; it was an advanced climb and the route was not easy to find. Secretly they longed to do it guideless but mountain wisdom, accumulated over the years, prevailed; uncertain weather and guide books printed only in Italian were not the best basis for an ascent such as the Spigolo del Velo. They looked around for a guide, had the good fortune to engage Giacomo Scalet and discovered that this would be his fiftieth ascent by this route. He was very willing to take them, proved to be a delightful companion and enjoyed the day as much as they did. The Spigolo del Velo is a steep, exposed and extremely strenuous climb with surprising chimneys and not a few awkward moments. Nea's description of the focal-point of the ascent is worth recording.

'The crux of the climb is getting across what I remember as a fathomless chasm and somehow attaching oneself to the sheer wall on the far side. You stand on the brink, let yourself fall forwards, and it seems ages before you reach the other side. And

K

there you are, arching across very much beyond the point of no return, looking and feeling like the Bridge of Sighs!'

In spite of, or perhaps because of, all this Nea and Denise described it as an 'intensely happy climb' which they found thoroughly satisfying. Of such calibre are the mountaineering mothers and daughters of the second half of the twentieth century.

Nea Morin had one more great climb that summer – not with her daughter but nevertheless very much *en famille*. Need it be said that the peak involved was the Meije, that sublime creature that calls its women admirers back not once but again and again.

With her sister-in-law Micheline, Nea joined up with Janet Roberts in the Dauphiné and immediately set out from La Bérarde to walk up to the already overcrowded Promontoire Hut. It was twenty-five years almost to the day since Nea had made the first *cordée féminine* traverse of the Meije. Now Nea and Janet were to make what they thought was almost certainly the first British feminine traverse. Micheline, meanwhile, was going to climb with the eighteen-year-old son of a G.H.M. friend. On paper it sounds a curious assortment; in practice it proved to be a happy and successful arrangement.

Every climb has its unexpected hazards; was there ever an ascent that went without incident from start to finish! The hut was so crowded that none of them could sleep; to add to Janet's discomforts she was violently sick before they started. Climbing behind Nea she felt thoroughly miserable for the first two hours. However, after constantly reminding herself that in 1888 'Katy' Richardson had climbed the peak by leaving La Bérarde at 9 p.m. and that in 1899 Gertrude Bell had to start from the Etançons valley, she came to the conclusion that her lot was a good deal better than theirs and life began to look a little less cheerless.

When one climbs behind Nea, as those of us who have done so know well, even stiff pitches seem comparatively easy; Nea was obviously on the top of her form and Janet began to enjoy herself exceedingly. Certainly as time went on the Meije seemed to become more and more formidable, but they were in phase with the mountain and every climber is aware of the joy and sense of security that this brings – even if, for some, it is a rather rare occurrence. Nea remembered the route well, and if it became tricky Micheline yelled directions from afar. The Pic Zsigmondy is the crux of the climb, the point from which there can be no going back. Here it was impossible to haul the rucksack; it had to be carried by Nea while Janet stuck their single ice-axe in her belt. A diagonal crack leads up and across the gendarme from right to left and curves out of sight round an enormous bulge on to the ice-coated steep north face of the mountain. It is thought to be an impressive experience by most climbers; it was something rather more than this for two guideless women, encumbered with rucksack and ice-axe; cool heads and complete concentration were essential where the sense of exposure was so intense. They succeeded without any untoward incident and with this problem safely behind them were able to enjoy walking side by side over the points of the summit ridge.

The weather, which had been perfect, broke badly for the descent, which became something of an anti-climax – cold, wet and misty, with the rope becoming damp and heavy and awkward to manage. For the last part of the snow descent Janet decided on a sitting *glissade* (a swift although unusual manoeuvre) while Nea, Micheline and Guy, the schoolboy, descended in more orthodox style firmly grasping their ice-axes. At last the whole party was safely down and it was decided by all that not one but two records had been achieved. It was virtually certain that this was the first British women's party and there seemed to be no doubt whatever that this must be the first time that the Meije had been climbed by three ladies in their fifties accompanied by a schoolboy.

Miriam Underhill returned to the Alps in 1951 after an absence of nineteen years; with her came her fourteen-year-old son Bobby who had already had his preliminary introduction to climbing in the mountains of New England. They decided on Grindelwald for Bobby's first alpine season; it was an excellent choice; Miriam's great guide Adolf Rubi was still engaged in

active guiding and was delighted to take on the second generation
of Underhills. Nea Morin and Denise were also at Grindelwald
so once again there was a well-assorted family party. Adolf Rubi
jumped at the opportunity to take the young people under his
wing; he took them up the Kingspitze with Denise last on the
rope and Bobby as middleman. Bobby, obviously a born mountaineer, soon discovered the art of managing the rope; drawing it
in and paying it out as if he had been doing it all his life.

The next year the Underhills came over *en famille*. Robert
Underhill could no longer bear to get mountain news secondhand
from his wife; he abandoned the work that had detained him in
the previous year and decided that not only Bobby but Brian, the
younger son, should be in the party.

The first port of call had to be Grindelwald to link up with
Adolf Rubi. They embarked on a considerable climbing programme for all four of them and when the parents decided on an
occasional rest day Adolf insisted on taking the boys off for
training. They went rock climbing on the boulders behind the
hotel; they practised ice-climbing on the glacier; cramponing up
seracs and step-cutting on ice walls. Nothing was too trivial for
Adolf, who was thrilled to have two such apt and ready pupils.

From Grindelwald they went on to Zermatt – this, of course,
was a 'must'. Miriam maintains that she will want to go to Zermatt
even when she can no longer walk at all; for her it was a real thrill
when the train rattled out of the last avalanche tunnel into the
station and her two sons came face to face with the Matterhorn
for the first time. It was the first time, too, that Miriam had seen
it since she returned with Alice Damesme from their record-
making manless ascent. She was very touched when the older
guides strolling in the village street hurried to greet her, calling
'Miriam' as they came.

Miriam and her husband climbed the Matterhorn together; it
was the fourth time for Robert and the third time for Miriam and,
they decided simultaneously, the last time for both of them. The
mountain, they felt, was getting over-crowded. They preferred
to remember it as they first knew it – remote and rather aloof;
something to be revered.

The parents had renounced future climbs on the Matterhorn but naturally the sons had still to climb it and a promise was made for the next year. Thus, in 1953, back to Zermatt they came once more with sights set on the mighty mountain.

Strange as it may seem to non-mountaineers who hear the Matterhorn mentioned *ad nauseam* there *are* other mountains to be climbed from Zermatt: great and exciting peaks, some of which even Miriam had not had time to do in the days of her youth. The faithful Adolf Rubi was in attendance from the day they arrived and was prepared to climb constantly, Sundays included if need be. Where should they go first? Castor and Pollux won the day and before they set out from Zermatt the Lyskamm had been added to the trip – a delectable trio indeed.

Bobby, it was decided, would come along with his mother and thus add three to his growing list of four-thousanders. Owing to the dangerous condition of the glaciers at that particular time Adolf thought it prudent to take a second guide: 'just in case someone fell into a crevasse'. Someone did. It was the second guide; but he was an expert and extricated himself without assistance from anyone.

The party spent the night at Testa Grigia and started out in a rosy dawn. Everything was just as it should be; the snow was hard and crisp; the sun swept the mist from mountain and valley and the glorious panorama of peaks stretched for a hundred miles in each direction.

All day they climbed up and down, always well above 12,000 feet. They skirted the Breithorn on the Italian side to the Zwillinge Pass and climbed Pollux by the south-east ridge and Castor by the north-west face. In the afternoon they reached the Sella Hut and, owing to the vast crowds of climbers arriving, were only just in time to be allotted a bunk apiece. The dormitory was airless and more than a little odorous; Miriam reported that she was thankful when Adolf called them at 3 a.m.

The Lyskamm lived up to its great reputation and gave them all and more than they asked of it. Miriam led on the rocks, just to prove to herself that she could still do so; Adolf led on snow and ice up to the corniced summit ridge; the view was perfection.

The descent of the Lyskamm is usually difficult, involving several hours of step-cutting to the Felikjoch; this year, however, the snow was so compact that they merely wore crampons and had no need to cut a single step; they could hardly believe their luck.

Like all great expeditions these wonderful three days came to an end. As Miriam sat in the little mountain train which carried them down from Roten Boden to Zermatt she thought back to the glowing days of twenty years ago when guideless ascents were her goal. It never occurred to her then that in days to come she would have two sons to share the bliss of high adventure.

Whatever interesting ascents one may undertake in the Zermatt district – and there are enough to fill a lifetime – there is absolutely nothing to compare with the first ascent of the Matterhorn, even by the easiest and most usual route. More difficult ascents fade into insignificance, at any rate temporarily, until the Matterhorn has been achieved.

Bobby went first; guides will seldom take more than one client on their rope on the Matterhorn; Adolf Rubi conformed to this custom. He took Bobby up on what turned out to be the finest day of the season, warm and cloudless with unimpeded views; altogether a grand trip.

Brian went a few days later and conditions were a very different story. But it was a very special day; so much so that for a moment one must become personal. There were three ropes of good friends and it was the first time for all of us. Brian with Adolf Rubi; Nea Morin leading her son Ian (thus making one more record for a first British feminine lead) and myself with Bernard Biner (we had been trying to do the Matterhorn ever since I was at school).

We were unlucky with the weather. We knew it was too warm, even when we started in the dark. It was thundering furiously before we reached the Solvay Refuge Hut and lightning raced along the surrounding peaks. Many parties turned back but not those led by Bernard, Adolf and Nea; they judged the ascent to be possible and on we went. The roof was smothered in far more ice than is usual; Bernard, wearing crampons, hacked out steps for me in my vibrams. I knew the others were ahead but in the swirling mist I could see no sign of them. Suddenly two figures appeared, descending, and Brian's voice rang out, 'Stick it, only ten minutes to the top.' A few seconds later Nea showed up with Ian, in hot pursuit to keep Adolf in view. 'You're almost there but you won't see a thing' – and we didn't! After all those years of waiting Bernard and I could scarcely see each other, let alone the surrounding mountains. But we did not care; we had done it – Bernard and I together, that was all that mattered. And as a sort of bonus the ascent had included the presence of the sons of two of my best climbing friends. Could anyone ask for more!

That night, by invitation of Miriam and Robert, we all celebrated at the Mont Cervin Hotel. I was still in my climbing gear; the Monte Rosa had given me such a roaring welcome on my return that there had only been time to wash. Ronald, my husband, did his best to make up for my sartorial deficiencies and anyway no one cared what anyone wore. Miriam and Robert, Bobby and Brian, Nea and Ian and Ronald and I danced and drank and ate and talked, with occasional interludes for mountain songs, until well after midnight. It was a day to remember – a real mountain day.

And that is the right note on which to end this chapter. There is rather a special atmosphere about family climbing; somehow it is all done just for the fun of it; everyone is gay and relaxed; everyone speaks the same language; the joy and the challenge and the sheer exultation of the mountains is all that matters; records may or may not be created, if they are it is a bonus, an added dimension. The dominant theme is the sharing of deep and very personal experiences with those whom one loves in a world of incomparable beauty.

Chapter 7

Wider Horizons

The human race is ever moving on; men – and women – seldom take time off to rest on their laurels; no sooner has one goal been reached, the next ambition achieved, and they press on again seeking new fields to conquer. Women mountaineers are no exception; manless parties, mother and daughter ropes, no longer make news; most of the major alpine problems have been solved – in the 1950s women climbers were away to other great mountain ranges in other parts of the world.

In 1950 the American climber Elizabeth Cowles (Partridge) was the first and only woman to join the American Houston Expedition to Nepal. Betsy Cowles is a remarkable woman and a particularly delightful person to meet in the mountains; in spite of her great achievements she still retains the pristine simplicity and youthful zest of someone setting out on a first adventure. In 1950 she was already a grandmother twice over. An earlier chapter has told of her feats many years before in the Sierra Nevada and the Andes. No one was in the least surprised that the Houston Expedition decided to include her in their party. Until 1950 Nepal had been virtually closed to foreigners, but political events in China and Tibet had brought about a gradual change and in the spring of that year Oscar Houston, a member of the American Alpine Club, was granted permission by the Maharajah to take a small party into the region south of Everest. It was a very small party judged by later standards (the only other original members were Dr Charles Houston and Anderson Bakewell) but at Kathmandu they met up with Bill Tilman, who had of course had vast experience in the Himalayas. They persuaded him to make the team up to five.

It was the first American Expedition to Everest and it set out in October from Dharan, a small town in Eastern Nepal. The aim of the expedition was not to attempt to reach the summit of Everest but to explore the possibilities of an ascent from the south.

By now, of course, the team had been joined by quite an army of Sherpa porters and coolies carrying the gear; not to mention a soldier escort and a large number of hangers-on intent on seeing the fun. Betsy was the first western woman the locals had set eyes on; to her, the soul of modesty, it seemed a pity that on such an occasion it had to be herself and not some more exotic being.

The first night was spent in Camp at a glorious spot over-looking the Tamur valley; it was Betsy's first glimpse of the Himalayas. Across the northern skyline Chamlang, Makalu and Kanchenjunga held court; unchanging and yet ever-changing in the kaleidoscopic colours of early dawn, late afternoon and moon-lit evening. She was spellbound by the beauty around her but she looked in vain for Mount Everest – it was not until seventeen days later and 125 miles farther on that the party was granted that vision.

The route lay across country – over five great ranges, across six rivers and on the roughest of tracks; always going up and down, up and down. Betsy Cowles had the same approach to the hills as Mrs E. P. Jackson and her ready pen matches that of her famous predecessor of seventy-five years earlier. However diffi-cult the route, however intimidating the conditions, she always found some fresh aspect of beauty in her surroundings. Food and coolie troubles threatened to delay the party and for a time things were tense; Betsy, however, concentrated on the delicious flowering trees and shrubs and the thrill of crossing the river in a twenty-foot canoe manned by three native oarsmen. The troubles passed without serious incident; they went safely over the pass and came after a long, long march of many days to the Sherpa village of Namche Bazar. It was the home of many of the Sherpa porters; their hospitality was boundless and much appreciated, but one theme, and one alone, was uppermost in the minds of the members

of the party – Everest. It was very near; somewhere behind the
great cloud curtain it was hiding; they felt its presence as the
Zermatters feel the presence of the Matterhorn.

The next day it snowed interminably; they struggled on,
knowing that, if the weather had finally broken, their plans would
be laid almost, if not quite, in ruins. The party reached Thyangboche; it was decided that Charles Houston and Bill Tilman with
a few Sherpas should go on up towards the mountain; the other
three would remain at a small house in the grounds of the lamasery
to await their return in five days. The advance party set out and
still it snowed – and snowed.

The next morning all was transformed; a glorious day and a
scene of indescribable beauty. Ten miles up the valley Mount
Everest soared up into the blue arch of the sky; Nuptse and
Lhotse stood in front like silent attendants. Betsy described the
days at the lamasery as pure delight. All around rose line upon
line of tapering summits, with those delicate ridges and fluted
ice-faces that are so characteristic of the Himalayas. In the
lamasery itself, where twenty-five lamas lived permanently, there
was a warm and friendly spirit. They were thoughtful and very
generous, extremely interested in everything that their visitors
said, did, ate and wore. The Head Lama, aged only sixteen,
received them and invited them to sip Tibetan tea while they
watched Lamaistic rites – the first time for any American woman.
They enjoyed it all but, as Betsy wrote, 'it was the mountains we
loved the most'. At all times of the day and night they watched
Everest – always aware that here before them was the highest
point of all the earth's surface.

After five days, amid great excitement at Thyangboche, the
advance party returned safely, weary but in good heart. The
story they had to tell was disappointing; there appeared to be no
feasible means of approach to Everest from this side. They had
made most arduous explorations by several routes and had
climbed to nearly 19,000 feet on the slopes of Pumo-Ri but
always the answer to their quest seemed to be 'No'.

So that was that and the very next day they started the long
trek back to the outside world. It was a cheerful trip in spite of

the disappointment; they were all in perfect physical condition, well-acclimatised to great height. The loyal and happy spirit which had grown up among the members of the team made it a harmonious party. Betsy Cowles maintained that the happy days together among the mountains of Eastern Nepal would be a joy to remember for ever.

It is more than twenty years since the American Houston Expedition blazed the trail through Nepal towards Everest; since then a great many women have done a great many things in the Himalayas. Women had triumphed and will continue to triumph in these, the greatest of all mountain ranges. But it will always be remembered that Betsy Cowles was the first of the modern pioneers and the only woman included in the American Reconnaissance team. She has since married the famous American General Partridge.

A year later, back in the Alps – which, incidentally, are far from being played out as is sometimes suggested – an English woman distinguished herself by making, with a man friend, a new and guideless ascent on the tremendous east face of Monte Rosa. Mary Hingley, daughter of a well-known Alpine Club father and the mother of three young children, was at Zermatt looking round for a first-class climb to complete her holiday, of which there were only two and a half days left. To her and her friend Peter Nock the Santa Caterina on Monte Rosa seemed an obvious choice.

They were lucky in the weather; at 1.15 on a marvellous starry morning, they set out from the Bétemps Hut on what proved to be, for Mary Hingley at any rate, the best climb yet. They made good progress and reached the rocks above the Jaegerjoch at 7.15 a.m. Here they had an hour's rest and some food in preparation for the Santa Caterina which really begins from here, at a height of about 13,000 feet. The climb is divided into four distinct rock towers; the vertical height is about 1,500 feet. Mary reported that the most serious difficulties were encountered on the first tower. There was about 250 feet of climbing involved and they had the misfortune to get on the wrong route, being tempted to leave the straight and narrow way by an attractively wide ledge. They retraced their steps and took the correct, and much more difficult, route which entailed, among other things, crossing a smooth slab of twenty-five feet; to their joy they discovered a solitary *piton* here which helped considerably and they eventually reached the crest of the tower. The second tower proved to be short and easy, giving them a little respite to prepare for the third, which was a quite different problem. They were obliged to climb for some considerable distance up the very edge of the tower on a series of steep, and horribly loose, blocks; having survived this a diagonal crack took them without much difficulty on to a snow-ridge and so to the fourth and last tower. This was only 80 feet and they were soon up it and at the foot of the final snow-slope which runs up to the summit of the Nordend of Monte Rosa.

When they reached this slope they had been climbing for five-and three-quarter hours; they took a long, long rest and some much-needed food. The snow-slope presented no difficulties and could have been done in about forty-five minutes. Mary wrote later that at that point she felt more like a very ancient cart-horse than a climber and took a good deal longer than the allotted time to reach the summit. That, in spite of her engaging honesty, is of little significance; the climb itself – the first guideless ascent of the Santa Caterina – ranked as one of the great climbs of the season. For Mary 'the day remains a perfect memory'.

Three years later, in 1955, Mary Hingley led a rope of three generations, consisting of herself, her father and her younger daughter, on the Grooved Arête of Tryfan in North Wales. Just another instance of family mountaineering and an event which probably gave her as much pleasure as the ascent of Santa Caterina.

With so much mountaineering interest being centred on the Himalayas in the 1950s it must not be forgotten that great deeds were being done by women climbers in other parts of the world. In the Andes in 1951 there was a Franco–Belgian Expedition to the Cordillera Blanca of Peru, the primary object of which was to climb Alpamayo (20,080 feet), regarded by some as the most beautiful mountain in the world. In the party there were two women – Claude Kogan and Nicole Leiniger. Both had important ascents in the Alps to their credit and Claude Kogan, climbing alone with her husband, had actually led up the grim south ridge of the Aiguille Noire de Peuteret.

On Quitaraju (20,276 feet) Claude and Nicole succeeded in reaching the summit and were the first feminine party to do so, although not quite the first women to reach that height. The next year Claude returned to the Andes with the great French climber Bernard Pierre and together they made the first ascent of Salcantray (20,000 feet). Much more will be heard of Claude Kogan in this chapter; indeed the triumph, and ultimate tragedy, of her climbing career would make a book in itself.

In Kenya Clare Graaff and her husband Jan, who live in South Africa, did the Mackinder route up Batian by the Diamond Glacier – the first ascent by a woman. This couple were also active in the Kangra Himalayas. They set out up the Duhangan Nala to attempt Deo Tibba, a well-known peak in the northern part of the Kulu. Deo Tibba (19,687 feet) is not considered to be very high for the Himalayas but it had been unsuccessfully attempted five times since 1912 and so presented a worth-while challenge. After a variety of weather conditions, including heavy snowfalls, Clare Graaff with her husband, a friend Ken Berrill, and two porters, succeeded in making the first ascent of this interesting peak, which has since attracted many climbers.

Home again in South Africa Clare presented her husband with a daughter in 1953 and later followed up this important domestic achievement by climbing several of the Ruwenzori peaks, including the Margherita; her ascent was probably the first by a woman.

Meanwhile other women were exploring other new regions and the intrepid Eleanor Baillie, a member of the Ladies' Alpine Club well known for seeking adventure in the most unlikely places, climbed in Iceland. She reached the summit of Esja, 'the thousand coloured mountain', and nearly lost her life in one of the island's ferocious glacial rivers. Fortunately she survived to bring back a fascinating account of this new and interesting mountain region.

The greatest event in mountaineering history since Whymper's ascent of the Matterhorn in 1865 was, of course, the successful British Expedition which reached the summit of Mount Everest on 29th May 1953. The whole world was thrilled and everyone was agreed that the British deserved to be the first to tread that elusive summit. In this country the sense of elation was stupendous; that the climax of the years of courageous endeavour should come in Coronation Year and that the news should actually arrive on Coronation Day made the magnificent success artistically complete. Thousands will never forget the placards that greeted us as we trudged through the rain at daybreak to take our places on the processional route – 'All this and Everest too'. For mountaineers those words gave an even greater significance to an historic occasion.

Times had greatly changed since General Bruce's Expedition left for Everest in 1922. The Second World War was not far behind us; food rationing was still in force; life had barely returned to normal. The Ladies' Alpine Club had given no dinner and presented no badges to be taken on the 1953 expedition. The Club did, however, send a telegram of congratulations to Sir John Hunt and our President was invited to the Government Reception for the team at Lancaster House; a reception unique in mountaineering history for the number of V.I.P.s present.

At the meeting in the Royal Festival Hall when Sir John Hunt gave his first lecture on the Expedition women mountaineers were there in force. During the course of his speech Sir John read a letter he had received from two schoolgirls:

'Dear Colonel Hunt – We send our heartiest congratulations to the Everest Team. We want to tell you that we have decided that we will try to be the first women to reach the summit of Everest; but we think we must wait for a while as we are not yet eighteen . . .'

Amid vociferous applause Sir John went on, '... of all the thousands of letters which I have received I think that this has given me the most pleasure'. The hearts of his women listeners warmed to him; this seemed like the green light to go ahead with the many Himalayan plans already being formulated, knowing that such plans would get a sympathetic hearing when they were brought before the committees that can do so much to make or mar a project.

Perhaps it is significant that in 1953, when the whole world was applauding the exploits of British mountaineers, a woman should, for the first time, be appointed as a professional guide.

Gwen Moffat is a natural mountaineer who took to climbing almost by accident, having deserted from the A.T.S. In the hills she found something to satisfy her rather rebellious spirit; she began as a stormy petrel who had much to learn and, through no fault of her own, much to suffer. Usually hard up, in her early days she tried her hand at writing about mountains, with some success, in order to keep the wolf from the door; she picked up odd jobs in mountain regions for the same purpose. But gradually, in a hard school, she became an expert climber, prepared to tackle any big problem in the Alps or in her own country and was quite soon elected a member of the Pinnacle Club. She learned a lot about mountaineering and a lot about life, as anyone who reads her three remarkable books can discover. After her marriage she took over the charge of a hostel in the mountains; it was desperately hard work but all the time she was gaining experience in every aspect of her craft.

Once more there were financial difficulties; there had been bouts of bad health; there was a young daughter to provide for and money was not easy to come by. Suddenly a friend suggested that she should try to qualify for a guide's certificate. It was a challenging idea and, at first, quite overwhelming. It would mean a regular income and work which she loved and for which she was eminently suited. But would she ever attain the required standard? She – a woman – when no one had so far ever given a thought to the possibility of a woman mountain guide. Considerations such as these were not the kind to deter one with the questing spirit of Gwen Moffatt. She managed to discover just what would be required of her and set to work to fit herself for the task.

Qualifications for a guide's certificate have to be of the highest order. The applicant must have done hard rock climbs under good and adverse conditions; expeditions on snow and ice are another requirement; there must be knowledge and practical experience of mountain rescue; navigation and route finding are of great importance and there must be specialised knowledge of at least one mountain district in the British Isles. The task looked formidable but bit by bit Gwen covered the ground. At last she put in her application, not knowing in the least what her chances were. While she was awaiting the result she once more fell ill and was rushed off to hospital for an operation. When she was well on the road to recovery her mother brought her a large envelope. It contained not one but two certificates from the British Mountaineering Council: Grade I for rock climbing of a high standard, Grade II for mountaineering. Her joy was complete and recovery was immediately accelerated.

Gwen Moffat is now a fully accredited guide with the certificate of the British Mountaineering Council and the Association of Scottish Climbing Clubs. Her professional engagements take her to Wales, the Lake District and Scotland and – she is still the only woman guide.

Her daughter Sheena has become a keen rock climber and Gwen herself has had the distinction of being one of the very few women elected to the exclusive Alpine Climbing Group – the others being Denise Evans, daughter of Nea, Dr Nancy Smith and Janet Rogers.

It may be that it will still be many years before another woman qualifies as a professional guide but Gwen Moffatt has proved that it is possible for women to do so; she will go down to history as a plucky and rather remarkable pioneer.

In retrospect 1953 stands out as an eventful mountain year, even apart from the great, glowing triumph of Everest. It produced, as we have seen, the first professional woman guide; it also included a spectacular feminine achievement in Kashmir.

Bernard Pierre organised a small party to the Nun-Kun *massif* whose object was to reach the summit of Nun (23,410 feet), the highest point between Gahrwal and Nanga Parbat and the culminating point of the *massif*. Included in the party was Claude Kogan, who had already so distinguished herself in the Ardennes, the Alps and the Andes. The party made several attempts on the peak and suffered a number of frustrating set-backs. A good route had been found, the main difficulties had been surmounted and success was in sight when a sudden change in the weather made further progress impossible. On the descent they unfortunately started an avalanche; Claude Kogan and a Swiss missionary, Pierre Vittoz, escaped almost unscathed but Bernard Pierre and most of the other climbers and porters were badly bruised and shaken. When it was possible for another attempt to be made only Claude and Pierre Vittoz were fit to climb; it fell to them to make the bid for the summit, sent on their way with the generous blessing of the bitterly disappointed Bernard. The climb went smoothly; Claude led up the last steep snow slopes and found the summit ridge just broad enough for her to walk arm-in-arm with Pierre Vittoz to the top. Bernard Pierre was overjoyed at their success and Vittoz described Claude as the best climber of them all.

Success in the Himalayas is a heady wine; those who have sipped it long for more. In 1954 Claude was back again, this time with the great Raymond Lambert. In their attempt on Cho Oyu in Nepal they reached just under 25,000 feet and were only 1,700 feet from the summit when they had to turn back on account of the weather conditions. This still remains the greatest height ever reached by a European woman. The next year with Raymond Lambert, and his friend Gauchet, Claude successfully achieved the first ascent of Ganesh Himal (24,300 feet) and became firmly established in the eyes of the mountain world as a Himalayan virtuoso.

L

The spring of 1955 marks an important milestone in the annals of women mountaineers. In April of that year the first 'Ladies Only' Expedition set sail for the Himalayas. It was composed of four members of the Ladies' Scottish Climbing Club – Esmé Speakman, Monica Jackson, Elizabeth Stark and Evelyn Camrass; the first three are also members of the Ladies' Alpine Club.

These women found making the decision to go to the Himalayas the hardest part of the whole venture; it meant leaving husband, home and family and the relinquishing of good jobs. Once the decision was made, however, and preparations were complete, everything went more smoothly and successfully than they had imagined could be possible. They had all had much experience in the Alps and in Scotland; Esmé was the most experienced alpinist; Evelyn was a doctor and Monica, who had spent much of her life in India, spoke Hindustani fluently if, as Betty Stark reports, 'slightly ungrammatically'!

A special permit, backed by the Mount Everest Foundation through the Foreign Office, was required to climb in Nepal. Because they were women this was particularly hard to come by; they might be first-class climbers but this was no guarantee that they could cope with a drunken Sherpa. They applied for two permits; one for the Langtang Himal and another for the Jugal Himal. The Nepalese Government allowed only one expedition in any particular area at one time; unfortunately Raymond Lambert had already applied for, and received, permission for the Langtang; the ladies had to be content with the Jugal. They had just resigned themselves good humouredly to this *contretemps* when Esmé Speakman became ill and had to fall out. This was a real blow; Esmé's presence would always be regarded as an inspiration to any expedition; somehow they would have to manage without her, but all through the whole great adventure they always regarded her as still a member with them.

Monica, Betty and Evelyn arrived in Kathmandu on 10th April with plans carefully laid and preparations thought out in advance to the last detail. They were very well aware that any misfortune or accident would certainly be attributed to their sex. Not that they took themselves too seriously; all three were blessed with a strong sense of humour and this carried them through the moments of danger and discomfort inseparable from such an expedition. They were not entirely sure how the Sherpas would react to them; Sherpa women do not dominate the social order and they wondered if the men would be willing to take orders from 'memsahibs'. They soon found they had no need to worry; the Sherpas responded well to tact and good manners and seemed anxious to serve them and keen that the expedition should succeed in its purpose. The three women managed to combine firmness with kindness; they refused to budge on any decision that was of vital importance, but never stood on their dignity and gave way gracefully when it was necessary and possible.

The expedition left Kathmandu on 13th April accompanied by a liaison officer appointed by the Nepalese Government according to their usual custom. They found him a shy but most helpful and likeable young man, full of initiative and possessed of a prodigious appetite.

After six days they reached Tempathang, the nearest village to the mountains of the Jugal. Here they dismissed their Kathmandu porters, who were suitable only for work in the foothills, and engaged the local Sherpas, who were natural mountaineers.

It had always been intended that the expedition should be exploratory; most of the Jugal mountains are too difficult of approach for any but a much larger and more highly equipped party to attempt the summits. Their route led to the third and most easterly of the three glacier valleys of the Jugal Himal and they established their Base Camp on a high alp above it. They discovered this to be the Phurbi Chyachmbu Glacier; they explored it in detail and followed it up to the frontier between Nepal and Tibet. They discovered, too, a snowy dome rising above a smaller and subsidiary glacier. This, they decided, was the one mountain which it was within their powers to climb; it rose to a height of 22,000 feet and would give them a taste of real climbing, as distinct from glacier exploration.

They approached the mountain by the subsidiary glacier, which they christened the Ladies' Glacier. They had to find a way

through a complicated ice-fall and set up another camp at about
20,000 feet from which they could clearly see the route to their
summit. From here they ascended a snow couloir to a high col
overlooking Tibet and then strolled easily over the undulating
frozen slopes to the snow dome. They named it Gyalgen peak as
a tribute to Mingma Gyalgen, their Sirdar. He had shown much
skill and enterprise, particularly in ice-work and they had allowed
him to take his turn of leading.

Having captured their peak they succeeded in discovering the
approaches to all the glaciers of the Jugal Himal and the passes
between them. In doing so Monica and Betty reached an elevated
notch on the south ridge of Dorje Lapka, while Evelyn climbed
a peak of more than 17,000 feet overlooking the south-eastern
Jugal.

The limited time at their disposal at last reached its end, but
they were quite satisfied. They had not, of course, exhausted the
Jugal Himal but they had discovered a lot and this they hoped
might be useful to others. More important still they had learned
a great deal about the reactions of women at high altitudes and
this they knew would be invaluable for future all-women parties.
They found that on the whole they seemed to stand the cold
rather better than men and their powers of endurance seemed
greater. At their highest camp at 20,000 feet one member of the
party was able to sleep in pyjamas only – inside two down sleeping
bags. Their rate of acclimatisation varied. Monica, who is small,
light and wiry, acclimatised quickly and went fast at any altitude;
Evelyn acclimatised slowly; Betty was very sick at 16,000 feet
and thereafter encountered no further trouble.

All three found that the higher they went the less fearful they
became; at 20,000 feet they felt an absolute serenity and got on
even better than usual with each other. Since they had been led
to believe that the reverse would be true – and how often one
hears that altitude puts strains on relationships – they came to the
conclusion that such an unfortunate state of affairs must be
brought about by discomfort and boredom, and perhaps women
can shake these things off more easily. Above all, perhaps, this
women's expedition proved that it is possible for women to

control Sherpa porters, enlist their loyalty and support and climb happily with them. That this has been proved to be feasible has already been and will continue to be of the utmost importance to all future women's expeditions. It must have rejoiced the heart of Lord Hunt, who has such high hopes for women in the Himalayas.

The achievements of this small party are outstanding: Monica, Betty and Evelyn were moving in exceptionally difficult *terrain* and to climb a peak of 22,000 feet with no supporting party must surely be a record in itself. But they were not obsessed with record-making nor even with the fact that their all-woman party was the first of its kind. Anyone who reads their book *Tents in the Clouds* will realise how much they enjoyed themselves. They enjoyed the marches, the magnificent views and the happy, friendly Sherpas; most of all they enjoyed their highest camps, in the heart of the great snow mountains where neither man nor woman had ever set foot before. Could it be that it was their own attitude to the mountains that brought such unique success?

Momentous happenings among women climbers in 1955 were not confined to the great Himalayan ranges; at sea level, in fact in London, an event took place which was of historic importance in the mountain world, although of no significance whatever outside it. The Alpine Club and the Ladies' Alpine Club held a joint meeting at the Alpine Club premises in South Audley Street; the speaker was Claude Kogan just elected an Honorary Member of the Ladies' Alpine Club. Relations between the two clubs have always been cordial and have become increasingly so as the years have gone by. Women guests were always invited to the winter Alpine Club Reception and in recent times invitations have been extended by the Club to members of the Ladies' Alpine Club to some of the lectures given during the years. But never, in all the ninety-eight years of its existence, had the Alpine Club ever contemplated such a revolutionary suggestion as a *joint* meeting – the founding fathers must have turned in their graves. The A.C. was munificent; both Presidents were in the Chair (there were two chairs but this, of course, was unavoidable!).

Claude Kogan spoke to a packed house about her climbs on Alpamayo, Nun-Kun and Cho Oyu. Most of these climbs established records but they paled into insignificance beside the fact that Claude was the first woman ever to lift up her voice in the sanctuaries of the Alpine Club. It was an exceedingly happy evening; it may be that one day there will be another.

It soon became obvious that the 'ladies only' expedition to the Jugal Himal had opened a door through which others were eager to follow. Women came to see that there was much that a small, highly organised team could achieve and since there were no big financial grants likely to be forthcoming for women's expeditions in the foreseeable future it was better to plan within this framework.

In 1956 another group was ready – once more a team of four led by Mrs Joyce Dunsheath, with Hilda Reid, a theatre sister from a London hospital, Eileen Gregory (Healey), a biochemist, known to be a strong climber and keen camper, and Frances Delaney, a geologist working in French Equatorial Africa who had been yearning for a chance to visit the Himalayas. All these four are members of the Ladies' Alpine Club.

The party decided on the Kulu-Spiti-Lahul watershed in East Punjab as a suitable area for their explorations, and, travelling by various ways and from many directions, they all met up at Manali at the head of the Kulu valley. Almost from the first this expedition suffered misfortunes; the weather was uncertain all through; the going proved to be more difficult than had been anticipated and some members took quite a long time to acclimatise to altitude. But that is not the whole story; they battled bravely against enormous odds; they achieved a lot of survey work, especially of the Bara Shigri Glacier and they returned safely having won the respect and admiration of all for what they endured in order to obtain their results.

Eileen Gregory (Healey) stayed on in the Himalayas for another fortnight, and climbing only with two local Ladakhi porters, made the first ascent of Cathedral Peak (20,000 feet) in the Kulu; the first ascent of Chapter House (19,100 feet) in the same area and the third ascent and first feminine lead of Deo Tibba (19,688 feet) in the Kangra – a magnificent bag in two short weeks.

In the Alps in the same year some spectacular climbs were being done by a couple of young members of the Pinnacle Club. Denise Shortall and Rie Leggett concentrated on the Valais for their summer holiday; both were accomplished climbers and Rie Leggett had already done the complete traverse of the splendid rock ridge of the Scialouze, making a first *cordée féminine* with Nea Morin in 1954.

In the Zermatt district in 1956 they did the Rothgrat of the Alphubel; the Kanzelgrat of the Rothorn; the Wellenkuppe-Obergabelhorn-Arbengrat traverse and the Hörnli route on the Matterhorn. Each of these was a *cordée féminine*; the Obergabelhorn and the Kanzelgrat were almost certainly first ascents by a women's party and the ascent of the Matterhorn may well have been a first British women's rope. Denise and Rie do not seem to have bothered too much about records; they climbed for the fun of it; nevertheless it certainly appears to have been a pretty record-breaking holiday.

At least one more big climb by a woman was done in the Zermatt mountains that summer. Anna Roelfsema, always thirsting for more adventures, climbed the East Face of the Rothorn with Bernard Perren; it was only the second time this climb has been done by a woman.

There is never a dull moment in the alpine world; ever since men and women took to mountaineering in a big way there has seldom been a year that has not recorded a first ascent, some pioneer exploration or a *cordée féminine*. The year 1957 capped the lot for festivities, for it brought the Centenary of the Alpine Club and the Jubilee of the Ladies' Alpine Club. Both events were occasions of great celebrations in the Alps; the publication of special numbers of the respective Journals and culmination in the form of most exhilarating dinners.

The Ladies' Alpine Club Journal published fascinating reminiscences from the older members still surviving, some of them even still climbing. The photographs accompanying the articles were a joy to behold and gave glimpses of how our predecessors appeared at the turn of the century and even earlier.

The Jubilee President, Una Cameron, organised a Meet at Courmayeur in July and this enabled members to go on to join in the Alpine Club Centenary Meet at Zermatt in August.

We arrived at Zermatt to find Sir John Hunt (Lord Hunt) with most of his Everest team and a bevy of famous climbers from all over the world; there was a touch of poetic justice in the fact that John Hunt, leader of the Everest Expedition, should be the President of the Alpine Club in its Centenary Year. The A.C. did the L.A.C. proud; we were invited to participate in everything – except, of course, the Centenary Dinner at the Monte Rosa, which was strictly 'men only' and included many of the famous guides. However, those of us lucky enough to have A.C. husbands were later regaled with every detail of the memorable occasion. Meanwhile Lady Hunt invited the ladies to dinner at the Mont Cervin; we were all climbers in our own right; the talk was naturally of mountains and we spoke of the days, a hundred years ago, when wives came to Zermatt but could go no farther.

On the next day the Seiler family of hoteliers, who for more than a hundred years had cared for the bodily comforts of the Zermatt mountaineers, gave an open-air *raclette* party on the Riffelalp. This was a delightfully informal affair; *raclette* is the alpine repast *par excellence* and great honour is done to the recipients when such an invitation is extended. Enormous cheeses are melted at an open charcoal fire and each guest receives a portion on a platter, served with boiled potatoes and pickled onions. There is sparkling white wine to accompany the dish; this is a gastronomic necessity to ward off what would otherwise be inevitable indigestion.

The company assembled on this occasion must have been the greatest galaxy of alpine talent ever gathered together in one place. Relaxing on a rug with Sir John Hunt was Professor Noel Odell, the last man to see Mallory and Irvine alive on Everest in 1924; there was the famous French climber Bernard Pierre, and Eggler and Lützinger of the successful Swiss Everest Expedition.

Near by was Arnold Lunn in earnest conversation with Alfred Zürcher, one of the oldest and best known Swiss climbers, *persona grata* with all the British. Mr Sedgewick, a game old gentleman of eighty-six, the *doyen* of the Alpine Club, was consuming larger portions of *raclette* than anyone else and apparently thriving on it.

The Ladies' Alpine Club were there in force and those present included Ethel Blandy, daughter of Edward Whymper, Hermione de Freitas Martins from Madeira and Ursula Corning from America. Miss Edith Baring-Gould, aged eighty-seven, reigned supreme from her invalid chair, the timeless representative of the lady climbers of the Victorian age. Nor was the younger generation missing; Susan Hunt, already following the example of her famous father; Nigella Blandy, granddaughter of Whymper, and a host of future would-be members of both clubs aged from three to ten.

In the winter the celebrations continued in London. The President of the L.A.C. and several members, as well as those who happened to be A.C. wives, were invited to the Alpine Club's Centenary Reception in the beautiful Great Hall of Lincoln's Inn, which was attended by the Queen and the Duke of Edinburgh and many distinguished guests.

On 4th December the Ladies' Alpine Club held its Jubilee Dinner; in spite of one of the worst London fogs for years it was a gay, happy and elegant evening. The guests included the Ambassadors of Switzerland and Nepal; the Vice-President of the Alpine Club; Professor Noel Odell; Fräulein Gloor of the Swiss Ladies' Alpine Club; Claude Kogan; Anna Roelfsema and Miriam Underhill (both of whom were members who had travelled a long way to be present) and many more. The Swiss Ambassador, whose wife is a member of the Club, paid a graceful and generous tribute to our 'Faith to inspire, Courage to achieve and Loyalty to endure'. Emlyn Jones of the Alpine Club, replying for the guests, quoted an amusing speech by Douglas Freshfield at one of our club's first dinners, probably in 1907. 'In the confidence of after dinner we need not conceal that there are practical as well as sentimental grounds for our rejoicing. For by providing a safety-valve the Ladies' Alpine Club must diminish any risk of our meetings in Savile Row (at that time the A.C. headquarters) being interrupted by the alpine variety of Suffragette – should she exist! And may we not confidently hope that the committee of the new club will train up in the way in which they should a succession of damsels who will prove eligible brides for our younger members and become in due course of time the mothers of a race of twentieth-century climbers who will surpass our feats as much as we have surpassed those of the climbers of the eighteenth century'.

Lord Chorley, speaking on behalf of the Alpine Club, said, 'Mountaineering is a way of life to which women have contributed much. It would be a sad world without them. It is nice to have them with us, at least part of the time!' From the Alpine Club this was considered much.

The Jubilee Year did not consist only of feasting and merry-making. In between whiles Joyce Dunsheath pushed her way through the Iron Curtain and made the first ascent by an English-woman of Mount Elbrus in the Caucacus; Esmé Speakman also found an unclimbed route in the Alps and made a pioneer ascent on the South Face of the Grand Cornier. Meanwhile Eileen Gregory (Healey) and Monica Jackson made the first all-woman climb of the Boël route on the Aiguille Dibona.

Denise Morin aptly celebrated the Jubilee Year by marrying the Everest climber Charles Evans and indulging in a remarkable, but eminently suitable, honeymoon. They flew to Kathmandu and followed the Everest route to Jumbesi; they spent three weeks at Dudh Pokri and climbed an 18,500 feet rock peak and also Katani Peak – both these were first ascents. They explored glaciers and valleys during the next few weeks and eventually returned safely to Kathmandu on Christmas Day.

From every point of view the Ladies' Alpine Club had good reason to be proud of its Jubilee Year.

Not many people, probably, would associate Yugoslavia with mountaineering – sun-bathing, water-skiing and skin-diving come first to mind when this Adriatic country is mentioned. However,

Yugoslavia can boast many mountains, as those who read Mrs F. S. Copeland's book *Beautiful Mountains* will discover. Fanny Copeland is not only a writer about mountains, she is herself a mountaineer of considerable experience. Having in the course of many years climbed most of the mountains of Yugoslavia, she established a record in 1958 by climbing Triglav (9,400 feet) at the age of eighty-six.

How did such an unusual event come about? Everyone wanted to know; the Press headlined the news and the *Daily Mail* produced a cartoon captioned 'Excelsior'. Fanny Copeland explained her ascent in a charming and most interesting letter addressed to the Ladies' Alpine Club. 'Triglav, Father Triglav', she wrote, 'is no mere mountain to the Slovenes; something of the prestige of divinity still clings to him.' She wished to climb him to show her undiminished respect for him and her gratitude for her return to good health after a serious illness in 1953. The summers, however, were poor and she was only slowly recovering from a dislocated knee; it was impossible to consider an ascent until 1958. Fortunately in that year the summer was exceptionally fine and she went up to the Aljaz Hostel to ask for somebody to accompany her while she went slowly up the mountain (her knee was still not quite normal). The leading guide of the district, a close personal friend, insisted on taking Fanny up himself; he also insisted that they should be roped. Joze Cop, the guide concerned, had the surprise of his life; he found his client as good as ever on rock. They reached the summit hostel without incident and Fanny Copeland decided to spend two days there before making a leisurely descent. In her letter she went on to say that she hoped, in the winter, to shuffle about on skis if the snow was good; it was quite obvious that this intrepid lady's mountain days were by no means done.

Mrs Copeland, a Scottish woman, had lived nearly forty years in Yugoslavia. She endured a most perilous existence during the Nazi occupation in the war and more than once nearly lost her life. She was awarded the O.B.E. decoration.

Another woman, Yugoslav by birth, was doing great things about this time. Mlle Nadja Fajdiga did the West Face of the

Grand Dru and the North West Face *directissime* of the Cima su Alto in the Dolomites. Both these ascents were done in 1959, but Mlle Fajdiga continued her alpine adventures and today is one of Yugoslavia's leading lady climbers.

There are fewer alpine tragedies among women than among men but 1959 was a year which brought Nea Morin in very close contact with disaster and tragic death to two other distinguished women mountaineers. In the spring a party left England for Nepal; its object was to attempt Ama Dablam, which lies in the Everest district. Ama Dablam has become known as the Matterhorn of Nepal; it is a dramatic peak dominating the valley from which it rises. It is not high for a Himalayan mountain – only 22,500 feet – but Lord Hunt has described it as appearing 'utterly inaccessible' and from every angle it looks completely fantastic, and utterly magnificent. Such a peak inevitably exerts a compelling power over questing climbers; as one after another the great Himalayan summits were reached by teams from various countries, an attempt on Ama Dablam became a 'must'.

The party that set out in 1959 consisted of five experienced men climbers – Emlyn Jones, as leader, Frederic Jackson, Mike Harris, George Fraser and Ted Wrangham – and one equally experienced woman, Nea Morin. There should have been two more ladies – Louise Emlyn Jones and Anne Wrangham – but in the end neither was able to come. Suddenly finding herself the only woman posed a problem for Nea; she seriously considered pulling out and going instead with the all-women's expedition which Claude Kogan was leading to Cho Oyu, and which Claude had begged her to join. The matter was finally decided by family considerations, as so often has to be the case where women are concerned. The Cho Oyu party was to leave in July; in August Denise, Nea's daughter, was expecting her first child; Nea decided for Ama Dablam, which would bring her home by midsummer.

For some years Nea had longed for a chance to go to the Himalayas; it would be a fitting climax to her climbing career. It still seems hard that from the very first she was dogged by bad luck. Only a week before she was due to fly to Kathmandu she

damaged her weak knee climbing on Harrison's Rocks; a physio-
therapist did all that could be done but she joined up with the
party well aware that she was not, and probably could not be,
completely fit. Fred Jackson, the team doctor, provided an
elastic knee cap and with a crew of seventy porters the party set
off on the 130-mile march towards Ama Dablam. Somehow Nea
covered the distance; taking care every step of the way; sometimes
struggling along an hour or two behind the rest but always
arriving at camp before nightfall; always gallant and always
cheerful.

In her superb book *A Woman's Reach* Nea confesses that she
must have cut a comic figure – clad in cotton slacks and an off-
white hat, limping along with an ice-axe in one hand and an
umbrella in the other, as a protection against sun and rain. She
insists that all along the route people kept speaking to her just to
find out if she was a man or a woman. However, probably no one
else has ever walked the 130 miles from Kathmandu to Base Camp
entirely by themselves!

In spite of her handicap and the fact that she was at times in
considerable pain, Nea was a useful member of the expedition.
While the main party went on to establish Base Camp she went
off on a medical survey with Fred Jackson; two nights were
spent at Thyangboche, where the Rongbuk Lama was staying
with his family; to their delight he allowed an examination of his
heart for research purposes. Base Camp was established at 16,000
feet on a splendid site with incredibly beautiful views of Lhotse,
Nuptse, and Everest, the whole wall rising in a great sweep of
10,000 feet. While some of the party were prospecting for feasible
routes, Nea was engaged in assisting to get 2,000 feet of fixed
rope secured across some dangerous slabs and helping to get
the loads up the first 200 feet. Frequently there were strong
winds and snow; it was slow and exhausting work but quite
essential.

Slowly but surely Camp I and then Camp II were established,
the latter at 19,240 feet. It is hard for those of us who have not
been on such an expedition to realise the weeks of manual work,
careful planning and concentration that have to be endured before

the actual ascent of the mountain can even begin. Several members of the party, including Nea, were unwell during this time but at last, on 13th May, everyone went up to Camp I. Nea, although still not completely fit, insisted on going to make sure that she could lead these pitches if it ever should become necessary. She came down again that night; it was snowing hard and she reached Base Camp just before dark.

By now the assault was on; Nea remained at Base Camp but when the rest of the party went up to Camps I and II she went up to help with the loads and then returned. By now she was feeling quite fit again. Three days later Mike, Ted and George, with a porter, went up to Camp III, and the next day Mike and George set out from Camp III taking a light assault tent with them. By this time Fred, the doctor, while taking tests from everyone else decided to test himself and found that he was showing signs of coronary thrombosis. He was greatly concerned lest he should become a liability and came down at once to join Nea at Base Camp.

On 19th May for most of the day Nea was able to watch Mike and George on the mountain, getting slowly higher; by the end of the day they had established Camp V at 21,000 feet. On the next day she watched them again and realised they were engaged in exploring a route; they came down late in the afternoon towards Camp V.

On 21st May George and Mike were going up the Ice Pyramid once more at a tremendous pace with George leading; at 8 a.m. Nea saw them reach the top of the Pyramid and by 8.30 they had both disappeared from view. She judged them to be at 21,500 feet, less than a thousand feet below the summit of Ama Dablam. To get a better view of what the rest of the climb involved Nea went up to a spot called Ambu Gyaljen; she could see there was still a long way to go and the route was by no means easy, although probably the major difficulties were over. She had hoped for a good view of what was going on but mist enveloped the upper part of the mountain and she could see nothing.

Back at Base Camp the mist suddenly disappeared and the night was brilliant with moonlight – the night before full moon. The next day, 22nd May, was fine; Nea watched all day; there was no sign of movement anywhere; the silence around her could be felt. She began to be uneasy and wrote in her diary, 'Getting worried ...'. That night she could not sleep; in the full moon Ama Dablam and Everest were quite incredible; but it was warm and the roar of avalanches was unceasing.

On 23rd May it was misty again and from Base Camp nothing could be seen of the mountain. The weather broke and snow began to fall; Fred and Nea, alone in camp, were getting desperately anxious. They heard nothing all day and decided that the next day they must start up to Camp I.

Meanwhile the rest of the party up at Camp III were already convinced that something was wrong; conditions were bad, with a lot of new snow; they had to come down from Camp III to Camp II while it was still possible to descend and still possible to put up an extra tent to accommodate them all.

At 6 a.m. on 24th May Nea was scanning the mountain and spotted the extra tent at Camp II. For a short time she and Fred took this to mean that everyone was safe and down at Camp II. Their relief was enormous, but it was short-lived. The mist came down again; they saw nothing and heard nothing all day. They were puzzled and desperately worried. How was it that they had not come down? Once more it snowed – harder than ever.

On 25th May they were out again at 6 a.m.; it was clear and they could see Camp II. The porters at Base Camp shouted up with tremendous power; they got an answer from the porters at Camp II; they reported that the news was 'All well, everybody coming down'. Strangely Fred and Nea were not convinced; something, somehow, warned them that things were far from well. Slowly, through the mist, they picked out Emlyn with a Sherpa and then Ted with another. The mist thickened; everyone from Base Camp went up a little way to meet the party; it seemed a lifetime before they appeared. Somehow the little crowd from Base Camp knew what to expect – 'We've lost Mike and George'; the British and the Sherpas stood silently looking up at the great mountain. Ama Dablam had taken its toll; there was nothing more to be said.

Unobtrusively and with much hard work the porters brought down what equipment they could in shocking conditions; they did a magnificent job. On 29th May it snowed heavily all day but the party laboured away to build a memorial cairn for Mike and George; Gadul, one of the porters, had worked for three days carving the names and dates with a screwdriver on a large, flat stone. No one will ever know what happened but Nea and all the party tried to hope that they had reached the summit and that disaster overtook them on the way down – no one knows, but hope springs eternal.

For Nea the whole expedition might have seemed to be a series of tragic disappointments; the injured knee that crippled her from the start; her inability to play as large a part as she would have liked to; the irreparable loss of her two friends; and finally, after the sad return, the onset of serious osteo-arthritis of the hip, which led to a big operation and virtually ended her serious climbing career. But in spite of everything she sees it differently. 'Even had I been able to foresee that it would end my climbing days', she wrote, 'I think I still would have taken the opportunity to go . . . just to have been a member of a Himalayan expedition, to have seen the transcendent beauty of these mountains, to have known some of the splendid people who live among them, were experiences which I never dreamed would come my way and for which I shall ever be grateful.' Perhaps there is something here which is the essence of every mountaineer's creed.

In July 1959 the *Expédition Féminine 1959 au Nepal*, under the leadership of Claude Kogan, left for the Far East. It was an international party; the three British members, Eileen Healey, Countess Dorothea Gravina and Margaret Darvall, came from the Ladies' Alpine Club; Switzerland was represented by Loulou Boulaz; Claudine Van der Stratten was from Belgium; Jeanne Franco, Dr Colette Le Bret and the photographer Micheline Rambaud were all French. At Kathmandu they were to be joined by two daughters and a niece of Tenzing: Pem Pem, Nima and Douma. Tenzing himself had promised to provide a special Sherpa in charge. It was hoped to reach Base Camp about 18th

September, leaving six weeks to explore the lesser heights as well as the main objective.

In spite of the wealth of talent and experience included in the team, this expedition was the target for considerable criticism from official circles both in Great Britain and in France even before it left Europe. Claude Kogan was well aware of this but she had confidence in herself and in her companions; also she had an account to settle with Cho Oyu. Five years earlier, when only 2,000 feet from the summit, she and Raymond Lambert had been forced to turn back. This was the greatest height ever achieved by a woman; if only Cho Oyu, 26,700 feet, could be the first great Himalayan peak to be climbed by a women's expedition! Incidentally, it was the height of Cho Oyu which was causing concern among the critics; at 26,700 feet oxygen would be advisable and the carrying of oxygen cylinders invariably entails many extra difficulties.

There never was a more enthusiastic expedition. Margaret Darvall and Dorothea Gravina had been talking about an approach to the Himalayas for years; Eileen Healey had already had a taste and was anxious for more; Loulou Boulaz, having done almost all that could be done in the Alps, was eager to explore new fields of adventure; Claudine Van der Stratten, at twenty-six, had all the youthful exuberance that would be expected of the youngest member.

The idea of this expedition was really conceived, most suitably, at the Ladies' Alpine Club Jubilee Dinner in 1957, at which Claude was a guest; the period of gestation was rather unusually protracted but the result was a remarkably mature and well-developed child. Seldom can a party have set out with plans better laid.

In the middle of August the European members met at Kathmandu and were at once joined by Tenzing with his daughters and his niece. There was a good supply of Sherpa porters and the British women in particular found it touching to watch them filing past Tenzing, bowing their heads to the ground as they do in their own temples. Tenzing has become the Sherpa's idol, but his modesty and simplicity remain unimpaired.

M

The long trek from Kathmandu began on 21st August and followed the usual Everest route to Namche Bazar. The expedition was accompanied by Sherpas and Sherpanis – women porters. They seemed to be nearly as tough as their menfolk, except on the unpleasant and unsafe bridges notorious in these parts. Here the Sherpanis became very feminine, giggling coyly and demanding that the men take their loads across. However, these bridges provided some happy memories of delicious bathes and sunbathes; Margaret Darvall wrote that Douma, Tenzing's niece, sat on a rock like a mermaid combing her long black hair.

Everyone was looking forward to the arrival at Namche Bazar, a name of legendary fame in all Everest stories. The Tenzing girls were for ever talking about it and comparing the people of the lower Nepalese valleys most unfavourably with the delightful types to be found at Namche Bazar. They made a ceremonial entry into the village with Claude leading her team mounted on horseback. The people were as happy and friendly as the Tenzings had promised and Namche certainly lived up to its glowing reputation.

For four days the party waited at Namche Bazar; the clouds were low and the weather was poor; the monsoon obviously was not yet finished. With his usual hospitality the Lama at Thyangboche sent an invitation for seven ladies to come up for a visit. This was an unforgettable experience in spite of the absence of any view. Women were not allowed to sleep in the monastery buildings, but after their interview with the Lama they were ceremoniously conducted to a most comfortable tent, where rich carpets covered the floor.

Refreshed by this unexpected luxury they set off from Namche Bazar in good spirits. Above the village they left the Everest route and turned west along a track bordered by occasional patches of blue gentians. For four days they climbed steadily up; on the third night they camped on the moraine beside the glacier; on the fourth day they reached the Nangpa La (19,050 feet). On this day, 14th September, they saw for the first time the wide purple plains of Tibet stretching out before them; from the top of the pass they were to enter this wonderful new country. They sat there, perched between Nepal and Tibet, waiting for their caravan of porters and supplies to catch up, feasting their eyes on a great rolling sea of Himalayan giants. The caravan came up; they moved on over the pass; almost immediately Cho Oyu came into view; it was the moment everyone had been waiting for.

Base Camp was established about two hours farther on, the site was a little lower than the Nangpa La; it was higher than they would have chosen for a Base but it was the only available spot and had already been used by a Swiss Expedition.

With Base Camp suitably erected and equipped preparations for Camp I had to be started. A fixed rope was arranged to assist the porters in getting the loads up a snow gully and it was not long before Claude, Claudine, Eileen and the Tenzing girls were sorting stores at Camp I. They returned to Base but on the following night Claude, Claudine, Jeanne and Eileen went up to sleep at the Camp. On the next day, 20th September, they were off again to set about the task of preparing Camp II. Claude and Claudine, who had acclimatised quickly, took up their sleeping bags in order to sleep up there if possible; Eileen and Jeanne went up only to acclimatise and came back to sleep at Camp I. Here they found Dorothea Gravina, Loulou Boulaz and Pem Pem Tenzing; but already the effects of high altitude were being experienced. Loulou was badly affected and even the lively Pem Pem had to remain in her tent with a headache.

On 22nd September Dorothea and Eileen set out for Camp II with a Sherpa; on the way they met Claude and Claudine coming down with two Sherpas having finished putting up the fixed ropes required for getting loads up to Camp II. This had been done by Claude and Claudine entirely on their own; the Sherpas had offered to help but Claude had explained that, as it was a women's expedition, they felt it right to do this work themselves. She was at all times very keen that her team should demonstrate that women had the ability to undertake all the responsibilities that a Himalayan expedition entails.

Dorothea and Eileen were delighted with the news and full of congratulations on this courageous feat. They went on up to Camp II, two more Sherpas arrived and they set about preparing supper – a slow business because at that height the powder-snow took literally hours to melt in the cooking-pans. A storm got up in the night and the cold was intense; six inches of snow drifted in to the centre of the tent; Dorothea and Eileen, snuggled in two sleeping-bags apiece and clad in down jackets and trousers succeeded in avoiding frost-bite – but only just.

Most of the next day was spent in trying to clear the Camp of the ravages of the storm. It was a difficult time; on the next day, when they were still working, a team of tired Sherpas arrived bringing up loads from Camp I. Their leader brought a worrying message from Claude; Loulou was seriously ill with altitude sickness, Margaret had burst a vein. Colette, the doctor, had insisted on their immediate evacuation to Namche Bazar. Colette herself was accompanying them with four Sherpas and three kitchen boys. This was serious news and at over 20,000 feet it can sometimes be harder to stand up to anxiety. They put the porters' loads in the ice-cave they had excavated and set off for Base Camp. At Camp I they met Claudine and Jeanne already on their way up to try to site Camp III.

Back at Base the news was more cheering. Loulou had been taken down on an improvised stretcher with Margaret following slowly. At Namche Bazar they were taken to the home of Gyaljen, one of the Sherpas, and were already recovering rapidly at the lower altitude. These glad tidings came in a little note from Colette brought up by the wood porters. There was never, of course, any hope that Loulou and Margaret would be able to come up and rejoin the expedition; they spent four weeks at Gyaljen's house, feeling bitterly frustrated but thankful that by then they were pronounced completely fit.

After a blissful rest day at Base Camp, with anxiety about their friends much relieved, the other members of the expedition went off up the mountain again. On 28th September Claudine was at Camp III; Claude, Nima and Douma were at Camp II; Jeanne and Dorothea were at Camp I; the Sherpas were distributed among the different camps. It was curious weather. The morning was blisteringly hot; in the afternoon it snowed; by sunset deep frost had gripped everything. Jeanne and Dorothea had just slid gratefully into their sleeping-bags when shouts were heard. They pulled on their boots and struggled out; through the thick mist they could dimly discern Nima, Douma and five Sherpas temporarily lost and moving perilously near a sinister-looking group of crevasses. By means of a 200-foot rope and a furious chorus of shouts they managed to direct the wanderers into Camp I. After a short rest they set off for Base in a snowstorm and were safely guided in by torches. Jeanne and Dorothea returned to their sleeping-bags and a night free from further disturbance.

The 29th September dawned a glorious day. A note came down to Camp I from Claude and Claudine, both now at Camp III, to say that they would go up to site Camp IV but would return to sleep at Camp III. Could Jeanne and Dorothea send up Sherpas with more food. This was arranged satisfactorily; Pem Pem then turned up to take over Camp I; Jeanne went down to Base and Dorothea went up to Camp II. The sun was blazing; the snow was soft; Dorothea reported that she and the Sherpas slid back at every step; conditions were about as frustrating as they could be. Camp II when they reached it seemed to be the acme of comfort and peace; they recovered at once and ate an enormous supper. Whether it was the supper or the altitude Dorothea never knew but in the night the Sherpas began to complain of pains and headaches; she produced some lurid-looking pills; to her relief recovery was swift and miraculous!

The next morning, the last day of September, the Sherpas went up to Camp III with the urgent loads requested by Claude and Claudine. Dorothea remained at Camp II quite alone – she loved it; the weather was perfect; there was plenty to do sorting loads and clearing up the Camp and whenever she stopped for a rest there was the whole incomparable panorama spread out on all sides for hundreds of miles. Northwards Tibet stretched away to the horizon; to the west was Nangpa La and beyond it mile upon mile of great snow-peaks glittering in the sun; over Everest a storm was raging but at Camp II there was peace and contentment; it was a day for a mountaineer to remember.

At sunset Dorothea put a large pan of snow to heat; the equivalent, she suggested, of putting on the kettle. Soon there were shouts from above and below – welcome travellers returning. Pem Pem and a Sherpa were on their way up, another Sherpa was coming down. He brought a note from Claude at Camp III; Claudine had gone up with two Sherpas to establish Camp IV; she would return to Camp III for the night and the next day they would both go up to Camp IV. That would be 1st October; if the weather was good and looked settled they would try for the top on the second; if that was hoping for too much they would at least make tracks towards it. Finally, would Dorothea go up to Camp III, take a tent and enlarge the Camp. The last phase was about to begin; nerves were tense but hopes were high; no one knew better than Dorothea – an older and very mature climber – how much was at stake.

In the night the weather deteriorated; on 1st October it was, to say the least, extremely uninviting. However, it did not seem bad enough to prevent the trip up to Camp III and Dorothea and one Sherpa, loaded with stores and the tent, set off, following the marker flags placed by Claude and Claudine on the ice-cliff. It began to snow; they found a sheltered hollow containing a few stores; this, they decided, could not possibly be Camp III; they christened it Depot 3 and went on up weaving across a deeply crevassed area, still just able to make out the flags and the track. Soon they came out on the vast open face of Cho Oyu, sweeping up to the summit. There was still no sign of Camp III; it was snowing hard; their tracks were already becoming obliterated. It was time for a temporary retreat; visibility was so bad that even the return to Depot 3 was an anxious business. Here they pitched the tent; anchored it with heavy stakes; piled the stores inside and went down as quickly as possible to Camp II – expecting and hoping that, in such weather, they would soon be followed by the advance party.

At Camp II they found all three girls from the lower party plus a large number of Sherpas. They packed into the ice-cavern for supper (it was a terribly tight squeeze which at least kept them warm) and then there arrived a Sherpa hot foot from Camp IV with two notes from Claude – the last they ever received from her. Claude explained that with this Sherpa down there was only one, Ang Norbu, remaining at Camp IV; they had taken the high altitude tent from Camp III to Camp IV as the Sherpas were too tired to dig an ice-cavern. The last note, written at 1.30 p.m., said that the weather was very bad but they were in safety at Camp IV and had enough food to last them. The next day they would stay in their sleeping-bags and rest; she would like Wangdi, the Sirdar, and a really strong Sherpa to come up the next day. There was no hint in either note of impending disaster.

The next morning the Sirdar came to discuss matters with Dorothea; they both felt uneasy but at that time neither of them thought seriously of avalanches. It had snowed most of the night and the weather showed no sign of improvement. Wangdi, the Sirdar, planned to get up to Camp IV as speedily as possible and hurry Claude and Claudine down before conditions got worse. Dorothea was worried for him but he insisted time and again: 'It is my duty.' At last Dorothea agreed and wrote a note for him to take to Claude – it was never received. Wangdi set off with Chewang, a particularly able Sherpa. She watched them anxiously as they disappeared up the ice-cliff, wishing she could go with them but knowing that they were much faster than she could be and that speed was all-important just then.

Wangdi had asked that all camps should be cleared to Base so that those above Camp II could move down quickly. Dorothea saw at once that it was her job to see that this was done and, above all, to get the three girls down to safety as speedily as possible. They began the descent; the snow was deep and soft; it had turned unpleasantly warm – always a cause for alarm at high altitudes. Just above Camp I a small avalanche hissed by them. Dorothea became acutely anxious; it would be utterly impossible to go back to help anyone. At Camp I they picked up Jeanne and Eileen and hurried on; as they reached the col avalanches thundered down unceasingly; the whole party was racked with uncertainty.

That night, in the comparative safety of Base Camp, Dorothea and Eileen sat writing their notes in their little tent. Suddenly there was a faint cry from farther up the mountain; they rushed out, alerted the Sherpas and brought all the torches they had.

Slowly the Sherpas brought in Wangdi; he was completely exhausted, his lips were swollen and his hands frozen; he could only murmur 'Chewang is dead'. Food and warmth brought him round sufficiently for him to be able to explain that they had just left Camp III (23,000 feet) when an avalanche started and swept them down. After two hours of struggle Wangdi freed himself; he tried to free Chewang but he was buried too deep and was beyond help; somehow with unbelievable courage Wangdi had come down.

All night the avalanches continued; the expedition sheltering in Base Camp were utterly helpless; for the moment there was nothing they could do and although they tried to keep their courage up they knew there was very, very little to hope for.

By 3rd October the weather had cleared sufficiently for them to go up to the col; for the first time they had to rope up over the gullies. From the col they could scan the whole mountain; for two hours they searched every inch with powerful glasses. All hope faded; the news that Claude, Claudine and Ang Norbu were lost was sent by runner to Kathmandu.

On 6th October Dorothea, Jeanne, Colette and Eileen went up to Camp I; the next day they went on to Camp II; on 10th October Jeanne, Dorothea and a Sherpa went up to Depot 3 and then on to the site on Camp III. It had completely disappeared; only the end of Wangdi's rope still lay on the snow. They continued up, higher still, across the face of the mountain. Where Camp IV had been there was nothing, absolutely nothing – it was swept completely clean. All around great snow-peaks and fluted ice-ridges looked down upon them; the compelling summit of Cho Oyu pierced the deep blue sky. In silence they turned and came down.

As with all expeditions where tragedy has occurred the day-to-day work of winding things up had to go on. Camp II had to be evacuated and packed up; the same had to be done at Camp I. On a knoll between Camp I and Base they built a little memorial cairn to Claude and Claudine. Stores were packed, Base Camp was struck; on the trek back to Namche Bazar a happier note was struck when they were all reunited with Margaret and Loulou, now restored to full health. And so back to Kathmandu early in November, leaving their companions sleeping among the mountains, which were at their loveliest in the cool, crisp autumn air.

All her friends mourned Claudine Van der Stratten – so young, so gay, so courageous, with such a magnificent future before her. Perhaps to an idealistic climber like Claudine it would seem fitting that she should die with her leader.

In Claude Kogan the mountain world lost one of its greatest and most attractive climbers, and certainly the one most experienced in the Himalayas. Claude was small, fair and slender; she designed swimsuits at her own factory in Nice; no one would have imagined her to be a mountaineer. Of her outstanding achievements much has already been said. She had experienced tragedy in the sudden death of her husband immediately after their return from the Andes; her bereavement only served to strengthen her love for the hills. She never looked back – only forward and upward. She was lost when she was about to realise all her hopes. Claude loved life; perhaps she loved the mountains even more; if that were so 'nothing is here for tears'.

Just because this was an all-woman's party which met with disaster there was criticism of all kinds in the Press and in other quarters. This was not unexpected; women climbers have come a long way, but there is still far to go. The 1950s, for all their brilliant successes, ended in tragedy; women were not deterred, rather was their determination strengthened. The next decade, as we shall see, brought greater and even more exciting adventures; there will always be climbers to carry the torch of women's mountaineering to its ultimate destiny.

Chapter 8

From Strength to Strength

When historians, in years to come, look back on the 1960s they may not regard it as the most glorious decade in the history of western civilization; in the world of women's climbing, however, quite a galaxy of new stars appeared during this period while others, already observed, shone with an even greater brilliance.

In November 1960 news was received by the Ladies' Alpine Club that a team of Japanese women had been in the Northern Kulu of the Himalayas. In early October two members of the party, Miss K. Hamananka and Mrs M. Okabe, with two Ladakhi porters, had reached the summit of Deo Tibba (19,687 feet). This mountain had previously been climbed only by Clare Graaff and Eileen Healey; Eileen was delighted to receive a postcard in November from New Delhi giving news of the success. The leader, Mrs Hosokawa, was also able to report that they had, in fact, reached the summit by a variant route.

In the Alps in the same year there was a mass feminine ascent of Monte Rosa. It was christened the Hundred-Woman ascent; unfortunately although some British women were invited none was able to accept. Actually 119 women set out from Gressoney-la-Trinité for the Gnifetti hut; there were 114 Italians, three Swiss and two Austrians; the youngest was reported to be fifteen years of age and the oldest forty-seven. All but seven reached the Gnifetti summit; there were guides and soldiers standing by in case of mishaps, but none occurred and there was much feminine satisfaction that no masculine assistance had to be solicited.

Another success in the Alps was Joan Busby's ascent of the South Face of the Obergabelhorn; in contrast to the alpine adventure mentioned above this was a one-woman, one-guide affair! Joan Busby is a member of the Ladies' Alpine Club who specialises in big ascents; she is also a hockey international and once sailed to Sweden in a Tall Ship as a member of an all-women crew.

The South Face of the Obergabelhorn is a real test of mountaineering ability; it was not chosen by Joan (she had requested something smaller) but by her guide Berni Perren, who loved an ascent of this grade when he could have a keen, first-class climber on his rope.

They set out in good weather and for some time it was possible to climb in a carefree manner, often both moving at once; but on a narrow ledge Berni stopped.

'Wait,' he said, 'now it begins.'

According to Joan, it certainly *did* begin and there were no more carefree moments for a long, long time; exposure was great and ever-present; holds were few and minute. There were signs of deterioration in the weather; speed became imperative. They came to perpendicular blue-grey walls of rock, destitute of good handholds; cracks and fissures which might have helped were jammed by patches of ice. In the great couloir which plunges precipitately straight from the Gabel Joan came up behind Berni, gripping the steps he had cut and obtaining a little extra security from the fact that the pressure of her hands caused her gloves to freeze to the ice.

They approached the crux of the climb – a difficult, exposed perpendicular chimney. Berni led it magnificently. Joan followed – equally magnificently! 'The exposure was breathtaking', she wrote, 'the climbing first-rate, and I knew a moment of supreme joy on realising that it was within my capabilities.'

The final pitch led out of the chimney and up exceedingly steep, difficult rocks leading to the small platform below the summit cornice – 'a perfect ending to a superb climb'.

There was great excitement in Zermatt when Joan returned safely from the South Face of the Obergabelhorn; we were glad to be there to join in her rejoicings and to congratulate her, and Berni, on a great performance.

But three days later tragedy struck. My husband and I, returning with Bernard Biner from a lazy trip to the Cima di Jazzi, saw a grave-faced guide hurry across to Bernard, obviously bringing bad news. Bernard's face went suddenly ashen. 'Berni?', he murmured in a dazed voice. We waited anxiously. Bernard turned to us. 'Berni Perren was killed in the night, driving his jeep near Staffelalp.'

His words stunned us. Such a short time ago Berni had returned unscathed from his stupendous adventure in the mountains; now he was gone, in a tragic motor accident.

We all attended his funeral and as the years go by we remember him as he was; so strong, so happy and such an outstanding climber and skier. But for those who had even the tiniest share in the rejoicings over that last great climb there will always be a shadow over the South Face of the Obergabelhorn.

Also in 1960 Joyce Dunsheath and Eleanor Baillie made a two-women expedition to Afghanistan, their main object being Mir Samir (19,880 feet). Before their preparations were completed the leader of a German party to this mountain warned them of its extreme difficulty; they realised that the ascent might be impossible but the wild and remote nature of the country attracted them and they decided to continue with their plans.

Their route to Afghanistan was interesting; by boat to Leningrad; by train through Russia, then across the desert in a lorry to Tabris where they got a train for Teheran. They flew, rather conventionally for them, to Kandahar and did the rest of the journey to Kabul in a local Afghan bus.

Here, after a fortnight, their stores and equipment caught up with them; their visas were extended and the permission to climb and take photos in the Hindu Kush reaffirmed. With everything now in order they set off in a ten-seater private bus with about half a ton of luggage for the village of Zeneh, where the roadhead was situated. Here they hired donkeys for transport and tribesmen to carry the loads. These last proved to be somewhat erratic and quite unlike the dependable Sherpas; in spite of this Base Camp was somehow established at a height of 12,500 feet, above the stream flowing down from Mir Samir. A week later a more responsible tribesman came up to see how they were faring and helped to site the next camp 1,000 feet higher up. Two days later a tent and provisions for five days were taken up to another site at 15,000 feet. The porters, who loathed the cold, retired precipitately from this Camp but Joyce and Eleanor, snug in their little tent, looked out on the lonely world and the starry sky, against which Mir Samir was etched in sharp relief.

After a reconnaisance of the route to the summit they decided that with one bivouac *en route* it might be possible, and they retired into their sleeping bags that night with high hopes. But the weather, as it so often does, took a hand in decision-making. The next morning they found themselves snowed in after a night of ceaseless storms. They had to make a quick descent to the Camp below, and fortunately two tribesmen turned up to help them down. That had to be the end –the porters refused to return to so inhospitable a spot. Perhaps Mir Samir would have been beyond the powers of such a small party, but it is always good to hitch one's wagon to a star. Their enterprising spirit was admirable. They came down to Kanjan, explored another valley, climbed some lesser peaks and eventually returned home – a little disappointed perhaps but not entirely displeased with their duo-expedition.

In 1961 the mountain fraternity was increased by a new and most welcome addition; a blind girl began climbing in the Alps. Since then the blind have become increasingly attracted to the mountains and an association of Blind Mountaineers has been formed. Colette Richard, a French girl, was the pioneer; she fell in love with the mountains and with extraordinary courage and determination succeeded in becoming an alpinist. In 1961 she wrote an article for the bulletin of the Paris-Chamonix section of the *Club Alpin Français*. In it she explained how as a child she was often taken to the mountains for a holiday and even at that time the magic of the hills got into her system. She devoured every mountain book that was translated into Braille and begged people to read her those she could not read for herself.

In 1959 she went with a friend on an excursion to Mont Joli and decided at once that she must have more of this. In 1960, with a sympathetic guide, she reached the snowy summit of Mont Tondu and a few days later they did the Col du Géant together. 'Rarely,' she wrote, 'have I experienced such happiness as on that day.'

Colette Richard thinks that for the blind their rock climbing must be rather limited, but snow presents no special problems; when the snow slope steepens one follows the track with one's hands. She admits that climbing must naturally be harder for blind people, but not more dangerous if proper precautions are taken and the climber is roped so that she can place a hand on the guide's rucksack in order not to deviate from the route. More use than usual must be made of crampons and ice-axe.

Colette maintains that to love mountains it is not necessary to see them; it is enough that they exist; that one breathes the pure mountain air and experiences the exquisite smell of the snow. Hearing is all-important; to hear the steps of the party on the snow; the regular crunch of the ice-axe being driven in; the noises of the glacier. The final paragraph of her article makes a fitting conclusion to the unique story of Colette Richard.

'Above all is the unique feeling of the *cordée*; the splendid companionship; the ambiance of the huts; the poetry of night in the mountains as the party sets out before dawn; the deep silence of high altitudes; all that one feels, imagines, divines. And there is the joy of living in an element in which I feel at home, of which I am queen, the joy of holding an ice-axe in my hand.'

No sighted person could have put it better; Colette spoke for us all – brilliant Himalayan 'tigresses' and commonplace traditional alpinists. That she, a blind girl, could write thus helps to elucidate a little more precisely the answer to the eternal question: 'Why do men – and women – climb'?

The summer climbing season of 1961 did not produce so many highlights as some other years but there were interesting ventures in new fields. Women, including Whymper's granddaughter Nigella Blandy, were climbing in Turkey, and also in Israel, Jorden and Ethiopia. And, to the great pleasure of the Ladies' Alpine Club, a special tribute was paid to Wren Robinson who, as Wren Corry, in 1933 brought down her guide single-handed when he broke his leg on the descent of Mount Goldsmith. The New Zealand Alpine Club named a tributary glacier of the Spencer Glacier below Goldsmith, 'Corry Glacier' and so wrote Wren's courageous feat into history.

The autumn of this year brought another Himalayan Expedition; one that, in some respects, marked a new milestone in women's mountaineering history, because it proved conclusively that with the backing of the Mount Everest Foundation it is possible to carry out a small women's expedition with the minimum of expense and very little publicity

Josephine Scarr and Barbara Spark were both twenty-four; both were experienced climbers and members of the Pinnacle Club. Jo Scarr would not mind in the least being described as 'mountain mad'; she just could not live without the mountains. At Cambridge, where she was reading Classics, she was much put out to find that the Cambridge University Mountaineering Club was strictly 'men only'. She did go with a party of these young men to climb in the Zermatt district and did some memorable routes but, being a woman, she always found herself at the bottom of the rope.

This was frustrating; Jo refounded the defunct Cambridge Women's Mountaineering Club and began to climb more and more with other girls, on *cordées féminines*. With Muriel Baldwin she made the first feminine east–west traverse of the Aiguilles Dorées (this included a bivouac) and the first feminine ascent of the north-west ridge of the Cimon della Pala in the Dolomites.

She came down from Cambridge, secured a job as a mountaineering instructor at a National Recreation Centre in North Wales and spent all her holidays climbing and skiing with like-minded girl-friends. One day she fell off the Kaisergebirge Wall in the

Austrian Alps; it was a very severe climb; mercifully she was scarcely hurt. But Jo learnt her lesson; she had reached the physical limit of her powers in rock climbing because, as always, a woman is limited by her arm-strength. If she looked for harder climbs she might kill herself; the only alternative was to seek fresh channels for her mountain enthusiasm; she set to work to find these channels.

In Barbara Spark Jo found a kindred spirit, restless to spread her wings and be off to find new fields of endeavour. Where should they go? India, New Zealand, Peru? The last two were beyond their pockets in fares. India would be cheaper, they could drive there. The next query: would their mountain experience be adequate for the Himalayas? They consulted a man-friend who knew a lot about the Himalayas and, which was perhaps even more important, a lot about *them*. His advice was that there were hundreds of Himalayan peaks waiting to be climbed, many of 20,000 feet or so and well within their capabilities. That was enough; they decided on the Himalayas and on the Kulu-Lahul area, which had unclimbed peaks only a few days' march from the roadhead.

They visited more climbing friends to get further advice; one and all urged them to make themselves into an 'Official' expedition with headed note-paper, a patron and a printed leaflet describing their plans. Only in this way could they hope to get help from firms and societies. Greatly daring and feeling impossibly presumptuous they named themselves 'The Women's Kulu Expedition 1961'. Another friend from the Alpine Club suggested the Bara Shigri area, which included two fine climbs – Lion and Central Peak. They could hardly wait to set out for India, but at that time their only funds were their own savings; more money must be raised for transport, supplies and equipment.

With a bit of luck and the help of a friendly bank manager they got a long wheel-base Land-Rover at half price; for food and equipment they wrote pleading letters to firms and manufacturers; the response was amazing. To cut costs even more, Barbara, an expert dressmaker, made sleeping bags and mountain clothing for themselves and their porters. But even so, when everything was totted up they had got less than £200 left for the return journey to India and incidental expenses. Somehow a grant must be procured. Charles Evans, husband of Denise, was consulted. His immediate reply was that they must certainly apply to the Mount Everest Foundation and the Royal Geographical Society.

Trembling with apprehension Jo went to London for an interview with these august bodies. She tiptoed into the room and peered nervously at the kindly row of faces before her. One old gentleman, well on in the grandfather class, looked at her thoughtfully and said, 'If you don't mind my saying so, you look very young and small to be going on a Himalayan Expedition, my dear.' To which Jo truthfully replied, 'Well, it's only a small expedition.'

Of course that settled it; no one could refuse her. After a week the Royal Geographical Society offered official support and the loan of surveying instruments; the Mount Everest Foundation sent a cheque for £150. Jo and Barbara sent up a cheer; their financial worries were solved.

Somehow their luck seemed to be in; before their preparations for the Kulu were complete there came an invitation from Countess Dorothea Gravina to join a women's expedition she was leading to Nepal in the following spring. This invitation was too tempting to refuse; somehow they would find jobs in India after their Kulu trip was over and so manage to exist until the next expedition came out. To help with the expenses which membership of that expedition would mean they got contracts for articles and photographs with newspapers and women's magazines. If one really wants to do anything a way will always be found! Before they left for the Kulu the Nepal party was completed; it included Denise Evans, Nancy Smith and Pat Wood, a climber well known to Jo and Barbara.

In North Wales, at the Climbing Centre where Jo had worked, they packed their supplies into the Land-Rover and at 10.30 p.m. on 22nd July 1961, after a farewell party with wine, folk music, presents and a cake decorated with marzipan mountains, a baby Land-Rover and a signpost marked 'Himalayas 8,000 miles', they were off. The shimmering dream had become a concrete fact.

They drove by way of Greece – staying just long enough to climb Olympus – along the Black Sea coast of Turkey, into Iran and down through Baluchistan to Quetta, Lahore and into India. Most nights they camped but occasionally they were lucky enough to sample the luxury of a Y.W.C.A. Hostel or beds in the house of a friend. A few miles from the border of Iran they saw the lovely, lonely, snow-capped peak of Mount Ararat and only just managed to restrain themselves from making an attempt on its 9,500 feet. The bargain Land-Rover behaved well, except for an endless series of punctures while crossing Iran. Early in September they reached New Delhi, collected their mail and their money and motored up the Grand Trunk Road through Simla into the mountains. Late one afternoon they drove up the last lap from Mandi to Manali; as they emerged into the Kulu valley the sun was setting; on either side rose pine-mantled slopes, but here and there was a hint of icy walls, glowing pink in the sunset – their first glimpse of the Himalayas.

At the village of Manali, 6,000 feet up, at the head of the Kulu Valley, Jo and Barbara took a temporary farewell of the Land-Rover. Here, at the little hotel picturesquely named Sunshine Orchards, they were introduced to their Ladakhi porters by the hotel manager, who also gave them the welcome news that their ponies would be ready in two days' time. The next visitor was the local police officer, a suspicious type, who was so concerned about their climbing programme and its possible political implications with neighbouring Tibet that he announced his intention of accompanying them. Unfortunately he could not start with them but he assured them in no uncertain terms that he would soon catch up with them. The trek to the Bara Shigri Glacier looked as if it might be interesting!

On 15 September they set off, full of hope and thankful that all the initial worries and irritations were over. Within two days they had crossed the Rhotang Pass and come down into the Chandra valley. Up this they toiled for five days under a blazing sun. In Camp each night the porters were most solicitous for their comfort, waiting on them hand and foot, preparing excellent meals and brewing gallons of tea – all of which was far more than they had dared to expect.

At first nothing whatever was heard of the famous police officer who was supposed to be following hot foot. He seemed to be quite well known in the district as the 'C.I.D. man'; to the porters, however, he was always the 'Seedyman'. Jo and Barbara were beginning to hope that he had been finally prevented from beginning his pilgrimage when news came that he was at Chatoru, only a day's march behind them. This was worrying; evidently this man had meant what he said; was it really going to be the end of their long-planned expedition? They sat outside their tent in brilliant sunshine looking at the long line of Himalayan peaks which perhaps they would never reach. Morale was pretty low – especially as the donkeys had disappeared temporarily and they could not move Camp without them. The next day the donkeys were discovered; the C.I.D. man was still missing; with all speed they set off to cross the Chandra River. Under cover of the great rocks they headed for the foot of the glacier; by evening they had arrived at the highest point the donkeys could reach and still they had not been arrested or challenged. They pitched the tents out of sight of the valley and settled down for a peaceful evening still hoping for the best. After all these threats the Seedyman never did turn up; they heard later that he had been told in Chatoru that they were bound for the Bara Shigri and not for Tibet; he decided to turn a blind eye and go home.

This might have been the end of their troubles had not Jo developed an enormous abscess on a front tooth which made her feel thoroughly ill. Something had to be done; fortunately there was an Indian doctor back in Chatoru; it meant a trek of thirty miles but there was no other way of relieving the rather dangerous situation. The party split up; Barbara and two porters remained at the Camp and began carrying loads up the glacier; Jo, with one porter and the pony-man went back to Chatoru. It was a dreary journey; they failed to reach Chatoru by nightfall and had to bivouac. In the morning they found Chatoru almost deserted;

everyone was packing up to leave for the winter. Mercifully the Indian doctor was still at the little Rest House. He was thrilled to see Jo – his first European visitor during the whole season. He lanced the abscess; gave her penicillin injections and pronounced her cured. Two days later she was joyfully reunited with Barbara in Camp, told her story and heard Barbara's tale of the terrors of the glacier. A good night's sleep restored them both to normal and together they prepared for the seventeen days they were to spend on the next and most exciting part of their great adventure.

The Bara Shigri proved to be the ugliest and most desolate of glaciers; the sparkling surface and dramatic deep blue crevasses familiar to the ordinary alpinist were non-existent; it was just a wilderness of rubble, rock and muddy sludge. On the second night they camped rather comfortably on a convenient sandy shelf above the glacier. While the porters went back for more loads Jo and Barbara explored the area above the Camp; after an hour's scrambling the valley widened out; ice-cliffs and the snout of a glacier emerged. Mist made vision difficult but they had seen enough to be certain that this was the glacier they had been searching for; *their* glacier, untrodden and unexplored. The height at which they stood was 16,000 feet – the highest they had ever been; they looked around them in awestruck silence, hardly able to take it all in. It was a great moment; their cup of happiness was full; they built a little cairn to mark the spot and slipped light-heartedly down the rocks back to Camp.

Each day they pressed on slowly and Jo and Barbara frequently camped alone at night while the porters went down for more loads. They enjoyed this immensely; it gave them the opportunity to survey and explore on their own during the day which was, after all, one of the chief purposes of the Kulu Expedition. They were longing to reach the snow basin at the top of the glacier; it was a five-hour trek from Camp through a labyrinth of crevasses; their legs ached and their throats were dry; when at last they got there they were almost too tired to realise that they had arrived.

The porters pitched the tents in the middle of the basin to be out of range of avalanches. They were now at a height of 18,000 feet and were beginning to feel the altitude; it was not until the next morning that they felt able to appreciate the scene. A mile away to the south was the snow peak of Lion mountain, 20,000 feet; above them and to the west was Central Peak, 20,600 feet, rocky and formidable. On the eastern side of the snow basin there was a line of smaller peaks, all unclimbed. One of these was a slender rock spire, 19,850 feet; it was close to the Camp; it was attractive and compelling; they were tired of glacier work and impatient to begin climbing; this peak would be just the job, they told themselves.

The next morning they set out. The altitude was affecting them and they had to stop for frequent rests – but they enjoyed themselves, oh, *how* they enjoyed themselves! Jo cutting steps in a steep ice-slope above a yawning *bergschrund* was supremely happy, aware that she had her own life entirely in her own hands; she was deliberately courting danger and in doing so she found satisfaction. In her delightful book *Four Miles High* she describes this feeling in simple, uninhibited language.

'There is no one and nothing to rely on but oneself, there is no luck or objective danger involved. It is sport for its own sake, with no reward of money or fame, no justification of social or scientific purpose. It is pointless, unnecessary, largely unjustifiable, and yet supremely satisfying. Mind and body combine to overcome difficulties deliberately sought out, and both awareness and effort are heightened by the calculated risks that must be taken.'

Slowly they moved up their chosen peak; at 19,000 feet they were desperately tired; another 300 feet and they decided to call it a day. They did not mind in the least that the summit still towered 500 feet above them; maybe they would tackle it again when they were fitter. Meanwhile it had been an unforgettable experience.

Lion and Central Peak had always been recognised by Jo and Barbara as an integral part of the expedition. These were well-known peaks, at that time unclimbed; to achieve these summits would mean that they had made a definite contribution to the development of Himalayan mountaineering, perhaps to the geography of the world!

It was decided that Lion should be attempted first; it was slightly lower than Central Peak and looked easier. The three Ladakhi porters had no acclimatisation problems since they lived always at 16,000 feet. For Jo and Barbara it was different; their legs felt like lead and after a dozen steps they had to stop, doubled over their ice-axes, gasping for breath.

The climbing itself was not difficult; in fact by alpine standards it was easy, just a snow-plod interspersed with a few rock scrambles. It lacked any interesting or dramatic moments and yet it was strangely compelling; they *had* to do it. Above the rock a broad snow slope led to the rounded summit; they dragged themselves up the last few feet and sank on to the summit rocks exhausted. Gradually the great truth flooded over them – they had climbed a 20,000 feet virgin peak! It was not an important mountain but to them it might have been Everest. In Camp that night they lay in their little tent looking out on Lion – it belonged to them and to no one else.

Two days later they set out once more, this time for Central Peak. The porters were drunk with the wine of success; they would have raced up Central Peak entirely on their own had Jo and Barbara not taken a firm line. By this time they were better acclimatised; the rock climbing was good and quite difficult at times. A narrow, steep-sided, airy ridge led to the summit; the climbing was so satisfying they did not want it to end. The top was a sharp point, capped by a flat block, like a child's drawing. They had arrived. Central Peak, 20,600 feet, was theirs as well as Lion. One of the porters produced a thermos of hot tea, chocolate biscuits and raisins; a summit party was held. All around stretched mile after mile of peaks sparkling in the crisp, clear air; there can never have been a more satisfying party held against such a breath-taking décor.

They got back to Camp in the afternoon; the porters suggested that they should pack up and go down to Base; everyone thought it was a good idea. As they plodded down they turned for one last look. The snow basin still glowed in the sun, long purple shadows swept down from Lion and Central Peak; the unclimbed spire was burnished with pink and gold. The light faded, turned swiftly to palest pink and was gone; the last half mile had to be completed in darkness.

Lion and Central Peak had been climbed; their chosen glacier had been explored and surveyed; they had six days in hand – a kind of bonus with which they could do exactly as they pleased. Away across the Bara Shigri Glacier was a fine chain of peaks, only two of which had been climbed; it was certain that there would be something interesting there with which to end the season. Supplies for five days were packed and Jo and Barbara set out with the porters on a rubble-strewn track towards a mountain they had christened Snow Dome. After much exploration and much serious thought it was decided that Snow Dome was impracticable. However, to the north of it a large rocky peak rose immediately above their Camp; perhaps this would be possible – at any rate it was worth trying. They turned in for an early night, snug in their sleeping bags beside their roaring primus. Jo explains in her book how curiously remote everything seemed, almost as though they were on a different planet from the rest of the world. She had expected that such a situation would be ideal for discussing deep questions of all kinds – politics, philosophy, religion perhaps. But somehow it never happened like this; her mind never felt really clear; only the immediate mundane problems, such as drying socks, seemed important; even sustained conversation was too much of an effort.

On a warm, cloudless morning Jo and Barbara with two of the porters began the trek to the rocky peak which was their chosen objective. They did not know at that time that its height was 20,495 feet; had they done so they might have decided against it and thus missed the hardest and best climbing of the whole trip. They had made a reconnaissance on the previous day which gave them a good start; their progress up the snow was rapid and, as the rock became steeper and more difficult, they were delighted to find that they were scarcely affected by the altitude and could climb quickly and easily.

Eventually, of course, difficulties were experienced. They were obliged to do a lot of route-finding, which wasted precious time; the wind rose and thick clouds gathered. They laboured on and by mid-afternoon could just see the summit fifty yards ahead and only fifty feet above them. But it was late, too late; there were only three hours of daylight left and the descent to Base would be long and at times dangerous. It was a difficult decision to make, but one of the tenets of the mountaineer's creed is that one must never be afraid to turn back. They were unanimous in deciding to return; fifty feet in 20,000 is very little and they had had a glorious day's climbing. It was a wise decision; the descent proved to be very difficult; it was almost dark when they reached the most delicate section of the rock climbing. The night was black and bitterly cold; the descent took seven hours and it was 10.30 p.m. before all four of them crowded into one tent for hot soup and brandy. It was a grand moment; the return to safety, warmth and comparative comfort is always one of the best experiences connected with a difficult climb. They had no regrets; it was a perfect finale to the Women's Kulu Expedition.

Jo and Barbara were lucky; life might have seemed a little flat after such a thoroughly absorbing few weeks but they were happy in the knowledge that in the not-too-distant future there would be more adventures to look forward to. In March they would join up with Dorothea Gravina's women's expedition to Nepal; their farewell to the mountains was only temporary. Meanwhile they decided on a fortnight in Kashmir for a much-needed rest before they drove on in the Land-Rover to take up the teaching posts they had been offered in Delhi for the winter.

The women's expedition to Nepal, which, in the annals of Himalayan history, has become known as the Jagdula Expedition 1962, was concerned with mapping and climbing in the Kanjiroba Himal in West Nepal, a remote area off the beaten track. There had been considerable mountaineering activity in adjoining areas but none in the Kanjiroba range itself. This added a spice of excitement pleasing to everyone.

The party was picked and led by Countess Dorothea Gravina, a climber of very great experience. In the little leaflet printed for fund-raising purposes Dorothea described herself, at the age of fifty-six, as 'leader in years if nothing else' and explained that she had been knocking about among mountains all her life. She modestly omitted to mention that not only had she a climbing record that compared favourably with most of the contemporary 'tigresses' but that she had also, with remarkable courage and skill, taken over the leadership of the Cho Oyu expedition after Claude Kogan was killed.

Other members of the party were Denise Evans (née Morin) aged twenty-nine, who had spent her honeymoon climbing in the Himalayas and who, earlier, had shared with her brother the leadership of a party to Greenland. Denise was in charge of food – something that deserved a capital F. Next came Dr Nancy Smith, aged thirty-seven, who was official doctor to the expedition. She had been climbing in England and the Alps for twenty years. Then there was Patricia Wood, aged twenty-seven, who was a dentist. She was a fine climber, quiet and dependable, and took over responsibility for the equipment. The remaining two members, of course, were Jo Scarr and Barbara Spark, both full of experience and enthusiasm after their Kulu adventures. The Pinnacle Club had agreed to sponsor the expedition.

The party met in March in Delhi; Jo and Barbara were already there eagerly awaiting the travellers. Dorothea Gravina and Pat Wood arrived first, having travelled overland in a Hillman Husky. Denise and Nancy turned up shortly after by plane and the party was complete.

After a whirl of excitement in New Delhi they set off by car for Rapaidiha and Nepelgan, where the liaison officer and the Sherpas were waiting. From here the first stages of the approach march began through the hot forests and plains of the Terai. The heat here was tremendous and it was not until they climbed into the Manhabharat range that they experienced the comfort of a cool Camp. Denise Evans has said that this Camp, perched on a grassy knoll, reminded her of the eve of battle in *Henry V*. There were ponies everywhere, the dusky-faced pony-men, wrapped in blankets, were hunched over their flickering fires while the Sirdar enlivened the night with stories of other parties and other expeditions. There seemed to be a sense of urgency, as if the offensive was about to begin.

They paid off the pony-men, recruited coolies and spent a week trekking through the magnificent Bheri gorges to Kaigon, the last village before the Jagdula and Kanjiroba ranges. From here the expedition split up for purposes of finding a reasonable route to the mountain they were hoping to climb. This mountain was unnamed, there was no local name for it and among themselves it was always known as Kanjiroba. Before the end of April everyone reassembled at a spot at 13,000 feet which became Lower Base Camp. Upper Base Camp was established, at the behest of the Sirdar, at 17,000 feet – he deemed this an excellent place at which to acclimatise; his puffing, panting memsahibs were not at first so sure! However, the plan seemed to work and on 29th April Dorothea and Nancy went with the Sirdar to prospect for a site for Camp I. By 1st May Camp I was fully established and two days later Camp II was successfully pitched at 18,000 feet at the foot of a snow slope.

Members of the expedition were now dispersed among all the Camps and on 4th May Jo Scarr went up with the Sherpas to search for a site for Camp III; Denise was to have gone too but the altitude was already temporarily taking its toll and she had to remain in Camp to rest. Jo came back with the exciting news that they had found a site from which, with any luck, the summit could probably be reached. Pat and Nancy came up to Camp II but Pat then succumbed to the altitude; she was put to bed to await the arrival of Dorothea and Barbara who were bringing up the rear; meanwhile Denise, Jo and Nancy went up to the proposed site of Camp III. They decided it was suitable and put up two tents, one for the Sherpas and one for themselves. The next day they set out on a tentative approach to the summit but two-thirds of the way up bad weather overtook them and they were forced to descend in a heavy snowstorm. During the night the blizzard became so fierce and things got so bad that they decided to go down and very soon everyone was once more back at Base Camp.

Sickness seems inseparable from Himalayan expeditions and this party was no exception. By the time the weather was fit for them to go up again to the higher Camps Dorothea was in bed with a sore throat and high temperature. Nancy Smith prescribed penicillin and extracted a promise that she would not leave her bed for two days and at last the rest of the party went up to Camp II.

It was the night of 12th May; Denise, Nancy, Jo and Barbara sat in the comfortable tent discussing ways and means of tackling the mountain. Everyone was self-effacing to a degree; they were all mad-keen to have a go; no one felt that her own claim was the particular one to be advanced. The Sirdar looked in to suggest that all five memsahibs should do it at once. He appeared to be serious and the idea was attractive. At that very moment a messenger arrived from Dorothea with a note begging them not to do anything rash. The effect was salutary; Dorothea, lying sick and alone would be remembering the tragedy of Cho Oyu; they had a duty to their leader and they had another big think. At last a decision was reached; Jo and Barbara were the best-acclimatised members of the party and therefore able to move faster if bad weather should set in. Let them go first with two Sherpas while Denise, Pat and Nancy made the second ascent with one Sherpa on the next day.

On the morning of 13th May Denise, Nancy, Pat, Jo and Barbara – everyone in fact except the unfortunate Dorothea – left for Camp III with three Sherpas. On 14th May Jo and Barbara with two Sherpas set out on a cold and windy day for the summit. In a matter of only a few hours they were back in Camp having achieved the peak in an amazingly short time. Everyone was astonished and overjoyed; Jo and Barbara were bombarded with questions and congratulations alternately as Denise, Pat and Nancy gathered round to hear the story. They reported that they reached the summit at 9.30. a.m. and the altimeter read 21,500 feet; they could hardly believe they had done it so easily. There were no special difficulties and they were not exhausted. After a meal Jo and Barbara went on down to Camp II; sadly, Denise had to go with them; she, too, had developed a fierce sore throat and a temperature of 105°. At Camp II Dorothea, now more or less recovered, was waiting with the Sirdar and they cared for Denise as best they could. Meanwhile the next day dawned brilliantly fine and they were all able to watch Nancy, Pat and the Sherpa reach the summit at 9 a.m. After this Denise was escorted down to Base by three Sherpas and retired to bed until her temperature had subsided.

When everyone had recuperated there were still about ten days before the homeward journey had to begin. Jo and Barbara took a Sherpa and spent a week exploring on the west side of Kanjiroba. The rest of the party set up a Camp in the Kagmara Lekh on the south side of Garpung Khola. From here Dorothea and Denise with two Sherpas, and Nancy and Pat with one, climbed Kagmara I, 19,710 feet. They then put up another Camp on the col between Kagmara I and Kagmara II and Dorothea and Pat made the first ascent of Kagmara II, 18,920 feet. By this time Jo and Barbara had rejoined the party and Jo with a Sherpa made the second ascent of Kagmara II. Finally Denise, Jo, Barbara and Nancy made the first ascent of Kagmara III, 19,100 feet.

There were now only a few days left and these were spent in explorations of remote regions, rarely visited by Europeans. The weather was unsuitable for the peaks but they crossed high cols and put up their Camps on lofty, exciting sites where the views extended for hundreds of miles and great mountains rose up on every side. This short finale was not an anti-climax; rather was it a fitting coda to a great adventure.

In the middle of June the expedition split up and the members made their various ways home by devious ways and means. Jagdula Expedition 1962 was voted a great success. The reputation of women mountaineers soared to even greater heights than hitherto.

In the Alps in 1962 an Australian woman climber, Faye Kerr, and her Swiss companion Dorothée Borys had a remarkable season. It was Faye Kerr's last alpine holiday before returning to Australia; she was determined to make the most of it.

In the Zermatt region Bernard Biner egged them on to climb classic routes they had never dared to dream of. Bernard was usually unerring in his estimation of a climber's capabilities and he made no mistake on this occasion. Added to this he insisted on introducing them to all his friends with great pride as his 'manless, guideless women climbings', a turn of phrase which delighted everyone since Bernard's English was known to be impeccable, unless he wished it to be otherwise!

Faye and Dorothée began with Monte Rosa – an old favourite – and made the first all-women traverse of Monte Rosa and the Lyskamm. They followed this with the first *cordée féminine* on the Z'mutt ridge of the Matterhorn. Yet another 'first feminine' record was their ascent of the Weisshorn by the North Ridge and descent by the East Ridge. On hearing of this escapade Bernard Biner rolled his eyes and murmured, 'You terrible girls.' This did not deter them in the least and they went off to do the complete traverse of the Sudlenz Spitze-Nadelhorn-Stecknadelhorn ridge – just one more feminine record. When Faye eventually left for Australia she took with her all that the Alps could give her and she left behind the memory of a remarkably fine climber that will not fade for a long time to come.

The year 1962 having been such a series of spectacular events 1963 seemed comparatively quiet. Not that women mountaineers were resting on their laurels; they were climbing in every part of the world where mountains are to be found – from Turkey to the Pacific coast of America, from New Zealand to Alaska – and some severe routes were recorded. In 1964, however, women hit the headlines again when the German climber Daisy Voog succeeded in scaling the North Face of the Eiger with Werner Bittner as guide. It was an historic event; the North Face of the Eiger is something that even the non-climbing public knows a little about; television has brought it to the family fireside. It was common knowledge that this route had demanded great sacrifices and still demanded great courage. That it should be done by a woman excited the admiration of all.

The Himalayas also came into the picture again. Joyce Dunsheath led the first Indian Women's Himalayan Expedition in the Garwhal Himalayas and three of the members climbed Mrigthuni, a peak of 22,400 feet – a foretaste of further adventures for Indian women in the years to come.

Women were by now firmly established in the Himalayas; women's expeditions to these great ranges were no longer regarded with surprise or suspicion; they still evoked interest; what would women climbers be doing next? And at the back of everyone's mind was the unasked question 'Could it be, would it be, Everest?'

Chapter 9

Invitation to Everest

The Year of The Alps – that was how Switzerland designated 1965; within a matter of weeks the theme had been taken up all over the world. Through the years many of us had wondered how, if at all, the centenary of the first ascent of the Matterhorn would be celebrated. In the far-off days between the wars when one was learning to climb it was something about which there was occasional speculation among one's older friends, but to the teens and twenties of those days life was so full and exciting; we lived for the present and thought only intermittently of an event destined to take place in the misty future of thirty years ahead. Slowly but surely, however, time caught up on us and suddenly everyone realised that great plans were afoot. Secretly and silently, for many years, the Swiss had worked for this day; plans were made on a world-wide scale; the results exceeded the most optimistic expectations.

For women climbers the event had a particular significance. Edward Whymper, hero of the great Matterhorn epic, married late in life. His only child was born just three years before his death and proved to be a daughter, Ethel. When the centenary celebrations were planned they centred on Ethel Blandy, as she had become, as the guest of honour of the whole project. As we have seen, during the hundred years since 1865, women had been climbing regularly in the Alps and in many other parts of the world; progress had been quiet and unostentatious; they had never sought the limelight nor boasted of their ever-increasing achievements. But long before 1965 the world was aware that women mountaineers were making history in all the greatest mountain ranges; it seemed eminently suitable that a woman, and no less a person than Whymper's daughter, herself a climber of repute and worthy descendant of her famous father, should be the figurehead of the Matterhorn centenary celebrations.

Early in 1965 invitations went out to mountaineering clubs all over the world and governments were asked to send representatives. By July every road, railway, sea-route and air-flight seemed to lead to Zermatt. Each day brought a fresh contingent of climbers and women were as much in evidence as men. When the centenary week began on Sunday, 11th July, only one important and well-loved figure was missing: Bernard Biner, to whom this book is dedicated, had died suddenly on 9th April and for some of us a bit of Zermatt had gone with him. Many, many women mountaineers owed much to him; only a year before the Ladies' Alpine Club had made his Hotel Bahnhof the centre for their summer meet and Bernard and his sister Pauly had ensured its great success. He had been asked to be President of the Centenary Committee but had declined. Perhaps he had a premonition – as those who live among the mountains sometimes do – that his time had come. And so, when the curtain went up for this long-awaited event, Bernard was present only in spirit; but at his Hotel Bahnhof, *rendez-vous* of a host of climbers, his loyal sister displayed the Union Jack beside the Swiss flag as he would have wished – Bernard was an unashamed Anglophile. He lies among his ancestors in the village churchyard below the Matterhorn, and the grave on which we laid our flowers before the celebrations began seemed only a half-truth, so real was his presence among us. On the wall of the Hotel Bahnhof, above the balcony on which he always used to sit, there is now an unobtrusive blue plaque, placed there in memory of Bernard by his British friends to whom he gave so much and meant so much.

Although the arrangements for the Matterhorn centenary were on such a magnificent scale there was a delightful simplicity and informality about them that was typically alpine. The Centre Alpin de Zermatt gave a dinner at the Hotel Monte Rosa at which the leading members of all clubs were present. We dined by candlelight at tables decorated with alpine flowers and guests wandered about between courses greeting friends and clinking glasses.

A great pilgrimage took place to the Gornergrat led by Sir John (now Lord) Hunt. The ranks of the mountaineers were swelled by journalists, cameramen and TV reporters. We were under orders to bring back pieces of rock for a centenary cairn to be erected at the Riffelberg, from which so many of the early pioneers had set out. The cairn was built and our names were buried in a tin box for posterity.

Carillons of cowbells, mountain songs by the choir of Zermatt and finally the long, echoing notes of the alphorn summoned the great crowd of mountaineers to gather outside the old Riffelhaus for speeches and the introduction of the guests of honour. Descendants of Whymper, Hudson, Hadow, the Taugwalders and Michel Croz appeared on a small platform. The last to be introduced, and the heroine of the hour, was of course Ethel Blandy.

The Ladies' Alpine Club gave an informal cocktail party to which they invited their male appendages and members of other women's climbing clubs. An unrehearsed and unique event was a nine 'man-and-woman' ascent of the Rimpfischhorn, said to be the first mountain climbed by the Presidents of the Alpine Club and the Ladies' Alpine Club in the same party. Included in the expedition were two Greeks as well as Nigella Blandy, granddaughter of Whymper, and, of course, the two Presidents – Eric Shipton and Eileen Healey.

Wednesday, 14th July was the official memorial day of the first ascent of the Matterhorn. A huge crowd of climbers and their friends met on the Festival Square, the ice-rink in winter! The weather was perfect, the Matterhorn reigned supreme with the flag cloud flying. Mass was celebrated in German by the priests of Zermatt and my husband, a member of the Alpine Club and Bishop of Leicester, gave an address in English. This was followed by a procession to the village cemetery, where Sir John Hunt laid wreaths on the graves of those who perished in the Matterhorn disaster. When these solemn and rather touching rites had been completed a mammoth cocktail party took place at which mountaineers of all nations greeted their friends and exchanged their many stories. Meanwhile, throughout the whole of this day the first ascent was being commemorated on the Matterhorn itself. There was one party on the Hörnli Ridge, the route taken by Whymper in 1865, and another on the fearsome North Face. Until then the North Face had been scaled by only a handful of climbers, all of them men. On this most auspicious occasion, however, the party of three Swiss included a woman, Yvette Vaucher, climbing with her husband Michel and the Zermatt guide Oscar Kronig. Television cameras were trained constantly on the progress of the parties and those at home in England and America and many other parts of the world knew more about the climbing than did those in Zermatt. By evening news was received that both climbs had been safely completed; no accident marred the day and there was immense satisfaction that a woman had climbed the North Face for the first time.

As students of alpine history know, the Matterhorn was climbed from the Italian side by the great Italian guide Jean-Antoine Carrel and his party a few days after Whymper's successful ascent. Naturally the Italians wished to play their part in the centenary celebrations and it was arranged that Ethel Blandy and as many other guests as possible should cross the frontier to Breuil over the Théodule Pass or by the traverse of the Matterhorn summit. The whole affair was carried through with distinctive Italian panache. A very stylish sledge was provided for Ethel Blandy; the President and the Honorary Secretary of the Ladies' Alpine Club were less fortunate; the exciting snow cat on which they travelled all but tipped them out into a sizeable crevasse. This was an isolated incident and added colour to the day's activities; nothing was wanting to add comfort and even dignity to the journey. Provisions, reminiscent of the days of the pioneers, were packed in smart red and white gingham bags and the travellers partook of cold meats, chicken, cheeses, dessert and wine at the many halts which were called during the traverse of the pass.

Down in Breuil the festivities were continued on an equally lavish scale; there were banquets, firework displays and innumerable speeches. Ethel Blandy, still the guest of honour *par excellence*, was presented with a magnificent bouquet and won all hearts by placing it on Carrel's grave before she left for England. And so the long-planned celebrations of the centenary of the first ascent of the Matterhorn came to an end; women mountaineers had been in evidence in ways undreamed of a hundred years ago and the Matterhorn still cast its immortal spell over men and women alike – '*Le Cervin n'est pas quelque chose, c'est quelqu'un.*'

It has been said by a great Swiss climber that if the Matterhorn is considered to be the King of the Alps then the Dent Blanche is without doubt the Queen. Certainly this great and lovely mountain does seem to be something of a ladies' peak where difficult routes are concerned.

The Dent Blanche was climbed for the first time – by men, of course – in July 1862. Three years later Miss Meta Brevoort with her nephew and the Almer guides made the ascent by the same, that is the normal, route and was the first woman to reach the summit. In 1889 Mrs E. P. Jackson climbed the south-west face with her guides and made the first-ever descent by the Ferpècle ridge. In 1928, as has been described in an earlier chapter, the newly-married Ivor and Dorothy Richards made their epic first ascent of the North Ridge with Joseph Georges, *le skieur*, and his brother. Only a few days later Dr Maud Cairney of the Ladies' Alpine Club made the guided first ascent of the north-east face.

In 1966 the Swiss couple Michel and Yvette Vaucher, who the previous year had done the North Face of the Matterhorn, put up a splendid new route on the Dent Blanche, climbing without guides. It was an extremely tough expedition; the weather turned sour on them and they were out on the mountain for two days from 10th to 12th July. Yvette came through the cruel conditions virtually unscathed but Michel suffered badly with frost-bitten toes and Yvette needed all the skill she could muster on the descent. At times the situation became quite desperate but somehow they survived and had the satisfaction of knowing that they had achieved a fine new climb. Desperate situations were not new to Yvette and her husband; they were with Loulou Boulaz on her magnificent, although unsuccessful, attempt on the Eiger North Face in 1962. More will be heard of Yvette later in this chapter.

When all the great mountain ranges of the world have been opened up and explored it seems that there will still be some uncharted areas with hills to climb and new routes to be tried.

In the later 1960s women climbers were remarkably enterprising in reaching out to hitherto untried territory. Greenland had been the scene of many heroic happenings in the past – Nansen in 1888; Gino Watkins and Augustine Courtauld in 1930; the Odells a little later; but since Denise Morin and her brother Ian had led an expedition there in the 1950s there had been something of a lull.

In 1966 Myrtle Simpson with her doctor husband and two climbing friends crossed Greenland from coast to coast, across 4,000 miles of inland ice which sometimes rises to 9,000 feet and where gales and blizzards rage long and furiously. The party crossed the ice-cap without dogs or any mechanical aids for sledge-pulling; it was an outstanding achievement.

Myrtle Simpson describes the expedition in her lively book *White Horizons*.

In the next summer a party of members of the Ladies' Alpine Club, led by Joan Busby, spent a fascinating month climbing in Greenland. It was rough going; there were mischances, miscalculations and disappointments as well as moments of immense satisfaction. In spite of everything most of the party were eager to return and use their experience on another expedition. Joan Busby summed up the situation aptly when she declared, 'This is a man's world, and we are the first all-woman's party to enter it.'

In faraway Alaska there was also much mountain activity. Dr Grace Hoeman and her husband Vin, who lived at Anchorage in Alaska, made an expedition to Igckpak, the North-west Alaska Highpoint. This was real exploration; neither Igckpak nor the surrounding mountains were mentioned in previous exploration reports. The climbing was severe and more than once they wondered if they really would make the summit; but at last, first Vin and then Grace hauled themselves to the top. They had troubles enough on the descent and it was long after midnight when they limped into Base Camp and crept into the welcome warmth of their sleeping-bags.

For some years the Hoemans were the inspiration and focal-point of mountaineering in Alaska; they were experienced, first-class climbers, full of enthusiasm and with an intimate knowledge of the *terrain*. The mountaineering world was shocked when disaster overtook the American Dhaulagiri Expedition and seven members were swept away by an avalanche. One of the victims was Vin Hoeman. His death was a tragedy for Grace after only three years of married life. Among climbers in Alaska his death left a gap that could not be filled.

Grace Hoeman refused to be daunted by her bereavement; she at once set about organising a women's expedition to Mount McKinley, a mountain in which her husband had always had a very special interest. The party included Arlene Blum, Dana Isherwood and Margaret Young from San Francisco; Margaret Clark from New Zealand and Faye Kerr who came up once more from Australia. The expedition became known as the Denali Damsels – Denali being one of the original names of Mount McKinley. Like most of these northern expeditions it turned out to be a tough and unrelenting assignment; sickness and diabolical weather were two hazards with which the climbers had to contend. But success was ultimately theirs and unescorted damsels trod the summit of Mount McKinley for the first time. It was a great triumph and the honours certainly went to Grace, the leader.

Less than a year later Grace was dead, killed by an avalanche in a skiing accident on Eklutma Glacier in Alaska. Strange that both husband and wife should be buried by avalanches; strange too, and so sad, that Alaska should lose its two most brilliant climbers in the short space of two years. But, as one of Grace Hoeman's climbing friends wrote of her, 'She died as she had enjoyed most to live – in the mountains; and one cannot wish for more than that.'

Still in the arctic regions, the Ladies' Alpine Club organised a meet in Iceland. They made many surprising discoveries there; one dip in a sparkling stream taught them that the streams are not for bathing in – they all emerged blue and almost frozen. On the other hand hot pools, when available, made up magnificently for any lack of ablutions on other parts of the journey. It also became obvious that Iceland's central glaciers are more for looking at than climbing and that there is more walking and scrambling to be had than real rock climbing. All the inland travel had to be done by hired Land-Rovers. Driving was exhausting since the conditions on even the main roads are appalling. They drove across miles of endless desert, through rivers and streams. Land-Rovers tend to sink into the soggy ground and it was an everyday occurrence to see one being hauled out. Roadside ditches were also a menace and one of their Land-Rovers overturned and ignominiously spilled everyone into the ditch. It all sounds rather gloomy but this was not the final impression of members of the meet. There was much beautiful and unusual country. Daylight lasted for almost twenty-four hours and they found courtesy, kindness and much helpfulness wherever they went. It seems, however, that there is one absolute essential for Iceland – one must be terribly tough.

It is a far cry from the tundras of Iceland to the hot and steamy plains lying below the Himalayas but about this time there was yet another women's expedition on its way to these parts. Niki Clough, hearing that there were at least eight unclimbed peaks of over 20,000 feet in the little-known Padar Himalaya in the area south of Nun-Kun in Kashmir, gathered together a strong team which included the brilliant and indefatigable Janet Rogers. They succeeded in climbing Rocky Peak 17,700 feet, and a snow peak of 18,500 feet. Plans were being made for an attempt on a 21,000 feet peak when news came of the tragic death on Annapurna of Niki Clough's husband Ian and the attempt was at once abandoned.

Another splendid, but little noticed, climb in the Himalayas was the ascent of Annapurna III, 24,583 feet, by two Japanese women, Miss Nunko Tabei and Miss Hiroko Hirakwa. Since then it has been realised that Japanese ladies are rapidly coming into their own in the mountains and will soon be a force to be reckoned with.

In the Alps big things still continued to happen, one of the most outstanding being the ascent of the Eiger North Face by Christine de Colombel, a French girl from Paris. This was the second ascent by a woman and was a tremendous victory over adversity. Christine and her guide Jacques Sarnier were out on the mountain from 26th August to 2nd September but mercifully returned safely. Since then she has added to her list among other notable climbs, the Walker Spur on the Grandes Jorasses and the Whillans-Brown route on the West Face of the Blaitière.

In May 1968 the Swiss Ladies' Alpine Club (*Schweizerische Frauen Alpen Club*) celebrated its Jubilee. Climbers representing many of the women's mountaineering clubs gathered in Montreux to attend the festivities and to bring congratulations. S.F.A.C. now has fifty-six sections and 7,000 members and is one of the most cosmopolitan of all mountaineering societies.

In this same year, and in the same month, another gathering of women climbers took place in Switzerland at Engelberg. It proved to be one of the most important events of recent years; the results have been far-reaching and extremely successful.

The moving spirit behind this venture was Baronin Felicitas von Reznicek, author of the book *Von der Krinoline zum Sechsten Grad*. With the help of Rosli Häcki, of the Swiss Ladies' Alpine Club, the Swiss National Tourist Office and the hoteliers of Engelberg, women mountaineers, and the husbands of some of them, from ten different countries were invited for an 'Engelberg Week'. The object of this get-together was to form an association that would promote more contact between women mountaineers of all nations.

About fifty women from Austria, Britain, Czechoslovakia, France, Germany, Holland, Italy, Poland, Switzerland and Yugoslavia were able to be present. Many of the most famous

women climbers made a special effort to come; Loulou Boulaz
and Yvette Vaucher from Switzerland; Christine de Colombel
from France; Anna Roelfsema from Holland; Halina Krüger from
Poland; Sylvia Metzeltin-Buscaini from Italy and Barbara
Lipvosek-Scetinin from Yugoslavia; with Nea Morin, Margaret
Darvall, Eileen Healey and Esmé Speakman, making up the
British contingent, were all present. The hospitality was remarkable; there were fondu parties, film shows and colour slides; free
passes on the téléfériques gave skiers a great time on the Titlis;
there was rock-climbing on the Bettlerstock and a spectacular
champagne party on the summit of the Titlis. Here amid much
applause the formation of the international association, *Rendez-
Vous Hautes Montagnes*, was announced by Felicitas von
Rezniceck; those present were aware that a new chapter was
opening for all women mountaineers.

The *raison d'être* of the *Rendez-Vous Hautes Montagnes* is
simple. It has only one purpose – to bring together from all parts
of the world those who climb because they love the mountains,
so that they may meet, get acquainted and climb together. It is
primarily a women's organisation but men are not excluded.
There are two types of membership, 'passive' and 'aktive', or,
in colloquial English, 'moderates' and 'tigresses'; climbs are
arranged to suit both categories.

There is no membership fee; those who can, contribute to a
fund to help with costs and also to assist in some small way those
from countries with strict currency controls. In most cases
members pay their own expenses but those who need help can
always rely on at least some assistance; thus climbers who are
keen to come to a meet are seldom prevented by financial reasons
and the membership is wider and friendships are richer because
of this.

Politics and philosophies are strictly taboo. Those who come,
come to enjoy themselves in a happy unsophisticated atmosphere;
for once controversy, the bane of modern civilisation, is stilled.
There is just one passion that is common to all – the love of the
mountains and the joy of being among them. Nor is there any
sense of competition; 'moderates' and 'tigresses' meet solely as

mountaineers and above all as mountaineers who revere and respect the hills; the trendy notion of 'conquering' a mountain has no place in the *Rendez-Vous Hautes Montagnes*.

As might be expected, with such simplicity of organisation, R.H.M. has prospered exceedingly; meets are held in different centres every year. In 1969 the venue was Zermatt; the official headquarters were at the Monte Rosa Hotel, where the much-loved manageress Hildi Eberhardt, herself a member of R.H.M., made everyone welcome. At the Hotel Bahnhof another member, Pauly Biner sister of Bernard, looked after a large group of guests; her organisation and hospitality would have warmed her brother's heart. The fact that the hostesses were themselves so dedicated to the mountains contributed something special to the whole spirit of the meet.

The guests of honour for this year were Tenzing Norkey of Everest and his daughter Pem Pem, who had been a member of the Cho Oyu expedition. Pem Pem was now married and had become Mrs Pem Pem Tsherring. She delighted everyone in Zermatt as she had done in Nepal; Pem Pem's grace and charm are well-known; all who meet her are refreshed by the experience and her kindness of heart knows no bounds.

Climbing conditions were poor in Zermatt that year but no less than ten parties climbed the North Face of the Breithorn and there was a Polish *cordée féminine* on the Matterhorn. During the many parties members of R.H.M. met a Japanese woman doctor who had just done the Japanese route on the North Face of the Eiger *en cordée féminine* with another Japanese woman, Miss Yoshiko Wakayama. Before the meet ended Yvette Vaucher and her husband Michel arrived to join in the fun; afterwards Yvette disappeared with Loulou Boulaz to make the first 'all women's' ascent of the North East Face of the Piz Badile.

The following year the meet took place at Chamonix, when Jeanne Franco and her husband acted as hosts. This time there was much climbing; excellent routes were organised for 'tigresses' and 'moderates' and there were many opportunities for the extending of mountain friendships. By now there were many more countries involved and membership had increased to include women mountaineers from Spain, Russia, Bulgaria and the United States.

In 1971 the attractive Nadja Fajdiga agreed to organise the meet at Kranjsha Gora in her own country of Yugoslavia. Not many of those taking part had done much climbing in the Julian Alps and everyone was surprised and delighted at the severity of the climbs and the beauty of the mountain country – something which most members would probably never have experienced but for the R.H.M.

The R.H.M. now has a membership of about 300 and its frontiers have been extended to include Denmark, Norway, Sweden, Belgium, East Germany, India, Indonesia, Australia, Chile and Mexico; East meets West; colour and creeds count for nothing. Between sixty and eighty members gather at a centre each year and the host country does its best, by its programme of festivities, to present a true picture of itself to the guests. Centres are found farther and farther afield; in 1972 it is the turn of Czechoslovakia and the High Tatras; in 1973 it will be the Himalayas; and in 1974 Greenland. There seems no limit to the possibilities for good in an organisation such as the R.H.M. and it has certainly provided a great stimulus for women's mountaineering.

In 1972 the Ladies' Alpine Club was delighted to elect its first Indian member, Dr Meena Agrawal. Meena Agrawal is a member of the Himalayan Club of India and has served on the committees of the Bombay University Hikers' and Mountaineers' Society and the Climbers' Club of Bombay. She was Deputy Leader and doctor to the All-Women Himalayan Expedition to Kokthang in Sikkim and leader of the Ladies' Trisul Expedition in the Garhwal Himalayas, which succeeded in climbing Trisul, 23,360 feet.

Meena Agrawal came to England to take up a post in a hospital in the Midlands. It was not long before her love of climbing led her to seek like-minded companions; the result has brought much happiness to her and to the Ladies' Alpine Club.

The Royal Netherlands Alpine Club has recently produced a young virtuoso of whom much may be heard in the future. She is a girl named Marleen Schalkwijk who has already, among other outstanding successes, done the North East Face of the Piz Badile; Mont Blanc de Tacul and a complete traverse of the Grandes Jorasses in five days with a fellow student.

At the end of the 1960s the reputation of women mountaineers had probably never stood higher. Once more the current question cropped up – what about Everest? And now, at last, a partial answer could be given; the International Expedition of 1971 would include one woman the Swiss Yvette Vaucher, whose husband Michel was also selected for the party.

It need hardly be said that doubts were expressed and eyebrows raised concerning the wisdom of incorporating one woman in such a team; theoretical problems of all kinds were posed. Yvette succeeded in exploding them all. The fact that she was climbing with her husband was a help. Michel is greatly respected by all climbers. He teaches mathematics in a High School in Geneva. He is a brilliant climber and is gentle as well as strong. Michel and Yvette are devoted partners. She was a widow when she married him in 1963. Within a few years they had faced several pretty desperate mountain situations together, notably, as have been mentioned, the North Face of the Matterhorn and the North Face of the Dent Blanche. Yvette regarded these as an almost inevitable part of the married life of dedicated climbers. She once explained her creed very simply: 'I love Michel and I love mountains and that is why I am here.'

On the 1971 expedition, however, Yvette was not only Michel's wife; she was there in her own right and had her own special contribution to make. In spite of having trained as a parachutist she is not the tough masculine type. The fact that she was a woman could not be overlooked; it helped to keep standards a little higher than might otherwise have been the case. There was nothing of the prude about Yvette, but her presence in the all-male party had its effect on even those most prone to unfortunate lapses in conversation, manners and etiquette and for this the party as a whole was genuinely thankful. Yvette, for her part, maintained her essential femininity under all circumstances and was quietly grateful for small acts of chivalry as, for example, the establishment of a little latrine for her own especial use. Much of her life with Michel had been spent in the rather crude environment of climbing huts but this had never coarsened her; nor had her vast experience of the mountain world made her blasé or blunted her sensitivity; she was almost in tears at the unimaginable beauty of her first view of the Himalayas from the plane.

At Kathmandu Yvette was put in charge of the expedition postcards, all of which had to be autographed by each member of the team. It was no mean task to get a large group of men to settle down to signing several hundred cards. Yvette's bright smile and gentle encouragement had the desired effect, however, and even the most rebellious relented and did all that was required of them.

Yvette's presence on the expedition produced several pleasant little domestic interludes. For example, sun-hats were indispensable; sartorial elegance was not required or expected and most of the male headgear had only too obviously seen better days. Yvette struck a brighter note. Her floppy yellow towelling model, profusely decorated with flowers was entirely adequate for its purpose but produced a country cottage atmosphere which helped considerably when conditions were dreary.

Then there was the expedition mascot. During the early stages of the approach march one of the party bought a fluffy little Tibetan mongrel; this attractive little creature was immediately christened Chomolungma – the local name for Everest – and Yvette became its adopted mother. Chomo slept in the Vauchers' tent at night and covered the roughest stages of the journey in a rucksack. She grew up quickly into a noisy, boisterous puppy with a mind of her own. Unlike her Victorian predecessor, Tschingel, Chomo was anything but discreet; Tschingel had her *affaires de coeur* but kept the matter dark until the puppies actually arrived. Chomo, true to the permissive age into which she was born, knew no such restraints. The world's top dog she might be, but this heavy responsibility did nothing to prevent her from forming a clandestine alliance with an undesirable mongrel who had wandered up to Base Camp. The Vauchers were not inclined to invite the visitor into their tent. Chomo henceforth turned her back on them and sat outside in the moonlight with her boy-friend, where they made the night hideous with their howling. When the expedition could stand it no longer various missiles came hurtling through the air; in the ensuing stampede Chomo gave the boy-friend the slip and was found later comfortably curled up in the sleeping bag of another member of the expedition. Chomo's story ends rather abruptly; let us hope she has further mountain adventures when she reaches years of discretion.

The expedition was divided into two teams; Yvette and Michel were in the West Ridge team and at one time it was hoped that this whole team might reach the summit of Everest. Yvette played her part unostentatiously and with much expertise. She went up to Camp II and then, after acclimatisation, went on to help set up Camp III with some Sherpas and two other members of the expedition.

It was after this that endless misfortunes overtook the expedition. One after another members went sick; the weather broke and conditions became almost intolerable. Finally tragedy stepped in and one of the most popular members, Harsh Bahuguna, an Indian, died from exposure, despite the heroic endeavours of his friends to save him. In the teeth of the blizzard and through some of the worst weather ever experienced on Everest, Yvette assisted Michel and some of the still fit members to bring down the body of poor Harsh. She struggled along uncomplainingly, showing great reserves of strength and eventually came down the terrible and dangerous ice-fall, the most hazardous part of the journey, quite magnificently with no help from anyone. Everyone had loved Yvette from the beginning of the expedition; from now on they admired her too.

The next casualty was Michel himself who, it was feared, was suffering from phlebitis. The only course was a temporary return to Base Camp; Yvette went down with him; nursed him until the danger was past and then together they returned to the fray.

By now conditions on Everest and the whole position of the

party had deteriorated so much that routes had to be reconsidered. The Vauchers voted for the South Col route instead of the West Ridge. According to Dr Peter Steele one of the aims of the expedition was to put a woman on the summit of Everest; some thought that by the South Col this might still be achieved.

Sadly this was not to be, nor indeed were any of the carefully evolved plans to succeed. Until the question of reconsidering the routes came up it had been a happy expedition with few tensions and much comradeship. But in the end, after such a series of misfortunes, personal discontents began to show up; especially when a final recasting for a last attempt was made. It was then, and only then, that Yvette's morale broke under the strain. She was not the only one who suffered in this way, but just because she was a woman public attention, always seeking for something sensational, centred on her. Disappointed and despairing, desperately worried about Michel, she allowed her feelings to get the better of her and vented her wrath on Norman Dyhrenfurth, one of the two leaders, pelting him with snowballs as he came into his tent. It was a childish but short-lived outburst; Yvette was under great strain. If unsympathetic and undue prominence had not been given to the event by those who knew little about the situation the sorry story might have been kept within the family circle of the expedition. As it was, Yvette's reputation was temporarily tarnished; but time gradually effaces bitter memories; Yvette remains a great climber for whom very many still cherish a sincere affection and deep admiration. She will ride the storm and go on, we all hope, to still greater adventures.

And there is still time – all the time in the world. To quote Peter Steele again, 'Everest always wins; men challenge and even climb her but they never conquer,' and so it is with all mountains. It may be that Yvette will still have another chance but that does not matter so much; we shall all remember, and history will record, that in 1971 a woman was included in the International Expedition to Everest – and that woman was Yvette. She has paved the way for others; the world will not look in vain for future women mountaineers to follow where she has led.

Chapter 10

'Out to the Undiscovered Ends'

It is the end of 1972; time to stop and glance back at the unfolding, still unfinished, pageant of women's mountaineering. In 1808 the first woman stood on the summit of Mont Blanc; just over a hundred years ago Lucy Walker climbed the Matterhorn; in the 'naughty nineties' Mrs Aubrey Le Blond was pioneering winter ascents; by the first decade of the present century women had their own mountaineering clubs; the twenties and thirties saw a spate of *cordées féminines*; the fifties became the 'mother and daughter' era; Himalayan adventures crowded the sixties and in 1971 an Everest Expedition included, for the first time, a woman member. It is a story of adventure, courage, companionship, good fun, and, for many, incomparable joy. There are highlights in the many-hued kaleidoscope, and stars that gleam with a special brilliance; but through the years each woman climber, however undistinguished, has been a thread in the tapestry. The story is not ended and never will be while there are still hills to climb.

What of women mountaineers in the complicated, computerised world of today? And what of their future? Perhaps the present position is some guide to future developments. Women climbers are active in all parts of the world and their numbers increase year by year. There has been another expedition on Mount Everest and for the second time there was a woman in the team. Beth Burke is not a climber, although she is a skier; she is a nurse and that is why she was with the expedition. However, she marched from Kathmandu with the male members of the team and was stationed at Base Camp at 17,500 feet. She added to her nursing duties responsibility for the 'walky talky' radio communication with the higher camps and was later put in charge of the ordering and marshalling of supplies. Her husband Mick was a climbing member of the expedition and Beth herself earned an honoured place in the team. The weather once more denied the expedition the summit, nevertheless Lord Hunt was able to welcome them home as 'a happy band of heroes'.

Back in Europe there is a plethora of talented mountaineers climbing regularly in the Alps, eager for adventures farther afield when the opportunity occurs. Christine de Colombel, one of the heroines of the Eiger North Face, is at the height of her powers; the young Dutch climber Marleen Schalkwijk goes from strength to strength. Sally Westmacott, at the present time one of the most brilliant members of the Ladies' Alpine Club, with a remarkable record of ascents in mountain ranges all over the world, is the wife of Michael Westmacott, who was a member of the successful 1953 Everest team. She climbs in the summer, skis in the winter and goes ski-mountaineering in the spring. Sally still has many years of climbing before her and seems willing and able to tackle almost any mountain problem. With a climbing husband to aid and abet who knows what the future may hold?

Many of the great young climbers of the fifties and sixties have married and are busy with their families. But it would be quite in accordance with the best traditions for them to return to active mountaineering when home ties become less pressing. There may be chapters still to be written in the climbing biographies of Mrs Philip Flood (Jo Scarr), Mrs Christopher Wilson (Denise Shortall), Lady Evans (Denise Morin), Mrs Seitz (Betty Stark), Mrs Monica Jackson and Mrs Eileen Healey.

Meanwhile the veterans, the *virtuosi* of the thirties and forties, still continue to climb with almost unabated vigour. Dorothea Gravina, Loulou Boulaz, Margaret Darvall, Dorly Lehner and Esmé Speakman, to mention only a few, still plan impressive programmes every year, while the American Elizabeth Knowlton comes regularly to Europe to join the meets of the *Rendez-Vous Hautes Montagnes*. Perhaps the most persistent and indefatigable of this generation is Anna Roelfsema; her achievements over the last thirty years include the Younggrat of the Breithorn, the

Furggen ridge of the Matterhorn, the Teufelsgrat, the Ostwand of Monte Rosa, the Sudwand of the Obergabelhorn, the Ostwand of the Zinal Rothorn and the Viereselgrat of the Dent Blanche. Nearly every season she adds another to the list or goes back to recapitulate on one she has particularly enjoyed, and within the last two years she has been busy in the Julian Alps and the Himalayas. It is a magnificent record and the Ladies' Alpine Club has elected Anna an Honorary Member.

For sheer courage and tenacity Nea Morin is hard to beat. In 1963 she had a serious operation for osteo-arthritis of the hip. She now has one leg shorter than the other and, except for a 90 per cent forward movement, a completely stiff hip. But nothing stops Nea; in city streets she walks with a stick; in the mountains of North Wales, the Dolomites and Austria she continues to climb. She no longer leads and because of her disability she has almost had to learn to climb afresh, but no meet of the Ladies' Alpine Club or the *Rendez-Vous Hautes Montagnes* would be complete without her active participation, and, although skiing is now denied her, Nea can still be found winter walking around Zermatt.

Dorothy Pilley-Richards, now in her seventies and sadly crippled by a disastrous road accident caused by a drunken driver, still travels widely in the mountains. In an article which she wrote recently entitled *'Sunset Ascent'* she explains how climbs gradually have to become smaller and smaller as age creeps on, but the glory still awaits one on the summit – the glory of achievement and of thankfulness. She retains to a remarkable degree her gratitude for the past and hope for the future.

For Dorothy and Nea and many others like them the poet's lines still ring true;

> *I have not lost the magic of long days;*
> *I live them, dream them still;*
> *Still am I master of the starry ways*
> *And freeman of the hill.*
> *Shattered my glass ere half the sands were run*
> *I hold the heights, I hold the heights I won.*

P

So far we have been thinking of the 'tigresses', 'tigresses' of the past and of the present; women mountaineers owe them much; they project the image which, in these days, seems to be considered so important in all activities. But the mountain world, like all other 'worlds', is made up mainly of the 'moderates' – the ordinary climbers of whom no one hears a great deal. Each summer they set out for their favourite mountain region with rucksack, rope and ice-axe eager to try their skill, to test their strength, to come to grips with the particular mountain of their choice and, if possible, achieve the summit.

It is from among these quite ordinary women that the leading mountaineers of the future will emerge. Most people start as nobodies and among them there must always be some who will later become the 'tigresses' of their generation. They will not necessarily be the very young, although naturally this is usually the case; but middle-aged women are often magnificent mountaineers; their wide experience, seasoned maturity and proved powers of endurance ensure them a position of leadership much longer than in most other forms of sport.

But hard facts have to be realistically considered when trying to assess the chances of unlimited success for women mountaineers of the future. Up to the present there has been a majority view that oxygen would be required for the very highest peaks; one of the notable exceptions to this view is Professor Noel Odell, who claims that the summit of Everest could be reached without the aid of oxygen. But if such equipment has got to be carried then women are bound to be at a disadvantage; their limited arm strength makes them more dependent on balance and this means that even a heavy rucksack is an encumbrance; presumably an oxygen cylinder would be an intolerable burden as things stand at present. But methods may change; science, not to mention the will to win, may find new ways and means and the day may come when the question of oxygen may not be a final deterrent in reaching the greatest heights.

For the foreseeable future it seems that women are likely to attempt the highest mountains only in company with men. This means that they almost certainly will not be leading; men are, on the whole, better climbers than women and they have greater reserves of strength – although women are capable of greater endurance. If women should decide to lead an expedition to Everest it would have to be an all-women party and even then there would be male Sherpa porters – unless the little Sherpanis took over these duties!

It appears at first sight to be a complicated problem; in reality it is no problem at all. Of course women climbers would like to see a woman on the summit of Everest; of course they would like to be part of an all-women Everest Expedition – the greatest mountain in the world is the supreme challenge to all mountaineers. But women climbers are not worried; they seem to have an intuitive instinct that these things will one day be achieved. Indeed, even as these words are being written there is news from the Far East that the enterprising ladies of Japan have been given permission for an all-woman expedition to make an attempt on Mount Everest in the spring of 1975.

Probably this will be the next major step for women mountaineers; the way ahead winds out of sight and carries a big question mark. Certainly women climbers will go on and go forward; their history has been a saga of quiet progress and ever-widening horizons; their future lies in their own hands. Women climbers do not lack courage nor the questing spirit; the challenge of the hills is the same as it always has been and they will follow wherever it may lead them – perhaps to undreamed-of triumphs.

But whatever the future may hold it is certain that women will still *enjoy* the mountains – that is the common inheritance that all mountaineers, men and women, have shared down the ages; it is the bond that, in spite of all the differences, makes them one. It is the feel of the rope round one's waist, the firm, warm rock beneath the fingers, the crunch of snow under vibram soles, the response of body and mind to the problem posed and, above all, the sheer exhilaration of being among the mountains that brings climbers back year after year. Climbing calls for all that one has got in perseverance and endurance; but always the mountains give more than they demand; there is beauty and exaltation of spirit in abundance and peace that passes understanding. In the uncertainties of the late twentieth-century modern mountaineers are lucky; the mountains are changeless, eternal; 'there is much comfort in high hills' and one has only to climb even a small mountain to stand above the chaos, to sense the steadfastness of the hills and to see the world, if only for a fleeting moment, as God sees it. To quote a well-known mountaineer, 'A world that can give so much rapture must be a good world, a life capable of such feeling must be worth living.'

And so we leave our women mountaineers, with their faces set to the future and the lines from Flecker's *Hassan* for their watchword;

> *We are the pilgrims, master; we shall go*
> *Always a little further: it may be*
> *Beyond that last blue mountain barred with snow.*

Bibliography

Alexander Burgener, Adolf Fux, Hallwag, 1962.
Alpine Byways, Mrs H. Freshfield, Longmans, 1861.
Century of Mountaineering, A, Arnold Lunn, Allen & Unwin, 1957.
Climbing Days, Dorothy Pilley-Richards, Secker & Warburg, 1935.
Early Alpine Guides, The, Ronald Clark, Phoenix House, 1949.
Early Mountaineers, The, Frances Gribble, T. Fisher Unwin, 1898.
Four Miles High, Josephine Scarr, Gollancz, 1966.
Give Me The Hills, Miriam Underhill, Methuen, 1956.
History of Mountaineering in the Alps, A, C. E. Engel, Allen & Unwin, 1950.
Lady's Tour of Monte Rosa, A, Mrs Cole, London, 1859.
Mountain Holidays, Janet Adam Smith, Dent, 1946.
Mountain Memories, Sir Martin Conway, Cassell, 1920.
Peaks and Passes, Anna Pigeon and Ellen Abbott, Griffith, Fanne, Okeden and Welsh, 1885.
Space Beneath My Feet, Gwen Moffat, Hodder & Stoughton, 1961.
Swiss Letters, Frances Ridley Havergal, James Nisbet, 1882.
Tents in the Clouds, Monica Jackson and Elizabeth Stark, Collins, 1956.
They Came To The Hills, C. E. Engel, Allen & Unwin, 1952.
True Tales of Mountain Adventure, Mrs Aubrey Le Blond, T. Fisher Unwin, 1906.
Victorian Lady Travellers, Dorothy Middleton, Routledge, 1965.
Victorian Mountaineers, The, Ronald Clark, Batsford, 1953.
Woman's Reach, A, Nea Morin, Eyre & Spottiswoode, 1968.

Alpine Club Journal, various volumes
Journal of the Ladies' Alpine Club, 1913–1972
La Montagne, various issues

The above is not a complete bibliography but contains the main sources of information used.

Index

PRINCIPAL PEOPLE AND INSTITUTIONS

PRINCIPAL PEAKS AND PLACES